Embedded Systems Design

An Introduction to Processes, Tools, and Techniques

Arnold Berger

CMP Books
Lawrence, Kansas 66046

CMP Books
CMP Media LLC
1601 West 23rd Street, Suite 200
Lawrence, Kansas 66046
USA
www.cmpbooks.com

Developmental Editor:	Robert Ward
Editors:	Matt McDonald, Julie McNamee, Rita Sooby, and Catherine Janzen
Layout Production:	Justin Fulmer, Rita Sooby, and Michelle O'Neal
Managing Editor:	Michelle O'Neal
Cover Art Design:	Robert Ward

Distributed in the U.S. and Canada by:
Publishers Group West
1700 Fourth Street
Berkeley, CA 94710
1-800-788-3123
www.pgw.com

ISBN: 1-57820-073-3

CMP**Books**

*This book is dedicated to
Shirley Berger.*

Table of Contents

Preface

Why write a book about designing embedded systems? Because my experiences working in the industry and, more recently, working with students have convinced me that there is a need for such a book.

For example, a few years ago, I was the Development Tools Marketing Manager for a semiconductor manufacturer. I was speaking with the Software Development Tools Manager at our major account. My job was to help convince the customer that they should be using our RISC processor in their laser printers. Since I owned the tool chain issues, I had to address his specific issues before we could convince him that we had the appropriate support for his design team.

Since we didn't have an In-Circuit Emulator for this processor, we found it necessary to create an extended support matrix, built around a ROM emulator, JTAG port, and a logic analyzer. After explaining all this to him, he just shook his head. I knew I was in trouble. He told me that, of course, he needed all this stuff. However, what he really needed was training. The R&D Group had no trouble hiring all the freshly minted software engineers they needed right out of college. Finding a new engineer who knew anything about software development outside of Wintel or UNIX was quite another matter. Thus was born the idea that perhaps there is some need for a different slant on embedded system design.

Recently I've been teaching an introductory course at the University of Washington-Bothell (UWB). For now, I'm teaching an introduction to embedded systems. Later, there'll be a lab course. Eventually this course will grow into a full track, allowing students to earn a specialty in embedded systems. Much of this book's content is an outgrowth of my work at UWB. Feedback from my students about the course and its content has influenced the slant of the book. My interactions with these students and with other faculty have only reinforced my belief that we need such a book.

What is this book about?

This book is not intended to be a text in software design, or even *embedded* software design (although it will, of necessity, discuss some code and coding issues). Most of my students are much better at writing code in C++ and Java than am I. Thus, my first admission is that I'm not going to attempt to teach software methodologies. What I will teach is the *how* of software development in an embedded environment. I wrote this book to help an embedded software developer understand the issues that make embedded software development different from host-based software design. In other words, what do you do when there is no `printf()` or `malloc()`?

Because this is a book about designing embedded systems, I will discuss design issues — but I'll focus on those that aren't encountered in application design. One of the most significant of these issues is processor selection. One of my responsibilities as the Embedded Tools Marketing Manager was to help convince engineers and their managers to use our processors. What are the issues that surround the choice of the right processor for any given application? Since most new engineers usually only have architectural knowledge of the Pentium-class, or SPARC processors, it would be helpful for them to broaden their processor horizon. The correct processor choice can be a "bet the company" decision. I was there in a few cases where it was such a decision, and the company lost the bet.

Why should you buy this book?

If you are one of my students.

If you're in my class at UWB, then you'll probably buy the book because it is on your required reading list. Besides, an autographed copy of the book might be valuable a few years from now (said with a smile). However, the real reason is that it will simplify note-taking. The content is reasonably faithful to the 400 or so lectures slides that you'll have to sit through in class. Seriously, though, reading this book will help you to get a grasp of the issues that embedded system designers must deal with on a daily basis. Knowing something about embedded systems will be a big help when you become a member of the next group and start looking for a job!

If you are a student elsewhere or a recent graduate.

Even if you aren't studying embedded systems at UWB, reading this book can be important to your future career. Embedded systems is one of the largest and fastest growing specialties in the industry, but the number of recent graduates who have embedded experience is woefully small. *Any* prior knowledge of the field will make you stand out from other job applicants.

As a hiring manager, when interviewing job applicants I would often "tune out" the candidates who gave the standard, "I'm flexible, I'll do anything" answer. However, once in while someone would say, "I used your stuff in school, and boy, was it ever a *kludge*. Why did you set up the trace spec menu that way?" That was the candidate I wanted to hire. If your only benefit from reading this book is that you learn some jargon that helps you make a better impression at your next job interview, then reading it was probably worth your the time invested.

If you are a working engineer or developer.

If you are an experienced software developer this book will help you to see the big picture. If it's not in your nature to care about the big picture, you may be asking: "why do I need to see the big picture? I'm a software designer. I'm only concerned with technical issues. Let the marketing-types and managers worry about 'the big picture.' I'll take a good Quick Sort algorithm anytime." Well, the reality is that, as a developer, you are at the bottom of the food chain when it comes to making certain critical decisions, but you are at the top of the blame list when the project is late. I know from experience. I spent many long hours in the lab trying to compensate for a bad decision made by someone else earlier in the project's lifecycle. I remember many times when I wasn't at my daughter's recitals because I was fixing code. Don't let someone else stick you with the dog! This book will help you recognize and explain the critical importance of certain early decisions. It will equip you to influence the decisions that directly impact your success. You owe it to yourself.

If you are a manager.

Having just maligned managers and marketers, I'm now going to take that all back and say that this book is also for them. If you are a manager and want your project to go smoothly and your product to get to market on time, then this book can warn you about land mines and roadblocks. Will it guarantee success? No, but like chicken soup, it can't hurt.

I'll also try to share ideas that have worked for me as a manager. For example, when I was an R&D Project Manager I used a simple "trick" to help to form my project team and focus our efforts. Before we even started the product definition phase I would get some foam-core poster board and build a box with it. The box had the approximate shape of the product. Then I drew a generic front panel and pasted it on the front of the box. The front panel had the project's code name, like *Gerbil*, or some other mildly humorous name, prominently displayed. Suddenly, we had a tangible proto- type "image" of the product. We could see it. It got us focused. Next, I held a pot-luck dinner at my house for the project team and their significant oth- ers.[2] These simple devices helped me to bring the team's focus to the project that lay ahead. It also helped to form the "extended support team" so that when the need arose to call for a 60 or 80 hours workweek, the home front support was there.

(While that extended support is important, managers should not abuse it. As an R&D Manager I realized that I had a large influence over the engi- neer's personal lives. I could impact their salaries with large raises and I could seriously strain a marriage by firing them. Therefore, I took my responsibility for delivering the right product, on time, very seriously. You should too.)

Embedded designers and managers shouldn't have to make the same mis- takes over and over. I hope that this book will expose you to some of the best practices that I've learned over the years. Since embedded system design seems to lie in the netherworld between Electrical Engineering and Com- puter Science, some of the methods and tools that I've learned and devel- oped don't seem to rise to the surface in books with a homogeneous focus.

How is the book structured?

For the most part, the text will follow the classic embedded processor lifecy- cle model. This model has served the needs of marketing engineers and field sales engineers for many years. The good news is that this model is a fairly accurate representation of how embedded systems are developed. While no simple model truly captures all of the subtleties of the embedded develop- ment process, representing it as a parallel development of hardware and software, followed by an integration step, seems to capture the essence of the process.

What do I expect you to know?

Primarily, I assume you are familiar with the vocabulary of application development. While some familiarity with C, assembly, and basic digital

---

2.   I can't take credit for this idea. I learned it from *Controlling Software Projects*, by Tom DeMarco (Yourdon Press, 1982), and from a videotaped series of his lectures.

circuits is helpful, it's not necessary. The few sections that describe specific C coding techniques aren't essential to the rest of the book and should be accessible to almost any programmer. Similarly, you won't need to be an expert assembly language programmer to understand the point of the examples that are presented in Motorola 68000 assembly language. If you have enough logic background to understand ANDs and ORs, you are prepared for the circuit content. In short, anyone who's had a few college-level programming courses, or equivalent experience, should be comfortable with the content.

Acknowledgments

I'd like to thank some people who helped, directly and indirectly, to make this book a reality. Perry Keller first turned me on to the fun and power of the in-circuit emulator. I'm forever in his debt. Stan Bowlin was the best emulator designer that I ever had the privilege to manage. I learned a lot about how it all works from Stan. Daniel Mann, an AMD Fellow, helped me to understand how all the pieces fit together.

The manuscript was edited by Robert Ward, Julie McNamee, Rita Sooby, Michelle O'Neal, and Catherine Janzen. Justin Fulmer redid many of my graphics. Rita Sooby and Michelle O'Neal typeset the final result. Finally, Robert Ward and my friend and colleague, Sid Maxwell, reviewed the manuscript for technical accuracy. Thank you all.

Arnold Berger
Sammamish, Washington
September 27, 2001

Introduction

The arrival of the microprocessor in the 1970s brought about a revolution of control. For the first time, relatively complex systems could be constructed using a simple device, the microprocessor, as its primary control and feedback element. If you were to hunt out an old Teletype ASR33 computer terminal in a surplus store and compare its innards to a modern color inkjet printer, there's quite a difference.

Automobile emissions have decreased by 90 percent over the last 20 years, primarily due to the use of microprocessors in the engine-management system. The open-loop fuel control system, characterized by a carburetor, is now a fuel-injected, closed-loop system using multiple sensors to optimize performance and minimize emissions over a wide range of operating conditions. This type of performance improvement would have been impossible without the microprocessor as a control element.

Microprocessors have now taken over the automobile. A new luxury-class automobile might have more than 70 dedicated microprocessors, controlling tasks from the engine spark and transmission shift points to opening the window slightly when the door is being closed to avoid a pressure burst in the driver's ear.

The F-16 is an unstable aircraft that cannot be flown without on-board computers constantly making control surface adjustments to keep it in the air. The pilot, through the traditional controls, sends requests to the computer to change the plane's flight profile. The computer attempts to comply with those requests to the extent that it can and still keep the plane in the air.

A modern jetliner can have more than 200 on-board, dedicated microprocessors.

The most exciting driver of microprocessor performance is the games market. Although it can be argued that the game consoles from Nintendo, Sony, and Sega are not really embedded systems, the technology boosts that they are driving are absolutely amazing. Jim Turley[1], at the Microprocessor Forum, described a 200MHz reduced instruction set computer (RISC) processor that was going into a next-generation game console. This processor could do a four-dimensional matrix multiplication in one clock cycle at a cost of $25.

Why Embedded Systems Are Different

Well, all of this is impressive, so let's delve into what makes embedded systems design different — at least different enough that someone has to write a book about it. A good place to start is to try to enumerate the differences between your desktop PC and the typical embedded system.

- Embedded systems are dedicated to specific tasks, whereas PCs are generic computing platforms.
- Embedded systems are supported by a wide array of processors and processor architectures.
- Embedded systems are usually cost sensitive.
- Embedded systems have real-time constraints.

You'll have ample opportunity to learn about *real time*. For now, real-time events are external (to the embedded system) events that must be dealt with when they occur (in real time).

- If an embedded system is using an operating system at all, it is most likely using a real-time operating system (RTOS), rather than Windows 9X, Windows NT, Windows 2000, Unix, Solaris, or HP-UX.
- The implications of software failure is much more severe in embedded systems than in desktop systems.
- Embedded systems often have power constraints.
- Embedded systems often must operate under extreme environmental conditions.
- Embedded systems have far fewer system resources than desktop systems.
- Embedded systems often store all their object code in ROM.

- Embedded systems require specialized tools and methods to be efficiently designed.
- Embedded microprocessors often have dedicated debugging circuitry.

Embedded systems are dedicated to specific tasks, whereas PCs are generic computing platforms

Another name for an embedded microprocessor is a *dedicated* microprocessor. It is programmed to perform only one, or perhaps, a few, specific tasks. Changing the task is usually associated with obsolescing the entire system and redesigning it. The processor that runs a mobile heart monitor/defibrillator is not expected to run a spreadsheet or word processor.

Conversely, a general-purpose processor, such as the Pentium on which I'm working at this moment, must be able to support a wide array of applications with widely varying processing requirements. Because your PC must be able to service the most complex applications with the same performance as the lightest application, the processing power on your desktop is truly awesome.

Thus, it wouldn't make much sense, either economically or from an engineering standpoint, to put an AMD-K6, or similar processor, inside the coffeemaker on your kitchen counter.

That's not to say that someone won't do something similar. For example, a French company designed a vacuum cleaner with an AMD 29000 processor. The 29000 is a 32-bit RISC CPU that is far more suited for driving laser-printer engines.

Embedded systems are supported by a wide array of processors and processor architectures

Most students who take my Computer Architecture or Embedded Systems class have never programmed on any platform except the X86 (Intel) or the Sun SPARC family. The students who take the Embedded Systems class are rudely awakened by their first homework assignment, which has them researching the available trade literature and proposing the optimal processor for an assigned application.

These students are learning that today more than 140 different microprocessors are available from more than 40 semiconductor vendors[2]. These vendors are in a daily battle with each other to get the design-win (be the processor of choice) for the next wide-body jet or the next Internet-based soda machine.

In Chapter 2, you'll learn more about the processor-selection process. For now, just appreciate the range of available choices.

Embedded systems are usually cost sensitive

I say "usually" because the cost of the embedded processor in the Mars Rover was probably not on the design team's top 10 list of constraints. However, if you save 10 cents on the cost of the Engine Management Computer System, you'll be a hero at most automobile companies. Cost does matter in most embedded applications.

The cost that you must consider most of the time is system cost. The cost of the processor is a factor, but, if you can eliminate a printed circuit board and connectors and get by with a smaller power supply by using a highly integrated microcontroller instead of a microprocessor and separate peripheral devices, you have potentially a greater reduction in system costs, even if the integrated device is significantly more costly than the discrete device. This issue is covered in more detail in Chapter 3.

Embedded systems have real-time constraints

I was thinking about how to introduce this section when my laptop decided to back up my work. I started to type but was faced with the hourglass symbol because the computer was busy doing other things. Suppose my computer wasn't sitting on my desk but was connected to a radar antenna in the nose of a commercial jetliner. If the computer's main function in life is to provide a collision alert warning, then suspending that task could be disastrous.

Real-time constraints generally are grouped into two categories: *time-sensitive constraints* and *time-critical constraints*. If a task is time critical, it must take place within a set window of time, or the function controlled by that task fails. Controlling the flight-worthiness of an aircraft is a good example of this. If the feedback loop isn't fast enough, the control algorithm becomes unstable, and the aircraft won't stay in the air.

A time-sensitive task can die gracefully. If the task should take, for example, 4.5ms but takes, on average, 6.3ms, then perhaps the inkjet printer will print two pages per minute instead of the design goal of three pages per minute.

If an embedded system is using an operating system at all, it is most likely using an RTOS

Like embedded processors, embedded operating systems also come in a wide variety of flavors and colors. My students must also pick an embedded operating system as part of their homework project. RTOSs are not democratic. They need not give every task that is ready to execute the time it needs. RTOSs give the highest priority task that needs to run all the time it needs. If other tasks fail to get sufficient CPU time, it's the programmer's problem.

Another difference between most commercially available operating systems and your desktop operating system is something you won't get with an RTOS. You won't get the dreaded Blue Screen of Death that many Windows 9X users see on a regular basis.

The implications of software failure are much more severe in embedded systems than in desktop systems

Remember the Y2K hysteria? The people who were really under the gun were the people responsible for the continued good health of our computer-based infrastructure. A lot of money was spent searching out and replacing devices with embedded processors because the #$%%$ thing got the dates all wrong.

We all know of the tragic consequences of a medical radiation machine that miscalculates a dosage. How do we know when our code is bug free? How do you completely test complex software that must function properly under all conditions?

However, the most important point to take away from this discussion is that software failure is far less tolerable in an embedded system than in your average desktop PC. That is not to imply that software never fails in an embedded system, just that most embedded systems typically contain some mechanism, such as a *watchdog timer*, to bring it back to life if the software loses control. You'll find out more about software testing in Chapter 9.

Embedded systems have power constraints

For many readers, the only CPU they have ever seen is the Pentium or AMD K6 inside their desktop PC. The CPU needs a massive heat sink and fan assembly to keep the processor from baking itself to death. This is not a particularly serious constraint for a desktop system. Most desktop PC's have plenty of spare space inside to allow for good airflow. However, consider an embedded system attached to the collar of a wolf roaming around Wyoming or Montana. These systems must work reliably and for a long time on a set of small batteries.

How do you keep your embedded system running on minute amounts of power? Usually that task is left up to the hardware engineer. However, the division of responsibility isn't clearly delineated. The hardware designer might or might not have some idea of the software architectural constraints. In general, the processor choice is determined outside the range of hearing of the software designers. If the overall system design is on a tight power budget, it is likely that the software design must be built around a system in which the processor is in "sleep mode" most of the time and only wakes up when a timer tick occurs. In other words, the system is completely interrupt driven.

Power constraints impact every aspect of the system design decisions. Power constraints affect the processor choice, its speed, and its memory architecture. The constraints imposed by the system requirements will likely determine whether the software must be written in assembly language, rather than C or C++, because the absolute maximum performance must be achieved within the power budget. Power requirements are dictated by the CPU clock speed and the number of active electronic components (CPU, RAM, ROM, I/O devices, and so on).

Thus, from the perspective of the software designer, the power constraints could become the dominant system constraint, dictating the choice of software tools, memory size, and performance headroom.

Speed vs. Power

Almost all modern CPUs are fabricated using the Complementary Metal Oxide Silicon (CMOS) process. The simple gate structure of CMOS devices consists of two MOS transistors, one N-type and one P-type (hence, the term complementary), stacked like a totem pole with the N-type on top and the P-type on the bottom. Both transistors behave like perfect switches. When the output is high, or logic level 1, the P-type transistor is turned off, and the N-type transistor connects the output to the supply voltage (5V, 3.3V, and so on), which the gate outputs to the rest of the circuit.

When the logic level is 0, the situation is reversed, and the P-type transistor connects the next stage to ground while the N-type transistor is turned off. This circuit topology has an interesting property that makes it attractive from a power-use viewpoint. If the circuit is static (not changing state), the power loss is extremely small. In fact, it would be zero if not for a small amount of leakage current inherent in these devices at normal room temperature and above.

When the circuit is switching, as in a CPU, things are different. While a gate switches logic levels, there is a period of time when the N-type and P-type transistors are simultaneously on. During this brief window, current can flow from the supply voltage line to ground through both devices. Current flow means power dissipation and that means heat. The greater the clock speed, the greater the number of switching cycles taking place per second, and this means more power loss. Now, consider your 500MHz Pentium or Athlon processor with 10 million or so transistors, and you can see why these desktop machines are so power hungry. In fact, it is almost a perfect linear relationship between CPU speed and power dissipation in modern processors. Those of you who overclock your CPUs to wring every last ounce of performance out of it know how important a good heat sink and fan combination are.

Embedded systems must operate under extreme environmental conditions

Embedded systems are everywhere. Everywhere means everywhere. Embedded systems must run in aircraft, in the polar ice, in outer space, in the trunk of a black Camaro in Phoenix, Arizona, in August. Although making sure that the system runs under these conditions is usually the domain of the hardware designer, there are implications for both the hardware and software. Harsh environments usually mean more than temperature and humidity. Devices that are qualified for military use must meet a long list of environmental requirements and have the documentation to prove it. If you've wondered why a simple processor, such as the 8086 from Intel, should cost several thousands of dollars in a missile, think paperwork and environment. The fact that a device must be qualified for the environment in which it will be operating, such as deep space, often dictates the selection of devices that are available.

The environmental concerns often overlap other concerns, such as power requirements. Sealing a processor under a silicone rubber conformal coating because it must be environmentally sealed also means that the capability to dissipate heat is severely reduced, so processor type and speed is also a factor.

Unfortunately, the environmental constraints are often left to the very end of the project, when the product is in testing and the hardware designer discovers that the product is exceeding its thermal budget. This often means slowing the clock, which leads to less time for the software to do its job, which translates to further refining the software to improve the efficiency of the code. All the while, the product is still not released.

Embedded systems have far fewer system resources than desktop systems

Right now, I'm typing this manuscript on my desktop PC. An oldies CD is playing through the speakers. I've got 256MB of RAM, 26GB of disk space, and assorted ZIP, JAZZ, floppy, and CD-RW devices on a SCSI card. I'm looking at a beautiful 19-inch CRT monitor. I can enter data through a keyboard and a mouse. Just considering the bus signals in the system, I have the following:

- Processor bus
- AGP bus
- PCI bus
- ISA bus
- SCSI bus
- USB bus

- Parallel bus
- RS-232C bus

An awful lot of system resources are at my disposal to make my computing chores as painless as possible. It is a tribute to the technological and economic driving forces of the PC industry that so much computing power is at my fingertips.

Now consider the embedded system controlling your VCR. Obviously, it has far fewer resources that it must manage than the desktop example. Of course, this is because it is dedicated to a few well-defined tasks and nothing else. Being engineered for cost effectiveness (the whole VCR only cost $80 retail), you can't expect the CPU to be particularly general purpose. This translates to fewer resources to manage and hence, lower cost and simplicity. However, it also means that the software designer is often required to design standard input and output (I/O) routines repeatedly. The number of inputs and outputs are usually so limited, the designers are forced to overload and serialize the functions of one or two input devices. Ever try to set the time in your super exercise workout wristwatch after you've misplaced the instruction sheet?

Embedded systems store all their object code in ROM

Even your PC has to store some of its code in ROM. ROM is needed in almost all systems to provide enough code for the system to initialize itself (boot-up code). However, most embedded systems must have all their code in ROM. This means severe limitations might be imposed on the size of the code image that will fit in the ROM space. However, it's more likely that the methods used to design the system will need to be changed because the code is in ROM.

As an example, when the embedded system is powered up, there must be code that initializes the system so that the rest of the code can run. This means establishing the run-time environment, such as initializing and placing variables in RAM, testing memory integrity, testing the ROM integrity with a checksum test, and other initialization tasks.

From the point of view of debugging the system, ROM code has certain implications. First, your handy debugger is not able to set a breakpoint in ROM. To set a breakpoint, the debugger must be able to remove the user's instruction and replace it with a special instruction, such as a TRAP instruction or software interrupt instruction. The TRAP forces a transfer to a convenient entry point in the debugger. In some systems, you can get around this problem by loading the application software into RAM. Of course, this assumes sufficient RAM is available to hold of all the applications, to store variables, and to provide for dynamic memory allocation.

Of course, being a capitalistic society, wherever there is a need, someone will provide a solution. In this case, the specialized suite of tools that have evolved to support the embedded system development process gives you a way around this dilemma, which is discussed in the next section.

Embedded systems require specialized tools and methods to be efficiently designed

Chapters 4 through 8 discuss the types of tools in much greater detail. The embedded system is so different in so many ways, it's not surprising that specialized tools and methods must be used to create and test embedded software. Take the case of the previous example—the need to set a breakpoint at an instruction boundary located in ROM.

A ROM Emulator

Several companies manufacture hardware-assist products, such as ROM emulators. Figure 1 shows a product called *NetROM*, from Applied Microsystems Corporation. NetROM is an example of a general class of tools called *emulators*. From the point of view of the target system, the ROM emulator is designed to look like a standard ROM device. It has a connector that has the exact mechanical dimensions and electrical characteristics of the ROM it is emulating. However, the connector's job is to bring the signals from the ROM socket on the target system to the main circuitry, located at the other end of the cable. This circuitry provides high-speed RAM that can be written to quickly via a separate channel from a host computer. Thus, the target system sees a ROM device, but the software developer sees a RAM device that can have its code easily modified and allows debugger breakpoints to be set.

Figure 1   NetROM.

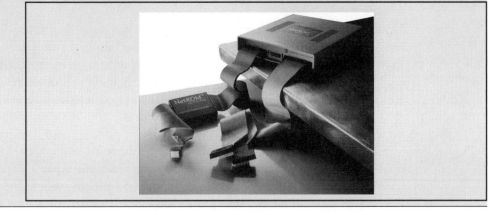

In the context of this book, the term *hardware-assist* refers to additional specialized devices that supplement a software-only debugging solution. A ROM emulator, manufactured by companies such as Applied Microsystems and Grammar Engine, is an example of a hardware-assist device.

Embedded microprocessors often have dedicated debugging circuitry

Perhaps one of the most dramatic differences between today's embedded microprocessors and those of a few years ago is the almost mandatory inclusion of dedicated debugging circuitry in silicon on the chip. This is almost counter-intuitive to all of the previous discussion. After droning on about the cost sensitivity of embedded systems, it seems almost foolish to think that every microprocessor in production contains circuitry that is only necessary for debugging a product under development. In fact, this was the prevailing sentiment for a while. Embedded-chip manufacturers actually built special versions of their embedded devices that contained the debug circuitry and made them available (or not available) to their tool suppliers. In the end, most manufacturers found it more cost-effective to produce one version of the chip for all purposes. This didn't stop them from restricting the information about how the debug circuitry worked, but every device produced did contain the debug "hooks" for the hardware-assist tools.

What is noteworthy is that the manufacturers all realized that the inclusion of on-chip debug circuitry was a requirement for acceptance of their devices in an embedded application. That is, unless their chip had a good solution for embedded system design and debug, it was not going to be a serious contender for an embedded application by a product-development team facing time-to-market pressures.

Summary

Now that you know what is different about embedded systems, it's time to see how you actually tame the beast. In the chapters that follow, you'll examine the embedded system design process step by step, as it is practiced.

The first few chapters focus on the process itself. I'll describe the design life cycle and examine the issues affecting processor selection. The later chapters focus on techniques and tools used to build, test, and debug a complete system.

I'll close with some comments on the business of embedded systems and on an emerging technology that might change everything.

Although engineers like to think design is a rational, requirements-driven process, in the real world, many decisions that have an enormous impact on the design process are made by non-engineers based on criteria that might have little to do with the project requirements. For example, in many projects, the decision to use a particular processor has nothing to do with the engineering parameters of the problem. Too often, it becomes the task of the design team to pick up the pieces and make these decisions work. Hopefully, this book provides some ammunition to those frazzled engineers who often have to make do with less than optimal conditions.

Works Cited

1. Turley, Jim. "High Integration is Key for Major Design Wins." A paper presented at the Embedded Processor Forum, San Jose, 15 October 1998.
2. Levy, Marcus. "EDN Microprocessor/Microcontroller Directory." *EDN*, 14 September 2000.

Chapter 1

The Embedded Design Life Cycle

Unlike the design of a software application on a standard platform, the design of an embedded system implies that both software and hardware are being designed in parallel. Although this isn't always the case, it is a reality for many designs today. The profound implications of this simultaneous design process heavily influence how systems are designed.

Introduction

Figure 1.1 provides a schematic representation of the embedded design life cycle (which has been shown *ad nauseam* in marketing presentations).

Time flows from the left and proceeds through seven phases:

- Product specification
- Partitioning of the design into its software and hardware components
- Iteration and refinement of the partitioning
- Independent hardware and software design tasks
- Integration of the hardware and software components
- Product testing and release
- On-going maintenance and upgrading

The embedded design process is not as simple as Figure 1.1 depicts. A considerable amount of iteration and optimization occurs within phases and between phases. Defects found in later stages often cause you to "go back to square 1." For example, when product testing reveals performance deficiencies that render the design non-competitive, you might have to rewrite algorithms, redesign custom hardware — such as Application-Specific Integrated Circuits (ASICs) for better performance — speed up the processor, choose a new processor, and so on.

Figure 1.1 Embedded design life cycle diagram.

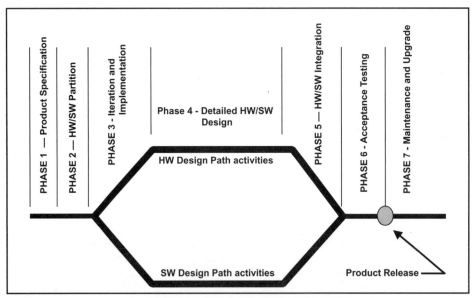

A phase representation of the embedded design life cycle.

Although this book is generally organized according to the life-cycle view in Figure 1.1, it can be helpful to look at the process from other perspectives. Dr. Daniel Mann, Advanced Micro Devices (AMD), Inc., has developed a tool-based view of the development cycle. In Mann's model, processor selection is one of the first tasks (see Figure 1.2). This is understandable, considering the selection of the *right* processor is of prime importance to AMD, a manufacturer of embedded microprocessors. However, it can be argued that including the choice of the microprocessor and some of the other key elements of a design in the specification phase is the correct approach. For example, if your existing code base is written for the 80X86 processor family, it's entirely legitimate to require that the next design also be able to leverage this code base. Similarly, if your design team is highly experienced using the Green Hills© compiler, your requirements document probably would specify that compiler as well.

The economics and reality of a design requirement often force decisions to be made before designers can consider the best design trade-offs for the next project. In fact, designers use the term "clean sheet of paper" when referring to a design opportunity in which the requirement constraints are minimal and can be strictly specified in terms of performance and cost goals.

Figure 1.2 shows the maintenance and upgrade phase. The engineers are responsible for maintaining and improving existing product designs until the burden of new features and requirements overwhelms the existing design. Usually, these engineers were not the same group that designed the original product. It's a miracle if the original designers are still around to answer questions about the product. Although more engineers maintain and upgrade projects than create new designs, few, if any, tools are available to help these designers reverse-engineer the product to make improvements and locate bugs. The tools used for maintenance and upgrading are the same tools designed for engineers creating new designs.

The remainder of this book is devoted to following this life cycle through the step-by-step development of embedded systems. The following sections give an overview of the steps in Figure 1.1.

Figure 1.2   Tools used in the design process.

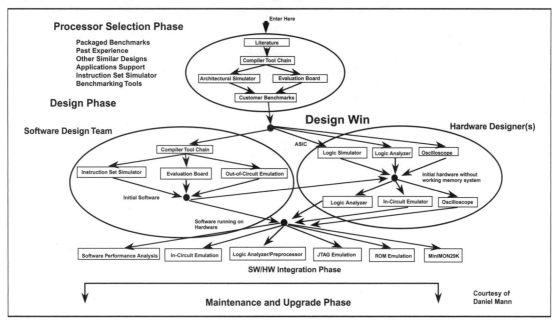

The embedded design cycle represented in terms of the tools used in the design process (courtesy of Dr. Daniel Mann, AMD Fellow, Advanced Micro Devices, Inc., Austin, TX).

Product Specification

Although this book isn't intended as a marketing manual, learning how to design an embedded system should include some consideration of designing the right embedded system. For many R&D engineers, designing the right product means cramming everything possible into the product to make sure they don't miss anything. Obviously, this wastes time and resources, which is why marketing and sales departments lead (or completely execute) the product-specification process for most companies. The R&D engineers usually aren't allowed customer contact in this early stage of the design. This shortsighted policy prevents the product design engineers from acquiring a useful customer perspective about their products.

Although some methods of customer research, such as questionnaires and focus groups, clearly belong in the realm of marketing specialists, most projects benefit from including engineers in some market-research activities, especially the customer visit or customer research tour.

The Ideal Customer Research Tour

The ideal research team is three or four people, usually a marketing or sales engineer and two or three R&D types. Each member of the team has a specific role during the visit. Often, these roles switch among the team members so each has an opportunity to try all the roles. The team prepares for the visit by developing a questionnaire to use to keep the interviews flowing smoothly. In general, the questionnaire consists of a set of open-ended questions that the team members fill in as they speak with the customers. For several customer visits, my research team spent more than two weeks preparing and refining the questionnaire.

(Considering the cost of a customer visit tour (about $1,000 per day, per person for airfare, hotels, meals, and loss of productivity), it's amazing how often little effort is put into preparing for the visit. Although it makes sense to visit your customers and get inside their heads, it makes more sense to prepare properly for the research tour.)

The lead interviewer is often the marketing person, although it doesn't have to be. The second team member takes notes and asks follow-up questions or digs down even deeper. The remaining team members are observers and technical resources. If the discussion centers on technical issues, the other team members might have to speak up, especially if the discussion concerns their area of expertise. However, their primary function is to take notes, listen carefully, and look around as much as possible.

After each visit ends, the team meets off-site for a debriefing. The debriefing step is as important as the visit itself to make sure the team members retain the following:

- What did each member hear?

- What was explicitly stated? What was implicit?

- Did they like what we had or were they being polite?

- Was someone really turned on by it?

- Did we need to refine our presentation or the form of the questionnaire?

- Were we talking to the right people?

As the debriefing continues, team members take additional notes and jot down thoughts. At the end of the day, one team member writes a summary of the visit's results.

After returning from the tour, the effort focuses on translating what the team heard from the customers into a set of product requirements to act on. These sessions are often the most difficult and the most fun. The team often is passionate in its arguments for the customers and equally passionate that the customers don't know what they want. At some point in this process, the information from the visit is distilled down to a set of requirements to guide the team through the product development phase.

Often, teams single out one or more customers for a second or third visit as the product development progresses. These visits provide a reality check and some midcourse corrections while the impact of the changes are minimal.

Participating in the customer research tour as an R&D engineer on the project has a side benefit. Not only do you have a design specification (hopefully) against which to design, you also have a picture in your mind's eye of your team's ultimate objective. A little voice in your ear now biases your endless design decisions toward the common goals of the design team. This extra insight into the product specifications can significantly impact the success of the project.

A senior engineering manager studied projects within her company that were successful not only in the marketplace but also in the execution of the product-development process. Many of these projects were embedded systems. Also, she studied projects that had failed in the market or in the development process.

Flight Deck on the Bass Boat?

Having spent the bulk of my career as an R&D engineer and manager, I am continually fascinated by the process of turning a concept into a product. Knowing how to ask the right questions of a potential customer, understanding his needs, determining the best feature and price point, and handling all the other details of research are not easy, and certainly not straightforward to number-driven engineers.

One of the most valuable classes I ever attended was conducted by a marketing professor at Santa Clara University on how to conduct customer research. I learned that the customer wants everything yesterday and is unwilling to pay for any of it. If you ask a customer whether he wants a feature, he'll say yes every time. So, how do you avoid building an aircraft carrier when the customer really needs a fishing boat? First of all, don't ask the customer whether the product should have a flight deck. Focus your efforts on understanding what the customer wants to accomplish and then extend his requirements to your product. As a result, the product and features you define are an abstraction and a distillation of the needs of your customer.

A common factor for the successful products was that the design team shared a common vision of the product they were designing. When asked about the product, everyone involved — senior management, marketing, sales, quality assurance, and engineering — would provide the same general description. In contrast, many failed products did not produce a consistent articulation of the project goals. One engineer thought it was supposed to be a low-cost product with medium performance. Another thought it was to be a high-performance, medium-cost product, with the objective to maximize the performance-to-cost ratio. A third felt the goal was to get something together in a hurry and put it into the market as soon as possible.

Another often-overlooked part of the product-specification phase is the development tools required to design the product. Figure 1.2 shows the embedded life cycle from a different perspective. This "design tools view" of the development cycle highlights the variety of tools needed by embedded developers.

When I designed in-circuit emulators, I saw products that were late to market because the engineers did not have access to the best tools for the job. For example, only a third of the hard-core embedded developers ever used in-circuit emulators, even though they were the tools of choice for difficult debugging problems.

The development tools requirements should be part of the product specification to ensure that unreal expectations aren't being set for the product development cycle and to minimize the risk that the design team won't meet its goals.

One of the smartest project development methods of which I'm aware is to begin each team meeting or project review meeting by showing a list of the project musts and wants. Every project stakeholder must agree that the list is still valid. If things have changed, then the project manager declares the project on hold until the differences are resolved. In most cases, this means that the project schedule and deliverables are no longer valid. When this happens, it's a big deal—comparable to an assembly line worker in an auto plant stopping the line because something is not right with the manufacturing process of the car.

In most cases, the differences are easily resolved and work continues, but not always. Sometimes a competitor may force a re-evaluation of the product features. Sometimes, technologies don't pan out, and an alternative approach must be found. Since the alternative approach is generally not as good as the primary approach, design compromises must be factored in.

Hardware/Software Partitioning

Since an embedded design will involve both hardware and software components, someone must decide which portion of the problem will be solved in hardware and which in software. This choice is called the "partitioning decision."

Application developers, who normally work with pre-defined hardware resources, may have difficulty adjusting to the notion that the hardware can be enhanced to address any arbitrary portion of the problem. However, they've probably already encountered examples of such a hardware/software tradeoff. For example, in the early days of the PC (i.e., before the introduction of the 80486 processor), the 8086, 80286, and 80386 CPUs didn't have an on-chip floating-point processing unit. These processors required companion devices, the 8087, 80287, and 80387 floating-point units (FPUs), to directly execute the floating-point instructions in the application code.

If the PC did not have an FPU, the application code had to trap the floating-point instructions and execute an exception or trap routine to emulate the behavior of the hardware FPU in software. Of course, this was much slower than having the FPU on your motherboard, but at least the code ran.

As another example of hardware/software partitioning, you can purchase a modem card for your PC that plugs into an ISA slot and contains the modulation/demodulation circuitry on the board. For less money, however, you can purchase a Winmodem that plugs into a PCI slot and uses your PC's CPU to directly handle the modem functions. Finally, if you are a dedicated PC gamer, you know how important a high-performance video card is to game speed.

If you generalize the concept of the algorithm to the steps required to implement a design, you can think of the algorithm as a combination of hardware components and software components. Each of these hardware/software partitioning examples implements an algorithm. You can implement that algorithm purely in software (the CPU without the FPU example), purely in hardware (the dedicated modem chip example), or in some combination of the two (the video card example).

Laser Printer Design Algorithm

Suppose your embedded system design task is to develop a laser printer. Figure 1.3 shows the algorithm for this project. With help from laser printer designers, you can imagine how this task might be accomplished in software. The processor places the incoming data stream — via the parallel port, RS-232C serial port, USB port, or Ethernet port — into a memory buffer.

Concurrently, the processor services the data port and converts the incoming data stream into a stream of modulation and control signals to a laser tube, rotating mirror, rotating drum, and assorted paper-management "stuff." You can see how this would bog down most modern microprocessors and limit the performance of the system.

You could try to improve performance by adding more processors, thus dividing the concurrent tasks among them. This would speed things up, but without more information, it's hard to determine whether that would be an optimal solution for the algorithm.

When you analyze the algorithm, however, you see that certain tasks critical to the performance of the system are also bounded and well-defined. These tasks can be easily represented by design methods that can be translated to a hardware-based solution. For this laser printer design, you could dedicate a hardware block to the process of writing the laser dots onto the photosensitive surface of the printer drum. This frees the processor to do other tasks and only requires it to initialize and service the hardware if an error is detected.

This seems like a fruitful approach until you dig a bit deeper. The requirements for hardware are more stringent than for software because it's more complicated and costly to fix a hardware defect then to fix a software bug. If the hardware is a custom application-specificc IC (ASIC), this is an even greater consideration because of the overall complexity of designing a custom integrated circuit. If this approach is deemed too risky for this project, the design team must fine-tune the software so that the hardware-assisted circuit devices are not necessary. The risk-management trade-off now becomes the time required to analyze the code and decide whether a software-only solution is possible.

The design team probably will conclude that the required acceleration is not possible unless a newer, more powerful microprocessor is used. This involves costs as well: new tools, new board layouts, wider data paths, and greater complexity. Performance improvements of several orders of magnitude are common when specialized hardware replaces software-only designs; it's hard to realize 100X or 1000X performance improvements by fine-tuning software.

These two very different design philosophies are successfully applied to the design of laser printers in two real-world companies today. One company has highly developed its ability to fine-tune the processor performance to minimize the need for specialized hardware. Conversely, the other company thinks nothing of throwing a team of ASIC designers at the problem. Both companies have competitive products but implement a different design strategy for partitioning the design into hardware and software components.

Figure 1.3   The laser printer design.

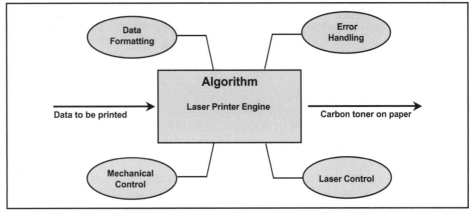

A laser printer design as an algorithm. Data enters the printer and must be transformed into a legible ensemble of carbon dots fused to a piece of paper.

The partitioning decision is a complex optimization problem. Many embedded system designs are required to be

- Price sensitive
- Leading-edge performers
- Non-standard
- Market competitive
- Proprietary

These conflicting requirements make it difficult to create an optimal design for the embedded product. The algorithm partitioning certainly depends on which processor you use in the design and how you implement the overall design in the hardware. You can choose from several hundred microprocessors, microcontrollers, and custom ASIC cores. The choice of the CPU impacts the partitioning decision, which impacts the tools decisions, and so on.

Given this *n*-space of possible choices, the designer or design team must rely on experience to arrive at an optimal design. Also, the solution surface is generally smooth, which means an adequate solution (possibly driven by an entirely different constraint) is often not far off the best solution. Constraints usually dictate the decision path for the designers, anyway. However, when the design exercise isn't well understood, the decision process becomes much more interesting. You'll read more concerning the hardware/software partitioning problem in Chapter 3.

Iteration and Implementation

(Before Hardware and Software Teams Stop Communicating)

The iteration and implementation part of the process represents a somewhat blurred area between implementation and hardware/software partitioning (refer to Figure 1.1 on page 2) in which the hardware and software paths diverge. This phase represents the early design work before the hardware and software teams build "the wall" between them.

The design is still very fluid in this phase. Even though major blocks might be partitioned between the hardware components and the software components, plenty of leeway remains to move these boundaries as more of the design constraints are understood and modeled. In Figure 1.2 earlier in this chapter, Mann represents the iteration phase as part of the selection process. The hardware designers might be using simulation tools, such as architectural simulators, to model the performance of the processor and memory systems. The software designers are probably running code benchmarks on self-contained, single-board computers that use the target microprocessor. These single-board computers are often referred to as evaluation boards because they evaluate the performance of the microprocessor by running test code on it. The evaluation board also provides a convenient software design and debug environment until the real system hardware becomes available.

You'll learn more about this stage in later chapters. Just to whet your appetite, however, consider this: The technology exists today to enable the hardware and software teams to work closely together and keep the partitioning process actively engaged longer and longer into the implementation phase. The teams have a greater opportunity to get it right the first time, minimizing the risk that something might crop up late in the design phase and cause a major schedule delay as the teams scramble to fix it.

Detailed Hardware and Software Design

This book isn't intended to teach you how to write software or design hardware. However, some aspects of embedded software and hardware design are unique to the discipline and should be discussed in detail. For example, after one of my lectures, a student asked, "Yes, but how does the code actually get into the microprocessor?" Although well-versed in C, C++, and Java, he had never faced having to initialize an environment so that the C code could run in the first place. Therefore, I have devoted separate chapters to the development environment and special software techniques.

I've given considerable thought how deeply I should describe some of the hardware design issues. This is a difficult decision to make because there is so much material that could be covered. Also, most electrical engineering students have taken courses in digital design and microprocessors, so they've had ample opportunity to be exposed to the actual hardware issues of embedded systems design. Some issues are worth mentioning, and I'll cover these as necessary.

Figure 1.4 Where design time is spent.

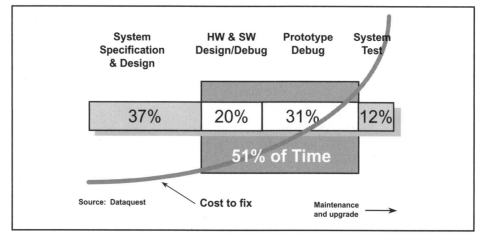

The percentage of project time spent in each phase of the embedded design life cycle. The curve shows the cost associated with fixing a defect at each stage of the process.

Hardware/Software Integration

The hardware/software integration phase of the development cycle must have special tools and methods to manage the complexity. The process of integrating embedded software and hardware is an exercise in debugging and discovery. Discovery is an especially apt term because the software team now finds out whether it really understood the hardware specification document provided by the hardware team.

Big Endian/Little Endian Problem

One of my favorite integration discoveries is the "little endian/big endian" syndrome. The hardware designer assumes big endian organization, and the software designer assumes little endian byte order. What makes this a classic example of an interface and integration error is that both the software and hardware could be correct in isolation but fail when integrated because the "endianness" of the interface is misunderstood.

Suppose, for example that a serial port is designed for an ASIC with a 16-bit I/O bus. The port is memory mapped at address 0x400000. Eight bits of the word are the data portion of the port, and the other eight bits are the status portion of the port. Even though the hardware designer might specify what bits are status and what bits are data, the software designer could easily assign the wrong port address if writes to the port are done as byte accesses (Figure 1.5).

Figure 1.5   An example of the endianness problem in I/O addressing.

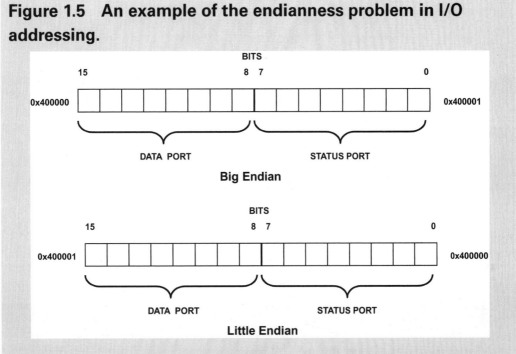

If byte addressing is used and the big endian model is assumed, then the algorithm should check the status at address 0x400001. Data should be read from and written to address 0x400000. If the little endian memory model is assumed, then the reverse is true. If 16-bit addressing is used, i.e., the port is declared as

```
unsigned short int * io_port ;
```

then the endianness ambiguity problem goes away. This means that the software might become more complex because the developer will need to do bit manipulation in order to read and write data, thus making the algorithm more complex.

The Holy Grail of embedded system design is to combine the first hardware prototype, the application software, the driver code, and the operating system software together with a pinch of optimism and to have the design work perfectly out of the chute. No green wires on the PC board, no "dead bugs," no redesigning the ASICs or Field Programmable Gate Arrays (FPGA), and no rewriting the software. Not likely, but I did say it was the Holy Grail.

> **Note**   Here "dead bugs" are extra ICs glued to the board with their I/O pins facing up. Green wires are then soldered to their "legs" to patch them into the rest of the circuitry.

You might wonder why this scenario is so unlikely. For one thing, the real-time nature of embedded systems leads to highly complex, nondeterministic behavior that can only be analyzed as it occurs. Attempting to accurately model or simulate the behavior can take much longer than the usable lifetime of the product being developed. This doesn't necessarily negate what I said in the previous section; in fact, it is shades of gray. As the modeling tools improve, so will the designer's ability to find bugs sooner in the process. Hopefully, the severity of the bugs that remain in the system can be easily corrected after they are uncovered. In *Embedded Systems Programming*[1], Michael Barr discusses a software architecture that anticipates the need for code patches and makes it easy to insert them without major restructuring of the entire code image. I devote Chapters 6, , and to debugging tools and techniques.

Debugging an Embedded System

In most ways, debugging an embedded system is similar to debugging a host-based application. If the target system contains an available communications channel to the host computer, the debugger can exist as two pieces: a debug kernel in the target system and a host application that communicates with it and manages the source database and symbol tables. (You'll learn more about this later on as well.) Remember, you can't always debug embedded systems using only the methods of the host computer, namely a good debugger and `printf()` statements.

Many embedded systems are impossible to debug unless they are operating at full speed. Running an embedded program under a debugger can slow the program down by one or more orders of magnitude. In most cases, scaling all the real-time dependencies back so that the debugger becomes effective is much more work than just using the correct tools to debug at full speed.

Manufacturers of embedded microprocessors also realize the difficulty of controlling these variables, so they've provided on-chip hooks to assist in the debugging of embedded systems containing their processors. Most designers won't even consider using a microprocessor in an embedded application unless the silicon manufacturer can demonstrate a complete tool chain for designing and debugging its silicon.

In general, there are three requirements for debugging an embedded or real-time system:

- Run control — The ability to start, stop, peak, and poke the processor and memory.

- Memory substitution — Replacing ROM-based memory with RAM for rapid and easy code download, debug, and repair cycles.

- Real-time analysis — Following code flow in real time with real-time trace analysis.

For many embedded systems, it is necessary also to integrate a commercial or in-house real-time operating system (RTOS) into the hardware and application software. This integration presents its own set of problems (more variables); the underlying behavior of the operating system is often hidden from the designers because it is obtained as object code from the vendor, which means these bugs are now masked by the RTOS and that another special tool must be used.

This tool is usually available from the RTOS vendor (for a price) and is indispensable for debugging the system with the RTOS present. The added complexity doesn't change the three requirements previously listed; it just makes them more complex. Add the phrase "and be RTOS aware" to each of the three listed requirements, and they would be equally valid for a system containing a RTOS.

The general methods of debugging that you've learned to use on your PC or workstation are pretty much the same as in embedded systems. The exceptions are what make it interesting. It is an exercise in futility to try to debug a software module when the source of the problem lies in the underlying hardware or the operating system. Similarly, it is nearly impossible to find a bug that can only be observed when the system is running at full speed when the only trace capability available is to single-step the processor. However, with these tools at your disposal, your approach to debugging will be remarkably similar to debugging an application designed to run on your PC or workstation.

Product Testing and Release

Product testing takes on special significance when the performance of the embedded system has life or death consequences attached. You can shrug off an occasional lock-up of your PC, but you can ill-afford a software failure if the PC controls a nuclear power generating station's emergency system. Therefore, the testing and reliability requirements for an embedded system are much more stringent than the vast majority of desktop applications. Consider the embedded systems currently supporting your desktop PC: IDE disk drive, CD-ROM, scanner, printer, and other devices are all embedded systems in their own right. How many times have they failed to function so that you had to cycle power to them?

From the Trenches

For the longest time, my PC had a nagging problem of crashing in the middle of my word processor or graphics application. This problem persisted through Windows 95, 95 Sr-1, 98, and 98 SE. After blaming Microsoft for shoddy software, I later discovered that I had a hardware problem in my video card. After replacing the drivers and the card, the crashes went away, and my computer is behaving well. I guess hardware/software integration problems exist on the desktop as well.

However, testing is more than making sure the software doesn't crash at a critical moment, although it is by no means an insignificant consideration. Because embedded systems usually have extremely tight design margins to meet cost goals, testing must determine whether the system is performing close to its optimal capabilities. This is especially true if the code is written in a high-level language and the design team consists of many developers.

Many desktop applications have small memory leaks. Presumably, if the application ran long enough, the PC would run out of heap space, and the computer would crash. However, on a desktop machine with 64MB of RAM and virtual swap space, this is unlikely to be a problem. On the other side, in an embedded system, running continuously for weeks at a time, even a small memory leak is potentially disastrous.

Who Does the Testing?

In many companies, the job of testing the embedded product goes to a separate team of engineers and technicians because asking a designer to test his own code or product usually results in erratic test results. It also might lead to a "circle the wagons" mentality on the part of the design team, who view the testers as a roadblock to product release, rather than equal partners trying to prevent a defective product from reaching the customer.

Referring to Figure 1.4, notice the exponential rise in the cost to fix a defect the later you are in the design cycle. In many instances, the Test Engineering Group is the last line of defense between a smooth product release and a major financial disaster.

Like debugging, many of the elements of reliability and performance testing map directly on the best practices for host-based software development. Much has been written about the correct way to develop software, so I won't cover that again here. What is relevant to this subject is the best practices for testing software that has mission-critical or tight performance

Compliance Testing

Compliance testing is often overlooked. Modern embedded systems are awash in radio frequency (RF) energy. If you've traveled on a plane in the last five years, you're familiar with the requirement that all electronic devices be turned off when the plane descends below 10,000 feet. I'm not qualified to discuss the finer points of RF suppression and regulatory compliance requirements; however, I have spent many hours at open field test sites with various compliance engineering (CE) engineers trying just to get one peak down below the threshold to pass the class B test and ship the product.

I can remember one disaster when the total cost of the RF suppression hardware that had to be added came to about one-third of the cost of all the other hardware combined. Although it can be argued that this is the realm of the hardware designer and not a hardware/software design issue, most digital hardware designers have little or no training in the arcane art of RF suppression. Usually, the hotshot digital wizard has to seek out the last remaining analog designer to get clued in on how to knock down the fourth harmonic at 240MHz. Anyway, CE testing is just as crucial to a product's release as any other aspect of the test program.

CE testing had a negative impact on my hardware/software integration activities in one case. I thought we had done a great job of staying on top of the CE test requirements and had built up an early prototype especially for CE testing. The day of the tests, I proudly presented it to the CE engineer on schedule. He then asked for the test software that was supposed to exercise the hardware while the RF emissions were being monitored. Whoops, I completely forgot to write drivers to exercise the hardware. After some scrambling, we pieced together some of the turn-on code and convinced the CE engineer (after all, he had to sign all the forms) that the code was representative of the actual operational code.

constraints associated with it. Just as with the particular problems associated with debugging a real-time system, testing the same system can be equally challenging. I'll address this and other testing issues in Chapter 9.

Maintaining and Upgrading Existing Products

The embedded system tool community has made almost no effort to develop tools specifically targeted to products already in service. At first blush, you might not see this as a problem. Most commercially developed products are well documented, right?

The majority of embedded system designers (around 60 percent) maintain and upgrade existing products, rather than design new products. Most of these engineers were not members of the original design team for a particular product, so they must rely on only their experience, their skills, the existing documentation, and the old product to understand the original design well enough to maintain and improve it.

From the silicon vendor's point of view, this is an important gap in the tool chain because the vendor wants to keep that customer buying its silicon, instead of giving the customer the chance to do a "clean sheet of paper" redesign. Clean sheets of paper tend to have someone else's chip on them.

From the Trenches

One can hardly overstate the challenges facing some upgrade teams. I once visited a telecomm manufacturer that builds small office phone systems to speak to the product-support team. The team described the situation as: "They wheel the thing in on two carts. The box is on one cart, and the source listings are on the other. Then they tell us to make it better." This usually translates to improving the overall performance of the embedded system without incurring the expense of a major hardware redesign.

Another example features an engineer at a company that makes laser and ink-jet printers. His job is to study the assembly language output of their C and C++ source code and fine-tune it to improve performance by improving the code quality. Again, no hardware redesigns are allowed.

Both of these examples testify to the skill of these engineers who are able to reverse-engineer and improve upon the work of the original design teams.

This phase of a product's life cycle requires tools that are especially tailored to reverse engineering and rapidly facilitating "what if ..." scenarios. For example, it's tempting to try a quick fix by speeding up the processor clock by 25 percent; however, this could cause a major ripple effect through the entire design, from memory chip access time margins to increased RF emissions. If such a possibility could be as easily explored as making measurements on a few critical code modules, however, you would have an extremely powerful tool on your hands.

Sometimes, the solutions to improved performance are embarrassingly simple. For example, a data communications manufacturer was about to completely redesign a product when the critical product review uncovered that the processor was spending most of its time in a debug module that was erroneously left in the final build of the object code. It was easy to find because the support teams had access to sophisticated tools that enabled them to observe the code as it executed in real time. Without the tools, the task might have been too time-consuming to be worthwhile.

Even with these test cases, every marketing flyer for every tool touts the tool's capability to speed "time to market." I've yet to hear any tool vendor advertise its tool as speeding "time to reverse-engineer," although one company claimed that its logic analyzer sped up the "time to insight."

Summary

Embedded systems projects aren't just "software on small machines." Unlike application development, where the hardware is a *fait accompli*, embedded projects are usually optimization exercises that strive to create both hardware and software that complement each other. This difference is the driving force that defines the three most characteristic elements of the embedded design cycle: selection, partitioning, and system integration. This difference also colors testing and debugging, which must be adapted to work with unproven, proprietary hardware.

While these characteristic differences aren't all there is to embedded system design, they are what most clearly differentiate it from application development, and thus, they are the main focus of this book. The next chapter discusses the processor selection decision. Later chapters address the other issues.

Work Cited

1. Barr, Michael. "Architecting Embedded Systems for Add-on Software Modules." *Embedded Systems Programming*, September 1999, 49.

Chapter 2

The Selection Process

Embedded systems represent target platforms that are usually specific to a single task. This specificity means the system design can be highly optimized because the range of tasks the device must perform is well bounded. In other words, you wouldn't use your PC to run your coffee machine (you might, but that's beside the point). Unlike your desktop processor, the 4-bit microcontroller that runs your coffee machine costs less than $1 in large quantities. It does exactly what it's supposed to do to — make your coffee. It doesn't play Zelda, nor does it exchange data with an Internet service provider (ISP), although that might change soon. Because the functionality of the device is so narrowly defined, you must find the optimal processing element (CPU) for the design. Given the several hundred choices available and the many variations within those choices, choosing the right CPU can be a daunting task.

Although choosing a processor is a complex task that defies simple "optimization" (see Figure 2.1) in all but the simplest projects, the final choice must pass four critical tests:

- Is it available in a suitable implementation?
- Is it capable of sufficient performance?
- Is it supported by a suitable operating system?
- Is it supported by appropriate and adequate tools?

Is the Processor Available in a Suitable Implementation? Cost-sensitive projects might require an off-the-shelf, highly integrated part. High-performance applications might require gate-to-gate delays that are only practical when the entire design is fabricated on a single chip. What good is choosing the highest performing processor if the cost of goods makes your product noncompetitive in the marketplace? For example, industrial control equipment manufacturers that commonly provide product support and replacement parts with a 20-year lifetime won't choose a microprocessor from a vendor that can't guarantee product availability over a reasonable span of time. Similarly, if a processor isn't available in a military version, you wouldn't choose it for a missile guidance system, no matter how good the specs are. In many cases, packaging and implementation technology issues significantly limit the choice of architecture and instruction set.

Figure 2.1 Choosing the right processor.

Considerations for choosing the right microprocessor for an embedded application.

Is the Processor Capable of Sufficient Performance? Ultimately, the processor must be able to do the job on time. Unfortunately, as embedded systems become more complex, characterizing "the job" becomes more difficult. As the mix of tasks managed by the processor becomes more diverse (not just button presses and motor encoding but now also Digital Signal Processor [DSP] algorithms and network processing), the bottlenecks that limit performance often have less to do with computational power than with the "fit" between the architecture and the device's more demanding tasks. For this reason, it can be difficult to correlate benchmark results with how a processor will perform in a particular device.

Is the Processor Supported by an Appropriate Operating System?   With today's 32-bit microprocessors, it's natural to see an advantage in choosing a commercial RTOS. You might prefer one vendor's RTOS, such as VxWorks or pSOS from Wind River Systems. Porting the RTOS kernel to a new or different microprocessor architecture and having it specifically optimized to take advantage of the low-level performance features of that microprocessor is not a task for the faint-hearted. So, the microprocessor selection also might depend on having support for the customer's preferred RTOS.

Is the Processor Supported by Appropriate and Adequate Tools?   Good tools are critical to project success. The specific toolset necessary depends on the nature of the project to a certain extent. At a minimum, you'll need a good cross-compiler and good debugging support. In many situations, you'll need far more, such as in-circuit emulators (ICE), simulators, and so on.

Although these four considerations must be addressed in every processor-selection process, in many cases, the optimal fit to these criteria isn't necessarily the best choice. Other organizational and business issues might limit your choices even further. For example, time-to-market constraints might make it imperative that you choose an architecture with which the design team is already familiar. A corporate commitment or industry preference for a particular vendor or family also can be an important factor.

Packaging the Silicon

Until recently, designers have been limited to the choice of microprocessor versus microcontroller. Recent advances in semiconductor technology have increased the designer's choices. Now, at least for mass-market products, it might make sense to consider a system-on-a-chip (SOC) implementation, either using a standard part or using a semi-custom design compiled from licensed intellectual property. The following section begins the discussion of these issues by looking at the traditional microprocessor versus microcontroller trade-offs. Later sections explore some of the issues relating to more highly integrated solutions.

Microprocessor versus Microcontroller

Most embedded systems use microcontrollers instead of microprocessors. Sometimes the distinction is blurry, but in general, a microprocessor is the CPU without any additional peripheral or support devices. Microcontrollers are designed to need a minimum complement of external parts. Figure 2.2 illustrates the difference. The diagram on the left side of the figure shows a typical microprocessor system constructed of discrete components. The diagram on the right shows the same system but now integrated within a single package.

Figure 2.2   Microcontrollers versus microprocessors.

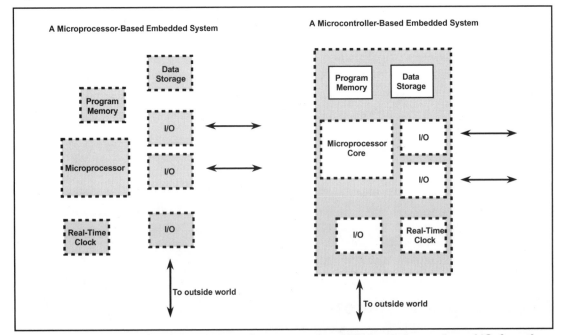

In a microprocessor-based system, the CPU and the various I/O functions are packaged as separate ICs. In a microcontroller-based system many, if not all, of the I/O functions are integrated into the same package with the CPU.

The advantages of the microcontroller's higher level of integration are easy to see:

- Lower cost — One part replaces many parts.
- More reliable — Fewer packages, fewer interconnects.
- Better performance — System components are optimized for their environment.

- Faster — Signals can stay on the chip.
- Lower RF signature — Fast signals don't radiate from a large PC board.

Thus, it's obvious why microcontrollers have become so prevalent and even dominate the entire embedded world. Given that these benefits derive directly from the higher integration levels in microcontrollers, it's only reasonable to ask "why not integrate even more on the main chip?" A quick examination of the economics of the process helps answer this question.

Silicon Economics

For most of the major silicon vendors in the United States, Japan, and Europe, high-performance processors also mean high profit margins. Thus, the newest CPU designs tend to be introduced into applications in which cost isn't the all-consuming factor as it is in embedded applications. Not surprisingly, a new CPU architecture first appears in desktop or other high-performance applications.

As the family of products continues to evolve, the newer design takes its place as the flagship product. The latest design is characterized by having the highest transistor count, the lowest yield of good dies, the most advanced fabrication process, the fastest clock speeds, and the best performance. Many customers pay a premium to access this advanced technology in an attempt to gain an advantage in their own markets. Many other customers won't pay the premium, however.

As the silicon vendor continues to improve the process, its yields begin to rise, and its profit margins go up. The earlier members of the family can now take advantage of the new process and be re-engineered in this new process (silicon vendors call this a *shrink*), and the resulting part can be sold at a reduced cost because the die size is now smaller, yielding many more parts for a given wafer size. Also, because the R&D costs have been recovered by selling the microprocessor version at a premium, a lower price becomes acceptable for the older members of the family.

Using the Core As the Basis of a Microcontroller

The silicon vendor also can take the basic microprocessor core and use it as the basis of a microcontroller. Cost-reducing the microprocessor core might inevitably lead to a family of microcontroller devices, all based on a core architecture that once was a stand-alone microprocessor. For example, Intel's 8086 processor led to the 80186 family of devices. Motorola's 68000 and 68020 CPUs led to the 68300 family of devices. The list goes on.

System-on-Silicon (SoS)

Today, it's common for a customer with reasonable volume projections to completely design an application-specific microcontroller containing multiple CPU elements and multiple peripheral devices on a single silicon die. Typically, the individual elements are not designed from scratch but are licensed (in the form of "synthesizable" VHDL[1] or Verilog specifications) from various IC design houses. Engineers connect these modules with custom interconnect logic, creating a chip that contains the entire design. Condensing these elements onto a single piece of silicon is called system-on-silicon (SoS) or SOC. Chapter 3 on hardware and software partitioning discusses this trend. The complexity of modern SOCs are going far beyond the relatively "simple" microcontrollers in use today.

Adequate Performance

Although performance is only one of the considerations when selecting processors, engineers are inclined to place it above the others, perhaps because performance is expected to be a tangible metric both absolutely and relatively with respect to other processors. However, as you'll see in the following sections, this is not the case.

Performance-Measuring Tools

For many professionals, benchmarking is almost synonymous with Dhrystones and MIPS. Engineers tend to expect that if processor A benchmarks at 1.5 MIPS, and Processor B benchmarks at 0.8 MIPS, then processor A is a better choice. This inference is so wrong that some have suggested MIPS should mean: Meaningless Indicator of Performance for Salesmen.

MIPS were originally defined in terms of the VAX 11/780 minicomputer. This was the first machine that could run 1 million instructions per second (1 MIPS). An instruction, however, is a one-dimensional metric that might not have anything to do with the way work scales on different machine architectures. With that in mind, which accounts for more work, executing 1,500 instructions on a RISC architecture or executing 1,000 instructions on a CISC architecture? Unless you are comparing VAX to VAX, MIPS doesn't mean much.

The Dhrystone benchmark is a simple C program that compiles to about 2,000 lines of assembly code and is independent of operating system ser-

---

1. VHDL stands for VHSIC (very high-speed IC) hardware description language.

vices. The Dhrystone benchmark was also calibrated to the venerable VAX. Because a VAX 11/70 could execute 1,757 loops through the Dhrystone benchmark in 1 second, 1,757 loops became 1 Dhrystone. The problem with the Dhrystone test is that a crafty compiler designer can optimize the compiler to blast through the Dhrystone benchmark and do little else well.

Distorting the Dhrystone Benchmark

Daniel Mann and Paul Cobb[5] provide an excellent analysis of the shortcomings of the Dhrystone benchmark. They analyze the Dhrystone and other benchmarks and point out the problems inherent in using the Dhrystone to compare embedded processor performance. The Dhrystone often misrepresents expected performance because the benchmark doesn't always use the processor in ways that parallel typical application use. For example, a particular problem arises because of the presence of on-chip instructions and data caches. If significant amounts (or all) of a benchmark can fit in an on-chip cache, this can skew the performance results.

Figure 2.3 compares the performance of three microprocessors for the Dhrystone benchmark on the left side of the chart and for the Link Access Protocol-D (LAPD) benchmark on the right side. The LAPD benchmark is more representative of communication applications. LAPD is the signaling protocol for the D-channel of ISDN. The benchmark is intended to measure a processor's capability to process a typical layered protocol stack.

Figure 2.3 Dhrystone comparison chart.

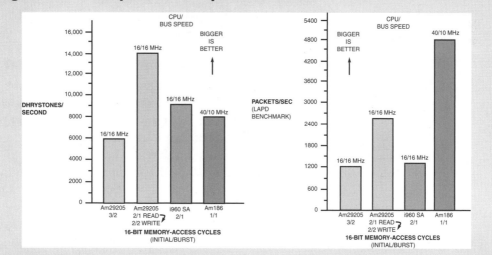

Comparing microprocessor performance for two benchmarks (courtesy of Mann and Cobb)[5].

Furthermore, Mann and Cobb point out that developers usually compile the Dhrystone benchmark using the string manipulation functions that are part of the C run-time library, which is normally part of the compiler vendor's software package. The compiler vendor usually optimizes these library functions as a good compromise between speed and code size. However, the compiler vendor could create optimized versions of these string-handling functions to yield more favorable Dhrystone results. This practice isn't necessarily dishonest, as long as a full disclosure is made to the end user.

A manufacturer can further abuse benchmark data by benchmarking its processor with a board that has fast static SRAM and then compare the results to a competitor's board that contains slower, but more economical, DRAM.

Meaningful Benchmarking

Real benchmarking involves carefully balancing system requirements and variables. How a processor runs in your application might be very different from its performance in a different application. You must consider many things when determining how well or poorly a processor might perform in benchmarking tests.

In particular, it's important to analyze the real-time behavior of the processor. Because most embedded processors must deal with real-time events, you might assume that the designers have factored this into their performance requirements for the processor. This assumption might or might not be correct because, once again, how to optimize for real-time problems isn't as obvious as you might expect. Real-time performance can be generally categorized into two buckets: interrupt handling and task switching. Both relate to the general problem of switching the context of the processor from one operation to another. Registers must be saved, variables must be pushed onto the stack, memory spaces must be swapped, and other housekeeping events must take place in both instances. How easy this is to accomplish, as well as how fast it can be carried out, are important in evaluating a processor that must be interfaced to events in the real world.

Predicting performance isn't easy. Many companies that blindly relied (sometimes with fervent reassurance from vendors) on overly simplistic benchmarking data have suffered severe consequences. The semiconductor vendors were often just as guilty as the compiler vendors of aggressively tweaking their processors to perform well in the Dhrystone tests.

From the Trenches

When you base early decisions on simplistic measures, such as benchmarks and throughput, you risk disasterous late surprises, as this story illustrates:

A certain embedded controller manufacturer, who shall remain nameless, was faced with a dilemma. The current product family was running out of gas, and it was time to do a re-evaluation of the current architecture. There was a strong desire to stay with the same processor family that they used in the previous design. The silicon manufacturer claimed that the newest member of the family benchmarked at twice the throughput of the previous version of the device (The clue here is *benchmarked*. What was the benchmark? How did it relate to the application code being used by this product team?). Since one of the design requirements was to double the throughput of the product, the design team opted to replace the existing embedded processor with the new one.

At first, the project progressed rapidly, since the designers could reuse much of their C and assembly code, as well as many of the software tools they had already purchased or developed. The problems became apparent when they finally began to run their own performance metrics on the new prototype hardware. Instead of the expected two-fold performance boost, their new design gave them only a 15-percent performance improvement, far less than what they needed to stay competitive in their market space.

The post-mortem analysis showed that the performance boost they expected could not be achieved by simply doubling the clock frequency or by using a more powerful processor. Their system design had bottlenecks liberally sprinkled throughout the hardware and software design. The processor could have been infinitely fast, and they still would not have gotten much better than a 15-percent boost.

EEMBC

Clearly, MIPS and Dhrystone measurements aren't adequate; designers still need something more tangible than marketing copy to use as a basis for their processor selection. To address this need, representatives of the semiconductor vendors, the compiler vendors, and their customers met under the leadership of Markus Levy (who was then the technical editor of *EDN* magazine) to create a more meaningful benchmark. The result is the EDN Embedded Microprocessor Benchmark Consortium, or EEMBC (pronounced "Embassy").

The EEMBC benchmark consists of industry-specific tests. Version 1.0 currently has 46 tests divided into five application suites. Table 2.1 shows the benchmark tests that make up 1.0 of the test suite.

Table 2.1 EEMBC tests list.

The 46 tests in the EEMBC benchmark are organized as five industry-specific suites.

EEMBC Test	
Automotive/Industrial Suite	
Angle-to-time conversion	Inverse discrete cosine transform
Basic floating point	Inverse Fast-Fourier transform (FFT) filter
Bit manipulation	Matrix arithmetic
Cache buster	Pointer chasing
CAN remote data request	Pulse-width modulation
Fast-Fourier transform (FFT)	Road speed calculation
Finite Impulse Response (FIR) filter	Table lookup and interpolation
Infinite Impulse Response (IIR) filter	Tooth-to-spark calculation
Consumer Suite	
Compress JPEG	RGB-to-CMYK conversion
Decompress JPEG	RGB-to-YIQ conversion
High-pass grayscale filter	
Networking Suite	
OSPF/Dijkstra routing	Packet Flow (1MB)
Lookup/Patricia algorithm	Packet Flow (2MB)
Packet flow (512B)	
Office Automation Suite	
Bezier-curve calculation	Image rotation
Dithering	Text processing

Telecommunications Suite	
Autocorrelation (3 tests)	Fixed-point complex FFT (3 tests)
Convolution encoder (3 tests)	Viterbi GSM decoder (4 tests)
Fixed-point bit allocation (3 tests)	

Unlike the Dhrystone benchmarks, the benchmarks developed by the EEMBC technical committee represent real-world algorithms against which the processor can be measured. Looking at the Automotive/Industrial suite of tests, for example, it's obvious that any embedded microprocessor involved in an engine-management system should be able to calculate a tooth-to-spark time interval efficiently.

The EEMBC benchmark produces statistics on the number of times per second the algorithm executes and the size of the compiled code. Because the compiler could have a dramatic impact on the code size and efficiency, each benchmark must contain a significant amount of information about the compiler and the settings of the various optimization switches.

Tom Halfhill[3] makes the argument that for embedded applications, it's probably better to leave the data in its raw form than to distill it into a single performance number, such as the SPECmark number used to benchmark workstations and servers. In the cost-sensitive world of the embedded designer, it isn't always necessary to have the highest performance, only that the performance be good enough for the application. In fact, higher performance usually (but not always) translates to higher speeds, more power consumption, and higher cost. Thus, knowing that the benchmark performance on a critical algorithm is adequate might be the only information the designer needs to select that processor for the application.

The source code used to develop the EEMBC benchmark suites was developed by various technical committees made up of representatives from the member companies. The EEMBC is on the right path and probably will become the industry standard for processor and compiler comparisons among embedded system designers.

Membership in the EEMBC is a bit pricey ($10K) for the casual observer, but the fee gives the members access to the benchmarking suites and to the testing labs.

Running Benchmarks

Typically, to run a benchmark, you use evaluation boards purchased from the manufacturer, or, if you are a good customer with a big potential sales opportunity, you might be given the board(s). All semiconductor manufacturers sell evaluation boards for their embedded microprocessors. These boards are essentially single-board computers and are often sold at a loss so that engineers can easily evaluate the processor for a potential design application. It's not unusual to design "hot boards," which are evaluation boards with fast processor-to-memory interfaces. These hot boards run small software modules, such as the Dhrystone benchmark, very quickly. This results in good MIPS numbers, but it isn't a fair test for a real system design.

When running benchmarks, especially comparative benchmarks, the engineering team should make sure it's comparing similar systems and not biasing the results against one of the processors under consideration. However, another equally valid benchmarking exercise is to make sure the processor that has been selected for the application will meet the requirements set out for it. You can assume that the manufacturer's published results will give you all the performance headroom you require, but the only way to know for sure is to verify the same data using your system and your code base.

Equipping the software team with evaluation platforms early in the design process has some real advantages. Aside from providing a cross-development environment early on, it gives the team the opportunity to gain valuable experience with the debugging and integration tools that have been selected for use later in the process. The RTOS, debug kernel, performance tools, and other components of the design suite also can be evaluated before crunch time takes over.

RTOS Availability

Choosing the RTOS — along with choosing the microprocessor — is one of the most important decisions the design team or system designer must make. Like a compiler that has been fine-tuned to the architecture of the processor, the RTOS kernel should be optimized for the platform on which it is running. A kernel written in C and recompiled (without careful retargeting) for a new platform can significantly reduce the system performance. Table 2.2 is a checklist to help you decide which RTOS is appropriate. Most of the factors are self-explanatory, but you'll find additional comments in the following sections.

Language/Microprocessor Support

Increasingly, RTOS vendors attempt to supply the design team with a "cradle-to-grave solution," which is also called "one-stop shopping." This approach makes sense for many applications but not all. To provide an integrated solution, the RTOS vendor often chooses compatible tool vendors and then further custom recrafts their tools to better fit the RTOS requirements. This means you might have to select the RTOS vendor's compiler, instead of your first choice. In other cases, to get the RTOS vendor's tools suite, you must choose from that vendor's list of supported microprocessors. Again, it depends on your priorities.

Table 2.2   Real-time operating system checklist. [4]

This checklist can help you determine which RTOS products are suitable for your project

Real-Time Operating System Checklist
✔ **Language/Microprocessing Support**
The first step in finding an RTOS for your project is to look at those vendors supporting the language and microprocessor you'll be using.
✔ **Tool Compatibility**
Make sure your RTOS works with your ICE, compiler, assembler, linker, and source code debugger.
✔ **Services**
Operating systems provide a variety of services. Make sure that your OS supports the services, such as queues, times, semaphores, etc., that you expect to use in your design.
✔ **Footprint**
RTOSs are often scalable, including only those services you end up needing for your application. Based on what services you'll need, the number of tasks, semaphores, and everything else you expect to use, make sure your RTOS will work in the RAM space and ROM space you have allocated for your design.
✔ **Performance**
Can your RTOS meet your performance requirements? Make sure that you understand the benchmarks the vendors give you and how they actually apply to the hardware you really will be using.
✔ **Software Components**
Are required components, such as protocol stacks, communication services, real-time databases, Web services, virtual machines, graphic libraries, and so on available for your RTOS? How much effort will be required to integrate them?

Real-Time Operating System Checklist
✔ **Device Drivers**
If you're using common hardware, are device drivers available for your RTOS?
✔ **Debugging Tools**
RTOS vendors may have debugging tools that help find defects that are much harder to find with standard source-level debuggers.
✔ **Standards Compatibility**
Are there safety or compatibility standards that your application demands? Make sure that your RTOS complies.
✔ **Technical Support**
Phone support is typically covered for a limited time after you purchase or on a year-to-year basis through a support contract. Sometimes application engineers are available. Additionally, some vendors provide training and consulting.
✔ **Source vs Object Code**
With some RTOSs, you get the source code when you buy a license. With others, you get only object code or linkable libraries.
✔ **Licensing**
Make sure that you understand how the RTOS vendor licenses their RTOS. With some vendors, run-time licenses are required for each board that you ship, and development tool licenses are required for each developer using the tools.
✔ **Reputation**
Make sure that you are dealing with a company with which you'll be happy.
✔ **Services**
Real-time operation systems provide developers with a full complement of features: several types of semaphores (counting, mutual exclusion), times, mailboxes, buffer managers, memory system managers, events, and more.

Tool Compatibility

To the RTOS vendors the world looks much like an archer's target. The RTOS and its requirements are at the center, and all the other tools — both hardware and software — occupy the concentric rings around it. Therefore, the appropriate way to reformulate this issue is to ask whether the tools you want to use are compatible with the RTOS. This might not be a serious problem because the RTOS is typically selected at the same time the processor is selected. Thus, the RTOS vendor has the opportunity to influence which additional tools are chosen. The RTOS vendor also has an opportunity to collect most of the available budget that has been allocated for tools procurement.

The developer should try, however, to create an environment in which all the development tool capabilities are leveraged to their maximum benefit. This does require cooperation between tool vendors, so the recommendation of the RTOS vendor is a good starting point but not the last word.

For example, an RTOS vendor might make the argument that its tools are so powerful that you don't need other specialized products, such as ICEs, real-time performance analyzers, and logic analyzers. This is a tempting thought because these more specialized development and debug tools usually are complex. However, plenty of hard evidence proves how subtle bugs can fall below the detection threshold of a software-only debug tool, and much time was wasted before the "big guns of debugging" were brought to bear on the problem.

Performance

Obviously, performance is a major issue that deserves a lot of research time up front. Most processor vendors have measured the context-switching times of various RTOS kernels with their silicon. Also, the silicon vendors try to appear "vendor-neutral" when it comes to recommending one RTOS vendor over another. They tend to let the data speak for itself. Also, because silicon vendors jealously guard the names of other customers, it's hard to get recommendations from other satisfied customers. Fortunately, if you are part of a large corporation with many other product-development divisions, it's relatively easy to find out what works and what doesn't.

Device Drivers

The availability of device drivers often is tied to the need to develop a board support package (BSP). The BSP consists of the set of drivers and the integration of those drivers into the RTOS kernel so that the RTOS operates smoothly with your hardware during development and in the field. You must be experienced to create a BSP because it can be an extremely difficult, defect-prone, and time-consuming activity. Many RTOS customers are influenced by the availability of a BSP for their hardware. This is particularly true if most of the processing hardware is a commercial off-the-shelf (COTS), single-board computer. Alternatively, the design team might choose to have the RTOS vendor's engineering team develop the BSP. Although it's an attractive alternative that can significantly reduce the development risks, it also can be costly (one BSP port cost a customer approximately $750K!).

Debugging Tools

Many debugging tool vendors believe the RTOS vendors have a "slash and burn, take no prisoners" attitude when it comes to the sale of debugging tools. Because the RTOS vendor is in the customer's decision process at an early stage, they have the opportunity to influence strongly how the development budget is apportioned. Although this can be self-serving because the RTOS vendor realizes a significant portion of its revenue from the sale of debugging tools, it also can be good for the customer. Debugging real-time software running under a commercial RTOS is not an easy process. In most cases, the user doesn't have visibility into the RTOS code itself, so the engineer must attempt to guess what's going on in the system. Having RTOS-aware tools is a great help in debugging this class of problems. If an RTOS vendor recommends its tool as the tool of choice, it's legitimate to question the assertion, but it's also important to ask other vendors about their abilities to debug code running under this RTOS.

Standards Compatibility

Because many embedded systems control devices that are mission critical, it makes sense to be sure the RTOS software you choose has already gone through a certification process and is deemed safe. For example, one RTOS vendor prominently advertises that its RTOS was chosen for the Mars Rover. This fact might or might not be relevant for your application, but it does convey a certain message about the reliability of the vendor's code base.

Technical Support

For most people, reading a technical manual is a painful experience. First, you're not even sure the information is in there. If the information happens to be in the manual, it's either hard to find or incredibly obtuse, so you phone the vendor. Don't underestimate the need for first-class tech support. Your next project could be at risk of failure without it.

Don't overlook consulting engineers.
Many consultants have developed more expertise with an RTOS than the vendor's internal engineering staff. I've worked with some who actually did much of the internal development for the RTOS vendor before seeking their fortune as an independent contractor. Consultants can be expensive, but they also can save your project.

Source Code vs. Object Code

Currently, a debate rages about using embedded Linux as a viable RTOS. Linux is freely available source code. Vendors who support this model sell you the support of the RTOS. They maintain versions, incorporate bug fixes as regular parts of their cycle, and sell consulting services to help you use it. They might also charge a licensing fee if you use their version of the code. It's too early to tell what Linux will achieve in the embedded marketplace. Product development teams have been able to get products to market using commercially available RTOSs that came as linkable libraries. As long you have faith that the RTOS vendor's code is defect free, that it supports your application needs, and that high-quality debugging tools exist that can work with it, you don't need the source code. However, most engineers have a strong urge to peek under the hood.

Services

One of the key reasons you choose an RTOS is that it provides already tested and integrated services. So, if you expect your target system to have an Ethernet communications link, you would most likely choose an RTOS that already has the support for the appropriate Ethernet protocol stacks. Also, you need to examine the overall system design to determine some of the fundamental design support issues. For example, do you expect to require communication of information between different tasks in your system? Are the data transfer rates generally equal, or are there variations in the rate of data generation and the rate of information consumption. If the data transfer rates are seriously mismatched, then you might need a message queue structure and a first-in, first-out (FIFO) buffer to level the loads. Conversely, you don't want to pay for complexity you don't need so scalability is also important.

Tool Chain Availability

Choosing the embedded design and debug development tools is as important as choosing the processor and RTOS. In some ways, the tool choices are even more important. If you don't select the right tools up front, when design decisions also are being made, debugging your design might take so long that the product will miss its market window. If you miss Comdex and are unable to show off your next generation of laser printer, for example, it might not be worth your while to continue the product development.

Multiprocessor designs are perfect examples of the necessity for debug strategies. Some telecommunications switches today contain more than 200 independent microprocessors, happily sending terabytes of data per second back and forth to each other. An engineering team has no hope of debugging such a system if they didn't design a debug strategy at the same time they designed the system.

When evaluating the tool chain, you should look for good, integrated coverage of these three broad categories:

- Compiler tools
- Hardware and software debugging tools
- Performance measuring tools

My Ideal Compiler

In an article written by Michael Barr[1], it's clear that the correct choice of a cross-compiler is more than just finding one that supports your target microprocessor. Your choice can be limited by hardware, RTOS, and debugging tool choices made by other team members. However, if you are able to choose without constraints, you should know how to compare cross compilers.

Features that improve the usability of a cross compiler include the following:

- In-line assembly — Although many cross compilers support the inclusion of assembly code as a separate "C-like" function, the best implementation is when in-line assembly code can be included in the compiler source file with the addition of the keyword asm. Whatever follows on that line or within the bracket-enclosed block that follows is assembled, not compiled.

- Interrupt function — The inclusion of the nonstandard keyword interrupt when used as a type specifier tells the compiler that this function is an interrupt service routine (ISR). The compiler then generates the extra stack information and registers saves and restores that are part of any ISR you write in assembly language.

- Assembly language list file generation — The assembly language list file contains C statements interspersed as comments with the assembly language instructions they generate, exactly as the processor would execute them. This feature is useful for manual code generation (and low-level debugging).

- Standard libraries — Many of the standard library functions that you expect to be included with your compiler are not part of standard C or C++; they might not be included with your compiler. This is particularly true of cross compilers, which are designed to be used with embedded systems. You should also be particularly careful that library functions are re-entrant.

- Startup code — Does the compiler include the assembly language code needed to establish the C run-time environment? This is the code that goes from RESET and ends with a JSR to main().

- RTOS support — Are your choices of compiler and RTOS compatible?

- Tools integration — Is your compiler choice compatible with the other tools (make utility, debugger, and so on) that you plan to use?

- Optimizations — Does the compiler support optimizations for speed and code size?

- Support for Embedded C++ (EC++) — To lower the overhead of C++ and make it more attractive for embedded system applications, the cross compiler should know the proper subset of the language it is restricted to use.

The inclusion of nonstandard keywords, such as asm and interrupt, tends to make the code nonportable. However, portability in embedded systems is often a hit or miss proposition, so relaxing the portability required in exchange for an application that works is a fair trade-off.

Compilers

A compiler can have a big effect on the apparent performance of a microprocessor, although it's not always obvious why. RISC processors are sensitive to the quality of object code generated by the compiler. To exploit the full potential of a RISC architecture, the compiler must know about the particular architecture. For example, the compiler might need to relocate instructions to follow delayed branches and certainly needs to be aware of the processor's particular register structure.

If you are coming to the field of embedded systems from the PC or workstation world, code-generating issues might be a new problem for you.

Suddenly, you might be forced to look at the assembly language output of your C compiler and count processor cycles, looking for ways to shave off microseconds here and there. Being informed about design decisions that might affect you can only help the product and the team, as well as improve your job security. However, challenging the selection choices of the system architects can be a career-defining moment, so use your newly acquired knowledge judiciously.

Choosing a compiler, however, is more than just a matter of choosing the best code generator. For embedded systems work, the compiler should support convenient access to particular features of the target hardware.

From the Trenches

One semiconductor manufacturer benchmarked three compilers — A, B, and C for this example — against each other with the same C code. The best and worst compiler differed by a factor of two. This is equivalent to running one processor with a clock speed of one-half the other processor!

In this case, the best code generator portion of the best compiler was written especially for this manufacturer's RISC architecture, while the worst compiler was a straight port from a classic CISC architecture. The CISC computer had 16 registers, and the RISC processor had 256 registers. The RISC processor could make up for its simpler instructions by keeping many variables nearby in the general-purpose register set. Because the CISC-based compiler did not take advantage of this feature, code generated by the compiler required many more memory accesses for the same code segment. External memory accesses require more clock cycles, so the code that it generated ran less efficiently than the optimized code.

Hardware and Software Debugging Tools

User preferences in software debugging tools tend to be highly personal. Some engineers must have the latest and greatest graphical user interface (GUI), whereas others like the speed and control of a text-based, command-line interface. Ideally, a modern debugger offers both types of interfaces, with the GUI automatically building and issuing the command-line interface as well. How the GUI connects to the target system, RTOS, and other debugging tools is covered in Chapter 6. Because it takes some amount of learning to gain experience with a debugger, embedded engineers (and their managers) put pressure on the tools manufacturers to port their debuggers to various "target agents." The target agent is usually the remote debug kernel, which resides in the target and communicates with the debugger. However, the target agent also can be:

- An ICE
- An interface to on-chip hardware debugging resources
- A ROM emulator
- A logic analyzer
- A performance analyzer

The customer benefits because the same debugger front end (DFE), or GUI, can be used with a variety of tools. So, the investment an engineer makes in learning the DFE for a debugger can be leveraged among several tools. The worst situation occurs when each tool has its own GUI, with no similarity to any other GUI, even from the same manufacturer!

The choice of the embedded design and debug development tools is every bit as important as the processor and RTOS choices. Perhaps, in some ways, the tool decisions are even more important. A case in point is the situation that exists today with multiprocessor designs. I am aware of some telecommunications switches containing over 200 independent microprocessors, happily sending terabytes of data per second back and forth to each other. How does an engineering team begin to debug this system? I would hope that they decided on a debug strategy at the same time as they designed the system.

Another example of the importance of the tool chain is the design effort required to develop an ASIC. In a speech[2.] to the 1997 IP Forum in Tokyo, Wilf Corrigan, the Chairman of LSI Logic, Inc., reported that design teams were finding that the effort required to develop an ASIC was five times greater than they had anticipated. Many ASICs had multiple, embedded processor cores in the design. Today, the tools that are the most appropriate for debugging systems-on-a-chip with multiple processors have yet to be invented (although I am aware of several vendors who are currently working on the problem.)

Other Issues in the Selection Process

From the previous discussion, it's obvious that many factors must be considered when choosing a specific microprocessor, microcontroller, or processor core for your application. Although implementation, performance, operating system support, and tool support impact the choice in nearly every project, certain other issues are frequently important. Three other issues frequently must be considered:

- A prior commitment to a processor family
- A prior restriction on language
- Time-to-market factors

A Prior Commitment to a Particular Processor Family

For some, the company's commitment to a specific family of devices might dominate the choice. For example, if your company has committed to using the 680X0 family from Motorola, your product evolution will track that of Motorola. As Motorola introduces a new microprocessor with higher speeds and better performance, you might then leverage their investment and enhance the performance of your products. The relationship creates a close cooperation between vendor and customer. Just as your customer might ask you for a vision of your product's life cycle, you ask the same question of your vendors.

Ideally, as a family of microprocessors grows and newer devices supplant older ones, the newer devices will continue to maintain degrees of code and architectural compatibility with the older ones. The desire to reuse existing software, tools, and tribal knowledge might be the major determining factor in the selection of the microprocessor or microcontroller, instead of which device has the best price/performance ratio at that time. The MC680X0 family maintains code compatibility back to the original MC68000 microprocessor, although the later devices (CPU32) are a superset of the original instruction set. Perhaps the Intel X86 family is an even better example of this phenomenon. Today's highest performance Pentium processor can still execute the object code of its 8086 processor, the device in the original IBM PC.

A Prior Restriction on Language

The language choice is important; however, sometimes you have no choice. If you are doing defense-related development, for example, you will probably be using Ada as your development language. Certain other industries have a strong preference for a particular language.

If your project is expected to leverage an existing body of source code written in language X, you'll either have to work in X or find a compiler/linker combination that supports mixed linking of the new language and modules in language X.

For many microprocessors — especially the more advanced, highly parallel architectures — some dialect of C and native assembler might be the only readily available languages.

Time to Market

Engineers tend to underestimate the business importance of market timing and often believe their design's superior performance or rich feature set will make it more successful in the marketplace. However, if the design team can't get the product to market fast enough to meet the competition because designing-in the selected processor took longer than anticipated, the processor selection was wrong. Some experts claim that just by missing your product's market introduction by as little as a month, you can lose up to 30% of the profitability of that product.

Members of Intel's Embedded Processor Division call this *time to money*. Time to money is the time from the start of a design project to the time the design ships in large quantities to the end users. No matter how impressive the performance of the latest processor, if you cannot efficiently design with it, it's a bad, or at least a risky, choice.

From the Trenches

I once managed a project that we designed using a large FPGA as a key element. The FPGA was a "bleeding edge" part, chosen for its speed, capacity, and number of I/O pins, which happened to be exactly the right amount for our design. Unlike an ASIC, an FPGA can be reprogrammed repeatedly without a $300K silicon-development charge. We planned to reload the FPGA with different functionality, as necessary for our application. So, instead of needing separate pieces of hardware for each feature, we would load different software images into the FPGA and change its behavior. The problem was that we had just enough I/O pins and no extra. If extra pins were available, we could have used them to bring several key internal (to the FPGA) nodes to the outside world, so we could observe its internal behavior. Unfortunately, the debug strategy was just to redo the FPGA software image. However, we didn't know what to change or why. I can remember watching several senior hardware designers standing around the board, staring at the FPGA as if they could determine whether the filament was lit.

There are all sorts of disciplined ways our designers could have avoided this problem. They might have taken the lead of the ASIC designers and allotted 50% of their total design time to creating simulation scenarios (called test vectors) so they could fully exercise the FPGA design in simulation, rather than in the target board. The reason ASIC designers spend so much time testing is that one failure could mean an ASIC re-spin costing thousands of dollars and months of time. However, our design team, because they could easily reprogram the FPGA, took the fast-track approach (after all, "it's only software") and lost a month in the process.

Additional Reading

- "Diversity, Thy Name Is RISC." *EDN*, 19 June 1997, S-25.
- Bourekas, Phil. "Architecting Modern Embedded CPUs." *Computer Design*, September 1998, 58.
- Bursky, Dave. "Tuned RISC Devices Deliver Top Performance."*Electronic Design*, 3 March 1997 (supplement), 9.
- Bursky, Dave. "16-Bit Embedded Controllers Open Up New Markets." *Electronic Design,* 3 March 1997 (supplement), 31.
- Bursky, Dave. "Novel Architectures, Parallelism Rule the Roost in Digital Circuits." *Electronic Design*, 6 March 2000 (supplement), 142.
- Cantrell, Tom. "Architecture Is Dead? Long Live Architecture!" *Computer Design*, September 1997, 108.
- Giovino, Bill. "Overlaps Between Microcontrollers and DSPs." *Embedded Systems Programming*, January 2000, 20.
- Grehan, Rick. "8-bit Microcontrollers Grow Up ... and Down." *Computer Design*, May 1997, 72.
- Grehan, Rick. "RISC Architects Address the Embedded World." *Computer Design*, July 1997, 90.
- Grehan, Rick. "DSPs No Longer on the Sidelines." *Computer Design*, October 1997, 105.
- Grehan, Rick. "16-bit: The Good, The Bad, Your Options." *Embedded Systems Programming*, August 1999, 71.
- Kohler, Mark. "NP Complete." *Embedded Systems Programming*, November 2000, 45.
- Leteinurier, Patrick and George Huba. "32-bit MCUs Gain Ground in Auto Control." *Electronic Engineering Times*, 17 April 2000, 92.
- Turley, Jim. "Choosing an Embedded Microprocessor." *Computer Design*, March 1998, 6.
- Turley, Jim. "Adapting to Bigger, Faster Embedded RISC." *Computer Design*, May 1998, 81.
- Turley, Jim. "Balancing Conflicting Requirements When Mixing RISC, DSPs." *Computer Design*, October 1998, 46.
- Turley, Jim. "32- and 64-Bit Processors: An Embarrassment of Riches." *Embedded System Programming*, November 1998, 85.
- Turley, Jim. "CPU Design Is Dead! Long Live CPU Design!." *Embedded System Programming*, March 1999, 13.
- Varhol, Peter. "Mainstream Processors Gain DSP Features." *Computer Design*, September 1997, 29.
- Yarlagadda, Krishna. "The Expanding World of DSPs." *Computer Design*, March 1998, 77.

Summary

Clearly, the selection of the right microprocessor, microcontroller, or SOC is a complex issue with many variables that need to be balanced to arrive at a solution. The chapters that follow discuss some of the other implications of these choices, but a detailed discussion of all the issues would require a book unto itself. Related articles in "Additional Reading" will help you research specific issues.

Two conclusions should be clear from just this chapter's discussion, however. First, it's important for those who are tasked with delivering the product to take an active interest in the selection process. Second, software and tool support must be an important part of the decision. The entire design team (including the software designers) must be involved in the selection because they are the ones who feel the pressure from upper management to "get that puppy out the door." If the task of selecting the best processor for the job is left to the hardware designers with little consideration of the quality of the software and support tools, it might not matter that you had the best paper design if you missed your market window with a product that never got out of the lab.

Works Cited

1. Barr, Michael. "Choosing a Compiler: The Little Things." *Embedded Systems Programming*, May 1999, 71.
2. Corrigan, Wilfred J. A speech at 1997 IP Forum in Tokyo, Japan. Reported in *EE Times*, 24 November 1997.
3. Halfhill, Tom R. "EEMBC Releases First Benchmarks." *Microprocessor Report*, May 2000.
4. Hawley, Greg. "Selecting a Real-Time Operating System." *Embedded Systems Programming*, March 1999, 89.
5. Mann, Daniel and Paul Cobb. "When Dhrystone Leaves You High and Dry." *EDN*, 21 May 1998.

Chapter 3

The Partitioning Decision

Designing the hardware for an embedded system is more than just selecting the right processor and gluing it to a few peripherals. Deciding how to partition the design into the functionality that is represented by the hardware and the software is a key part of creating an embedded system. This decision is not just an academic exercise nor is it self-evident. You don't just pick a processor, design the hardware, and then throw it over the wall to the software team. (Actually, many R&D labs still select a processor, design the hardware, and throw it over the wall, but the purpose of this chapter is to show you a better way.) The partitioning choice has significant impact on project cost, development time, and risk.

This chapter will explore the following:

- The hardware/software duality that makes the partitioning decision possible
- How the separation of hardware and software design imposes development costs
- How silicon compilation is making the partitioning decision more flexible but more risk-laden
- How future trends might radically alter your view of the partitioning decision

Hardware/Software Duality

Partitioning is possible and necessary because of the duality between hardware and software. For example, prior to the introduction of the 80486 by Intel, the hottest processor around was the 80386.

The 386 is an integer-only processor. To speed up your spreadsheet calculations, you purchased an 80387 numeric FPU processor. Systems without the FPU would detect that floating-point calculations were required and then simulate the presence of the FPU by branching to subroutines that performed the FPU functions, albeit much more slowly. The 387 performed floating-point calculations directly in hardware, rather than going through the much slower process of solving them in software alone. This difference often made the calculations 10 times faster.

This is an example of the partitioning problem. The 387 is more expensive than the 386. A cost-sensitive design won't include it because fast floating-point calculations are probably not a necessary requirement of a cost-conscious user. However, the absence of the 387 does not prevent the user from doing floating-point calculations; it just means the calculations won't be completed as rapidly as they could be if a FPU was available, either as a separate processor or as part of the processor itself (486).

For a second example, consider that any serious "gamer" (PC games player) worth his salt has the hottest, baddest video accelerator chip in his PC. Without the chip, software is responsible for the scene rendering. With the video accelerator, much of the rendering responsibilities are moved to the hardware. Without the accelerator, PC games don't have the same impact. They are slow and don't execute smoothly, but they do execute. A faster CPU makes a big difference, as you would expect, but the big payback comes with the latest graphics accelerator chip. This is another example of a partitioning decision, this time based upon the need to accelerate image processing in real time.

Recall Figure 1.3 of Chapter 1. It describes a laser printer as an algorithm. The algorithm is to take a digital data stream, a modulated laser beam, paper, and carbon-black ink (soot) as inputs and then output characters and graphics on a printed page. The algorithm's description didn't specify which parts were based on specialized hardware and which were under control of the software.

Consider one aspect of this process. The data stream coming in must be transformed into a stream of commands to the laser system as it writes its beam on the surface of the photosensitive drum that transfers ink to paper. The beam must be able to be turned on and off (modulated) and be steered to create the 1,200 dots per inch (dpi) on the page. Clearly, this can be accomplished in the software or in the hardware via a specialized ASIC.

The complexity of the partitioning problem space is staggering. To fully describe the problem space, you would need dimensions for multiple architectures, target technologies, design tools, and more. Today, many systems are so complex that computer-aided partitioning tools are desperately needed. However, Charles H. Small describes the partitioning decision process like this: "In practice, the analysis of trade-offs for partitioning a system is most often an informal process done with pencil and paper or spreadsheets."[1]

Ideally, the partitioning decision shouldn't be made until you understand all the alternative ways to solve the problem. The longer you can delay making the decision, the more likely you'll know which parts of the algorithm need to be in hardware and which can be performed adequately in software. Adding hardware means more speed but at a greater cost. (It isn't even that black and white, because adding more software functionality means more software to develop, more software in the system (bigger ROMs), and potentially a rippling effect back through the entire processor selection process.) Adding hardware also means that the design process becomes riskier because redesigning a hardware element is considerably more serious than finding a software defect and rebuilding the code image.

The fundamental problem, however, is that usually you can't debug your system until the hardware is available to work with. Moreover, if you delay the decision too long, the software team is left idle waiting for the hardware team to complete the board.

You don't literally need to have the hardware to begin testing. The software team always has a number of options available to do some early-stage testing. If the team is working in C or C++, it could compile and execute code to run on the team's PCs or workstations. Interactions with the actual hardware — such as reading and writing to memory-mapped I/O registers — could be simulated by writing stub code. Stub code is a simple function that replaces a direct call to non-existent hardware with a function call that returns an acceptable value so that the controlling software can continue to execute.

This method also works well with the evaluation boards that the semiconductor manufacturer might supply. Having the actual chip means that the code can be compiled for the target microprocessor and run in the target microprocessor's environment. In both cases, some incremental amount of code must be written to take the place of the non-existent hardware. Generally, this subcode (also called throw-away code) is based on some published hardware specification, so the danger of human error exists as well. If the degree of realism must be high, a large quantity of this throw-away code is written to accurately exercise the software, thus driving up the cost of the project. If the team can afford to wait for the actual hardware, the stub code can be cursory and skeletal at best.

Hardware Trends

In some ways, the partitioning decision was simpler in the past because hardware implementations of all but the simplest algorithms were too costly to consider. Modern IC technology is changing that fact rapidly.

Not too long ago, companies such as Silicon Graphics and Floating Point Systems made extremely expensive and complex hardware boxes that would plug into your DEC VAX or Data General Nova, and perform the hardware graphics and floating-point support that is now taken for granted in every desktop computer. Today, you can put entire systems on a single IC large enough, quantities of which can cost only a few dollars.

For example, AMD now produces a complete PC on a single chip, the SC520. The SC520 is designed around a 486 microprocessor "core" with all the peripheral devices that you might find in your desktop PC. Many of today's amazingly small and powerful communication and computing devices — such as PDAs, cell phones, digital cameras, MPEG players and so on — owe their existence to ASIC technology and systems-on-silicon.

Figure 3.1 shows how board-level designs are migrated to both a group of ASIC devices and discrete microprocessors or to complete systems on a single chip. This figure also shows a rough estimate of the number of equivalent hardware "gates" that are possible to design into the ASIC with the IC design geometries that are shown. Today, 0.18 micron geometries represent the mainstream IC fabrication capabilities. Soon, that number will be 0.13 micron geometries, and 0.08 micron technology is currently under development. Each "shrink" in circuit dimensions represents greater circuit density, roughly going as the inverse square of the geometry ratio. Thus, going from 0.35 micron to 0.18 micron represented a four-fold increase in the total gate capacity of the chip design. Shrinking geometries mean greater speed because transistors are ever more closely packed, and smaller devices can switch their states faster than larger devices. (My apologizies to the electrical engineers who are cringing while they read this, but without a complete discussion of capacitance, this is as good as it gets.)

Along with the shrinking geometries is the increasing size of the wafers on which the ASIC dies are placed. Because much of the cost of fabricating an IC can be attributed to processing a wafer, the larger the wafer, the more dies can be cut from the wafer and the lower the cost per die. Thus, the technology is rapidly building on itself. Advances in IC fabrication technology enable designers to create devices that run at even greater speeds with greater design complexity, thus providing even more opportunities for the design and deployment of SoS.

Figure 3.1 Evolution of SoS.

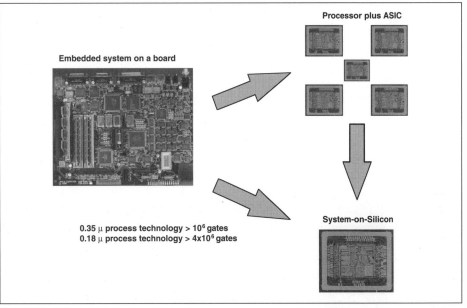

Board-level designs are migrating to processors plus ASICs and to complete systems on a single silicon die.

Much of the technology leap can be traced back to the work of Carver Mead and Lynn Conway[2] on silicon compilation detailed in their book entitled *Introduction to VLSI Design*. Prior to their efforts, IC design was a laborious process. ICs were designed at the gate level, and building complex circuits required huge design teams.

Silicon compilation changed all that. In a manner similar to the process used today for software development, a hardware design is created as source code, using C-like languages, such as VHDL or Verilog. These source files are then compiled, just as a C or C++ program might be compiled. However, the output is not object code, rather, it's a description language for how to build the IC, using the processes and design libraries of a particular IC vendor, or "silicon foundry." Thus, just as a C compiler parses your source code down to the appropriate tokens and then replaces the tokens with the correct assembly language blocks, the silicon compiler creates a description of the circuit block and interconnects between those blocks so that a foundry can fabricate the masks and actually build the chip. All modern microprocessors are fabricated using Verilog or VHDL.

"Coding" Hardware

The simple example in Figure 3.2 illustrates how closely hardware description languages relate to traditional programming languages. A logical AND function is represented in three forms. In the first, familiar to most software engineers, you declare that A and B are Boolean input variables, and C is the resultant Boolean output variable, whose value is determined by the function C = AND (A,B). Because A, B, and C are Boolean, they represent a single digital value on a wire or printed circuit trace.

Figure 3.2   Another view of hardware/software duality.

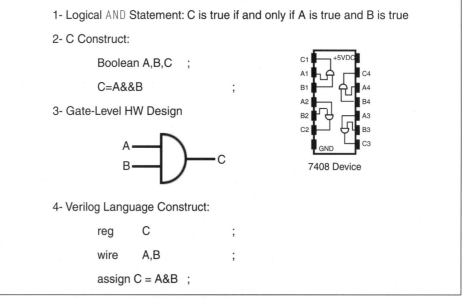

The basic AND **function is shown implemented as (2) a C construct, (3) a discrete hardware implementation using standard ICs, and (4) a hardware description language representation in Verilog.**

The hardware designer recognizes the function C = A AND B as a logical equation that can be implemented using a standard AND gate — such as the 7408 — which contains four, two-input AND gates in a single 14-pin package. Circuits such as the 7408 have formed the "glue logic" in millions of digital systems over the past 25 years.

The Verilog representation of the same logical function is the last construct and is less familiar to most. A and B are signals on wires, and C represents the "register" that stores the result, A AND B. All three systems implement the same logical function, and C is always true if A and B are both true. However, the hardware implementations will be significantly faster, even in this simple-minded example.

In the case of the C solution, A and B are perhaps local variables stored on the stack frame (local stack) of the function that is implementing the AND equation. Assuming a RISC processor with one operation per clock cycle and a cached stack frame, the processor must transfer both variables into separate registers (two instructions), perform the AND operation (one cycle), and then return the value in the appropriate register (more cycles). In the hardware implementation, the speed of the operation depends on either the propagation delay through the AND gate or, at worst, the arrival of the next clock signal.

Merging Hardware and Software Design

Because the hardware and the software design processes seem to be merging in their technology, you might wonder whether the traditional embedded design process is still the best approach. If the hardware design process and the software design process are basically identical, why separate the teams from each other? You've probably heard the phrase, "Throw it over the wall," to describe how the hardware design is turned over to the firmware and application software developers. By the time the software developers start finding "anomalies," the hardware designers have moved onto a new project.

Recently, several commercial products have come to market that attempt to address this new reality in the design process. "Hardware/software co-verification" is the term given to the process of more tightly integrating the hardware and software design processes. In hardware/software co-verification, the hardware, represented by Verilog or VHDL code, becomes a virtual hardware platform for the software. For example: Suppose the hardware specification given to the software team represents one of the hardware elements as a memory-mapped register block consisting of 64 consecutive 32-bit wide registers. (Registers can consist of various fields of width from 1 bit to 32 bits. Registers can be read-only, write-only, or read/write.)

In the absence of real hardware, the software developers write stub code functions to represent the virtual behavior of the hardware that isn't there yet. The software team usually spends a minimal amount of time and energy creating this throw-away code. Extensive software-to-hardware interface testing doesn't begin until real hardware is available, which is a lost opportunity. The later you are in a project when a defect is discovered, whether it is a hardware defect or a software defect, the more expensive it is to fix as illustrated in Figure 3.3.

Figure 3.3   Where design time is spent.

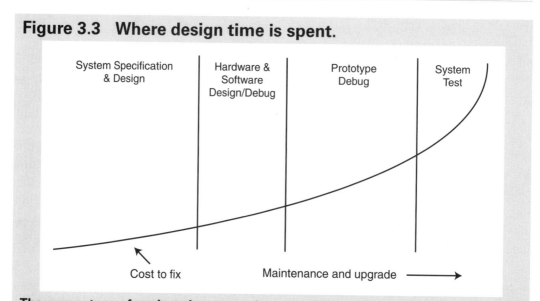

The percentage of project time spent in each phase of the embedded design life cycle. The curve shows the cost associated with fixing a defect at each stage of the process.

Slightly over half the time is spent in the implementation and debug (hardware/software integration) phase of the project. Thus, you can save a lot in terms of the project's development costs if you expose the hardware under development to the controlling software and the software under development to the underlying hardware as early as possible. Ideally, you could remove the "over the wall" issues and have a design process that continually exercises the hardware and software against each other from creation to release.

Figure 3.4 shows how the earlier introduction of hardware/software integration shortens the design cycle time. Much of the software development time is spent integrating with the hardware after the hardware is available.

Figure 3.4 Shortening the design cycle.

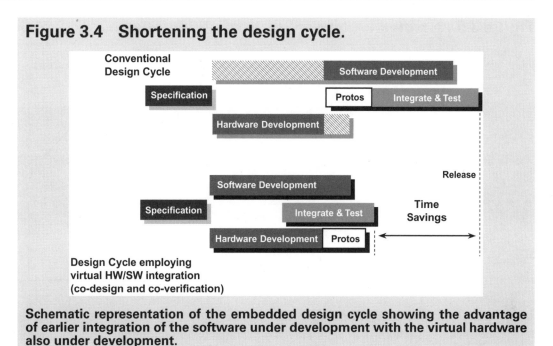

Schematic representation of the embedded design cycle showing the advantage of earlier integration of the software under development with the virtual hardware also under development.

The ASIC Revolution

Silicon compilation provided much more than a way for CPU designers to design better microprocessors and microcontrollers. Everyone who wanted to design an IC for any purpose could do so. Suddenly, anyone could design an IC that was specific to a particular function. Thus was born the ASIC. ASICs are the modern revolution in embedded-systems design. The chipsets that support the processor in your PC — the sound chip, the graphics accelerator, the modem chip — are all examples of ASICs that are widely used today. ASICs are also the technology of the SoC revolution that is still being sorted out today.

With silicon compilation, both hardware and software can be represented as compilable data files. Now, you can describe complete embedded systems in terms of a single software database. A portion of that software describes the fabrication of the hardware, and another portion of that software ultimately controls the hardware. The key point is that the distinction between what was once described as software and what was once described as hardware is blurring. Hardware design begins to look like software design that uses a different compiler (see Figure 3.5).

Figure 3.5 Hardware/software distinction blurring.

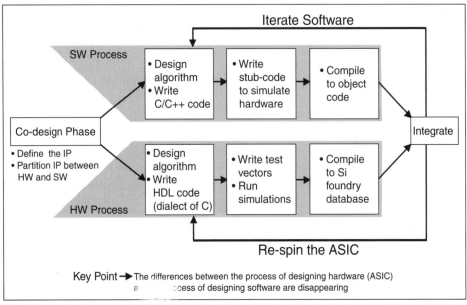

Hardware/software design flow. Notice the similarity between the activities followed by each design team.

Finally, just as the software designer can purchase a software library from a third-party vendor, the SoC designer can purchase hardware design elements, called intellectual property (IP) from third-party vendors as well. Several companies, such as Advanced RISC Machines, Ltd., sell the Verilog or VHDL description of their own RISC processors on a royalty basis. For example, you can't, in general, purchase an ARM 7 TDMI processor from a local electronic distributor in the same way that you can buy a Pentium processor or get a free sample from ARM. ARM doesn't manufacture the ARM 7 TDMI processor. ARM licenses the rights to fabricate the processor to several IC fabricators who can use the processor as part of an ASIC designed by (or for) their customer.

With all these similar problems, representations, and processes, it's reasonable to ask whether hardware and software design are really different creatures. Why can't you translate C or some other high-level programming language directly into VHDL instead of machine code? For that matter, why not compile C to assembly language and then use some advanced form of "linker" to generate VHDL for the portions of the design that you want to fabricate as hardware? In fact, development products already are available that can generate VHDL directly from C. Although these tools are still very expensive and are not for everyone, the ideal of system design languages and tools that can start from a high-level design description of a real-time system and then automatically generate the appropriate C++ or VHDL code is a reality today.

Fabless Chip Vendors

ARM is one of a growing number of "fabless chip vendors." These are traditional chip vendors in every way, except they lack the capacity to build their own products. ARM processors are designed to be included with other intellectual property to build entire embedded systems on a single silicon die. At the 1998 Microprocessor Forum, one of the speakers mentioned a system-on-silicon (SoS) containing 64 RISC processors. The following articles discuss the current state-of-the-art SoC technology:

- Wolfe, Alexander. "Embedded ICs: Expanding the Possibilities." *Embedded System Programming*, November 2000, 147.

- Gott, Robert A. "M-Core Poses Challenge to ARM in Low-Power Apps." *Computer Design*, June 1998, 14.

- Turley, Jim. "Mcore: Does Motorola Need Another Processor Family?" *Embedded System Programming*, July 1998, 46.

- Peters, Kenneth H. "Migrating to Single-Chip Systems." *Embedded System Programming*, April 1999, 30.

- Bursky. David. "Optimized Processor Blocks Eliminate the Gamble with RISC for SoC Designs." *Electronic Design*, May 2000, 81.

- Tuck, Barbara. "SoC Design: Hardware/Software Co-Design or a Java-Based Approach?" *Computer Design*, April 1998, 22.

- Tuck, Barbara. "Formal Verification: Essential for Complex Designs." *Computer Design*, June 1998, 55.

- Small, Charles H. "Mixed-Signal Methods Shift Gears for Tomorrow's Systems-on-a-Chip." *Computer Design,* October 1997, 31.

- Tuck, Barbara. "Integrating IP Blocks to Create a System-on-a-Chip." *Computer Design*, November 1997, 49.

- Kao, Warren. "Integrating Third-Party IP into the Design Process." *Embedded Systems Programming*, January 1999, 52.

ASICs and Revision Costs

At first glance, it might seem that the ability to compile directly to silicon would greatly simplify the partitioning decision. Instead of deciding up-front how to partition the problem, just write and test the entire solution in an appropriate design language. Then, based on cost and performance, choose which portions you will compile to firmware and which portions you will compile to silicon. Unfortunately, it's not that simple, primarily because it's very expensive to revise an IC. Consider the consequences of discovering a bug in such a solution. Now, of course, the bug in the software can be a defect in the hardware design description, as well as a defect in the control code. However, consider the implications of a defect that is discovered during the hardware/software integration phase. If the defect was in the "traditional" software, you fix the source code, rebuild the code image, and try again. You expect this because it is software! Everyone knows there are bugs in software.

From the Trenches

About 20 years ago, the part of HP that is now Agilent was rapidly moving toward instrument designs based on embedded microprocessors. HP found itself with an oversupply of hardware designers and a shortage of software designers. So, being a rather enlightened company, HP decided to send willing hardware engineers off to software boot camp and retrain them in software design. The classes were rigorous and lasted about three months, after which time the former hardware engineers returned to their respective HP divisions to start their new careers as software developers.

One "retread engineer" became a legend. His software was absolutely bulletproof. He never had any defects reported against the code he wrote. After several years, he was interviewed by an internal project team, chartered with finding and disseminating the best practices in the company in the area of software quality. They asked him a lot of questions, but the moment of truth came when he was bluntly asked why he didn't have any defects in his code. His answer was straightforward: "I didn't know that I was allowed to have defects in my code." In hindsight, this is just basic Engineering Management 101. Although he was retrained in software methods, his value system was based on the hardware designer viewpoint that defects must be avoided at all costs because of the severity of penalty if a defect is found. A defect might render the entire design worthless, forcing a complete hardware redesign cycle, taking many months and costing hundreds of thousands of dollars. Because no one bothered to tell him that it's okay to have bugs in his code, he made certain that his code was bug-free.

On the other side of the wall, the hardware designers have compiled their portion of the program into silicon. Finally, they get their first prototype chips back and turn them on. So far, so good, they don't cause the lights to dim in the lab. Even more exciting, you can see signals wiggling on the pins that you expect to see wiggling. With rising excitement, more tests are run, and the chip seems to be doing okay. Next, some test software is loaded and executed. Rats! It died.

Without spending the next 20 pages on telling the story of this defect, assume that the defect is found in the code and fixed. Now what? Well, for starters, figure on $300,000 of nonrecoverable engineering (NRE) charges and about two months delay as a new chip is fabricated. Start-up companies generally budget for one such re-spin. A second re-spin not only costs the project manager his job but it often puts the company out of business. Thus, the cost penalty of a hardware defect is much more severe than the cost penalty of a software defect, even though both designers are writing software.

(The difference between the hardware issues now and in the past is that board-level systems could tolerate a certain amount of rework before the hardware designer was forced to re-spin the printed circuit board. If you've ever seen an early hardware prototype board, you know what I mean. Even if a revised board must be fabricated, the cost is still bearable — typically a few thousand dollars and a week of lost time. In fact, many boards went into production with "green wires" attached to correct last minute hardware defects. Usually the Manufacturing department had something like a "five green wire limit" rule to keep the boards from being too costly to manufacture. This kind of flexibility isn't available when the traces on an IC are 180 billionths of a meter apart from each other.)

Sometimes, you can compensate for a hardware defect by revising the partitioning decision; simply repartition the algorithm back towards the software and away from the defective hardware element. This might be a reasonable compromise, assuming the loss of performance associated with the transfer from hardware to software is still acceptable (or the Marketing department can turn it into a new feature) and the product is not permanently crippled by it. However, suppose that a software workaround is not acceptable, or worse yet, the defect is not a defect in the hardware design *per se* but is a defect in the interpretation of the hardware/software interface. In this case, you have the option of attempting to correct the defect in software if possible. However, if the defect is pervasive, you might lose just as much time, or more, trying to go back through thousands of lines of code to modify the software so that it will run with the hardware. Even though repartitioning can't compensate for every hardware flaw, the cost penalty of a hardware re-spin is so great that every possible alternative is usually investigated before the IC design goes back to the vendor for another try.

Managing the Risk

Even though the hardware designer is writing software in silicon compilation, the expectations placed upon the hardware team are much greater because of what's at stake if the hardware is defective. In fact, the silicon fabricators (foundry) won't accept the design for fabrication unless a rather extensive set of "test vectors" is supplied to them along with the Verilog or VHDL code. The test vectors represent the ensemble of ones and zeros for as many possible input and output conditions as the engineer(s) can create. For a complex SoC, this can be thousands of possible combinations of inputs and outputs representing the behavior of the system for each clock cycle over many cycles of the system clock. The foundries require these vectors because they'll ultimately need them to test the chips on their automated testers and because they want some assurance from the customer that the chip will work. The foundries don't make profit from NRE charges; they want to sell the silicon that the customer has designed. This might be difficult for a software engineer to comprehend, but studies show that a hardware designer will spend 50 percent of the total project design time just in the process of design verification (creating test vectors). There are compelling arguments for investing a similar testing effort in software. At Microsoft, for example, the ratio of development engineers to test engineers is close to one.

Before submitting the design to the foundry, the hardware designer uses the test vectors to run the design in simulation. Several companies in the business of creating the electronic design tools needed to build SoS provide Verilog or VHDL simulators. These simulators exercise the Verilog or VHDL design code and use the test vectors as the I/O stimulus for the simulation. With these powerful and expensive tools, the hardware design team can methodically exercise the design and debug it in much the same way as a software designer debugs code.

Traditionally, these simulators are used by the hardware design team. Again, the question is what if hardware and software design are the same process? If the VHDL simulator was available during the entire development process, it could be used, together with the VHDL or Verilog representation of the hardware, to create a virtual test platform. This virtual hardware could be exercised by the actual embedded software, rather than artificially constructed test vectors. This would allow the traditional hardware/software integration phase to be moved earlier in the process (or even eliminated).

For the hardware developer, this would certainly enhance the hardware/software integration process and provide an environment for better communications between the teams. Furthermore, uncertainties and errors in system specifications could be easily uncovered and corrected. For the software team, the gain is the elimination of the need to write stub code. In fact, the team could test the actual code under development against the virtual hardware under development at any point in the design process, testing hardware/software behavior at the module level instead of at the system level, which could be a big win for both teams.

Co-Verification

This vision of embedded system design in which the hardware and software teams work closely together throughout the design process is not especially new, but it has become much more important as SoCs have become more prevalent in embedded system design. The key has been the development of tools that form a bridge between the software realm (code) and the hardware realm (VHDL or Verilog simulation). The formal process is called co-design and co-verification. The names are often used interchangeably, but there is a formal distinction. Co-design is the actual process of developing the hardware and controlling software together. Co-verification tends to focus on the correctness of the hardware/software interface.

To understand how the co-design system works consider Figure 3.6.

Figure 3.6 Memory bus cycle of microprocessors.

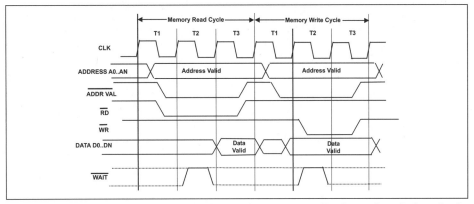

A memory bus cycle of a typical microprocessor. Each cycle of the clock, typically on a rising or falling edge, initiates different portions of the bus cycle.

In this particular example, which is representative of a generalized microprocessor, each processor bus operation (such as read or write) can be further subdivided into one or more clock cycles, designated as T1, T2 and T3. A hardware designer tasked with interfacing an ASIC design to a system containing this microprocessor might construct a set of test vectors corresponding to each rising and falling edge of the clock. Each vector would consist of the state of all the microprocessor's signals, all the address bits, all the data bits, and all the status bits, complete with any additional timing information. A set of these vectors could then be used to represent a bus cycle of the processor, reading from or writing to the ASIC.

If you can do this, it would be easy to write a program that would convert a C or C++ assignment statement into the corresponding set of test vectors representing that bus cycle to the ASIC. Consider the following code snippet

```
*(unsigned int* ) 0xFF7F00A6 = 0x4567ABFF;
```

This instruction casts the address 0xFF7F00A6 as a pointer to an unsigned integer and then stores the data value 0x4567ABFF in that memory location. The equivalent assembly language instruction (68000) might be

```
MOVE.L   #$4567ABFF, D0
LEA      $FF7F00A6, A0
MOVE.L   D0, (A0)
```

From the hardware viewpoint, the actual code is irrelevant. The processor places the address, 0xFF7F00A6 on the address bus, places the data value 0x4567ABFF on the data bus at the appropriate point in the T states, and issues the WRITE command. If you construct a simulation model of this processor, you could then automatically generate a set of test vectors that would represent the data being written to the ASIC in terms of a series of I/O stimulus test vectors written to the VHDL or Verilog simulator. The program that does the translation from C or assembly code to test vectors is called a bus functional model and is the key element of any hardware/software co-design strategy. In theory, a bus functional model can be built for any commercially available microprocessor or microcontroller or for an embedded core, such as the ARM 7 TDMI processor that was discussed earlier. Figure 3.7 is a schematic representation of the entire process.

To implement such a system, the C code snippets that actually access the hardware, such as in the example, must be replaced with a function call to the bus functional model. The function call contains all the information (read or write, address, data, bus width, and so on) necessary to construct a set of test vectors for the operation. On a read operation, the return value of the function is the result of the memory read operation.

If an Instruction Set Simulator (ISS) is used, assembly language code also can be used. The ISS must be able to trap the address accesses and then send the information to the bus functional model. A number of companies now offer such tools for sale (Seamless from Mentor Graphics, Eaglei from Synopsys, V-CPU from Summit Design are representative co-design and co-verification tools).

Figure 3.7 Conversion process.

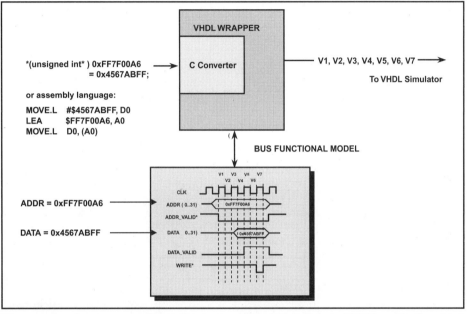

The conversion process from C or assembly language to VHDL or Verilog test vectors for ASIC simulation.

It would seem like this could be a boon to the SoC-development process. However, a number of challenges, both technological and economic, have prevented co-design and co-verification tools from achieving a broader market acceptance. For one, these tools are costly and complex to set up. For a team of software developers who are used to spending around $1,000 (or less) per user for a compiler and debugger, $50,000 per seat is a significant expense. Also, a VHDL simulator can cost $100,000 per seat; thus, it isn't the type of tool that is used to equip a team of developers.

Second, the throughput of an Hardware Description Language (HDL) simulator can be very slow relative to the execution speed of the software stimulus. Although the software might be able to run at 25 million instructions per second on the workstation, the speed can drop to under 100 instructions per second when communicating with the simulator. The HDL simulator is very computer intensive; it must recalculate the entire state of the system on each clock cycle, for each set of test vectors, including all timing delays and setups. For a complex design of a million gates or so, even a powerful workstation can be slowed to a relative crawl. So, how bad is it? Figure 3.8 gives some approximate values for the percentage of time that software actually communicates directly with the hardware for various types of software accesses.

Figure 3.8 Instructions communicating directly.

Software Type	I/O Density (percent)
RTOS	0.1 - 1.0
Application	1.0 - 5.0
Driver	1.0 - 10.0
Diagnostic	10.0 - 15.0
Initialization	10.0 - 25.0

* Courtesy of Mike Stanbro, Synopsys Inc.

Percentage of instructions (I/O density) that communicate directly with hardware (courtesy of Mike Stansbro, Synopsys Corporation, Beaverton, Oregon).

As you might expect, the initialization of the hardware, typically at boot-up or reset, has the highest percentage — as many as one in four instructions directly access the hardware. Application software and RTOS calls are the lowest, between 0.1 and 5 percent of the instructions. However, even if one instruction in a 1,000 must communicate with the simulator, the average slowdown is dramatic because the simulator is running many orders of magnitude slower than the software.

You might wonder whether any hard data indicates that co-verification is a viable technology. One case study[1] involves a manufacturer of telecomm and datacomm switching networks. The current design contained over one million lines of C source code. Prior to using the co-verification tools, the company's previous design experience was disappointing. The predecessor was late to market and did not meet its original design specification. The company used a commercial co-verification tool that was integrated with its

---

1.   Courtesy of Geoff Bunza, Synopsys Corporation.

Co-Verification and Performance

Figure 3.9 is a computer model that shows the expected performance of a co-verification system. This simulation, an Excel spreadsheet model, assumes that the HDL simulator is running on a dedicated workstation, located remotely from the software being executed. Latency is five milliseconds for the round-trip time on the network. This is fairly typical of the use model for a co-verification environment. The simulator is running at 100Hz, and the instructions are plotted per second on the Y-axis (into the paper) over a range of 1,000 to 10,000,000 instructions per second. The X-axis (left to right across the paper) is the I/O density plotted over a range of 5 percent down to 0.1 percent. The Z-axis is the resultant total throughput (instructions per second) for the simulation.

Figure 3.9   Throughput calculation.

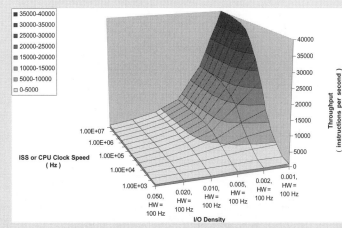

Throughput as a function of Software Clock Speed and I/O Density for Remote Call Latency = 0.005 Sec, where hardware simulation rate = 100 Hz. Low I/O Density view.

It is apparent from the model that after the I/O density rises above 1%, the throughput is entirely limited by the speed of the HDL simulator (lightest gray surface). Only when the I/O density drops below 0.2 percent does the throughput rise above 10,000 instructions per second.

RTOS of choice. The company focused its efforts on developing the hardware driver software while the ASICs were being designed and paid particular attention to verifying the correctness of the hardware/software interface specifications. As a result of this development strategy, product development time was cut from 16 months to 12 months, and the company realized a savings of $200,000–$300,000 in development costs. The company was so impressed with the results that it adopted hardware/software co-verification as the corporate standard design practice.

Additional Reading

You can find more information about co-verification and co-design in the following sources:

- Berger, Arnold. "Co-Verification Handles More Complex Embedded Systems." *Electronic Design*, March 1998 (supplement), 9.
- Leef, Serge. "Hardware and Software Co-Verification — Key to Co-Design." *Electronic Design*, March 1998 (supplement), 18.
- Morasse, Bob. "Co-Verification and System Abstraction Levels." *Embedded System Programming*, June 2000, 90.
- Nadamuni, Daya. "Co-Verification Tools: A Market Focus." *Embedded System Programming*, September 1999, 119.
- Sangiovanni-Vincentelli, Alberto, and Jim Rowson. "What You Need to Know About Hardware/Software Co-Design." *Computer Design*, August 1998, 63.
- Tuck, Barbara. "The Hardware/Software Co-Verification Challenge." *Computer Design*, April 1998, 49.
- Tuck, Barbara. "Various Paths Taken to Accelerate Advances in Hardware/Software Co-Design." *Computer Design*, September 1998, 24.

Summary

The advances made in ASIC fabrication technology have elevated the issue of system design to a much greater prominence. Previously, when systems were designed at the board level and hardware designers chose from the catalog pages of available devices, the portioning decisions were rather limited. New ASIC and SoC options have greatly complicated the partitioning decision and radically changed the risk associated with defects.

The solution might evolve from the same force that generated this complexity. I believe in the near future, you'll see a convergence of the hardware/software partitioning database with the hardware/software co-verification tools to form an integrated tool suite that will allow a complete design cycle from partition to integration in one continuous process. These tools will allow designers to delay many partitioning decisions until the impact can be explored using virtual hardware.

Whether it's sociological or traditional, embedded systems designers tend to draw a sharp distinction between the designers of hardware and the designers of software. Justified by this distinction, organizations have imposed varying degrees of separation between the teams. In an extreme case, the hardware might be built at a facility in another country and then shipped along with the hardware specification document to the software team for integration.

As hardware and software representations, tools, and processes converge, the justification will dwindle for this distinction — or for any separation between the teams.

Works Cited

1. Small, Charles H. "Partitioning Tools Play a Key Role in Top-Down Design." *Computer Design*, June 1998, 84.
2. Mead, Carver, and Lynn Conway. *Introduction to VLSI Systems*. Reading, MA: Addison-Wesley, 1980.

Chapter 4

The Development Environment

Modern desktop development environments use remarkably complex translation techniques. Source code is seldom translated directly into loadable binary images. Sophisticated suites of tools translate the source into relocatable modules, sometimes with and sometimes without debug and symbolic information. Complex, highly optimized linkers and loaders dynamically combine these modules and map them to specific memory locations when the application is executed.

It's amazing that the process can seem so simple. Despite all this behind-the-scenes complexity, desktop application developers just select whether they want a free-standing executable or a DLL (Dynamic Link Library) and then click Compile. Desktop application developers seldom need to give their development tools any information about the hardware. Because the translation tools always generate code for the same, highly standardized hardware environment, the tools can be preconfigured with all they need to know about the hardware.

Embedded systems developers don't enjoy this luxury. An embedded system runs on unique hardware, hardware that probably didn't exist when the development tools were created. Despite processor advances, the eventual machine language is never machine independent. Thus, as part of the development effort, the embedded systems developer must direct the tools concerning how to translate the source for the specific hardware. This means embedded systems developers must know much more about their development tools and how they work than do their application-oriented counterparts.

Assumptions about the hardware are only part of what makes the application development environment easier to master. The application developer also can safely assume a consistent run-time package. Typically, the only decision an application developer makes about the run-time environment is whether to create a freestanding EXE, a DLL, or an MFC application. The embedded systems developer, by comparison, must define the entire run-time environment. At a minimum, the embedded systems developer must decide where the various components will reside (in RAM, ROM, or flash memory) and how they will be packaged and scheduled (as an ISR, part of the main thread, or a task launched by an RTOS). In smaller environments, the developer must decide which, if any, of the standard run-time features to include and whether to invent or acquire the associated code.

Thus, the embedded systems developer must understand more about the execution environment, more about the development tools, and more about the run-time package.

The Execution Environment

Although you might not need to master all of the intricacies of a given instruction set architecture to write embedded systems code, you will need to know the following:

- How the system uses memory, including how the processor manages its stack
- What happens at system startup
- How interrupts and exceptions are handled

In the following sections, you'll learn what you need to know about these issues to work on a typical embedded system built with a processor from the Motorola 68000 (68K) family. Although the details vary, the basic concepts are similar on all systems.

Memory Organization

The first step in coming to terms with the execution environment for a new system is to become familiar with how the system uses memory. Figure 4.1 outlines a memory map of a generic microprocessor, the Motorola 68K (Even though the original 68K design is over 20 years old, it is a good architecture to use to explain general principles).

Figure 4.1 Memory map of processor.

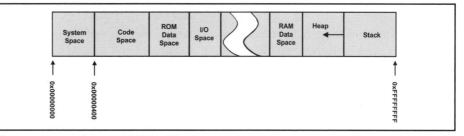

Memory model for a 68K family processor.

Everything to the left of I/O space could be implemented as ROM. Everything to the right of I/O space can only be implemented in RAM.

System Space

The Motorola 68K family reserves the first 1,024 memory locations (256 long words) for the exception vector tables. Exception vectors are "hard-wired" addresses that the processor uses to identify which code should run when it encounters an interrupt or other exception (such as divide by zero or overflow error). Because each vector consumes four bytes (one long word) on the 68K, this system can support up to 256 different exception vectors.

Code Space

Above the system space, the code space stores the instructions. It makes sense to make the system space and the code space contiguous because you would normally place them in the same physical ROM device.

Data Space

Above the code space, the ROM data space stores constant values, such as error messages or other string literals.

Above the data space, the memory organization becomes less regular and more dependent on the hardware design constraints. Thus, the memory model of Figure 4.1 is only an example and is not meant to imply that it should be done that way. Three basic areas of read/write storage (RAM) need to be identified: stack, free memory, and heap.

The Stack

The stack is used to keep track of the current and all suspended execution contexts. Thus, the stack contains all "live" local or automatic variables and all function and interrupt "return addresses." When a program calls a function, the address of the instruction following the call (the return address) is placed on the stack. When the called function has completed, the processor retrieves the return address from the stack and resumes execution there. A program cannot service an interrupt or make a function call unless stack space is available.

The stack is generally placed at the upper end of memory (see Figure 4.1) because the 68K family places new stack entries in decreasing memory addresses; that is, the stack grows downwards towards the heap. Placing the stack at the "right" end of RAM means that the logical bottom of the stack is at the highest possible RAM address, giving it the maximum amount of room to grow downwards.

Free Memory

All statically allocated read/write variables are assigned locations in free memory. Globals are the most common form of statically allocated variable, but C "statics" are also placed here. Any modifiable variable with global life is stored in free memory.

The Heap

All dynamically allocated (created by new or malloc()) objects and variables reside in the heap. Usually, whatever memory is "left over" after allocating stack and free memory space is assigned to the heap. The heap is usually a (sometimes complex) linked data structure managed by routines in the compiler's run-time package. Many embedded systems do not use a heap.

Unpopulated Memory Space

The "break" in the center of Figure 4.1 represents available address space that isn't attached to any memory. A typical embedded system might have a few megabytes of ROM-based instruction and data and perhaps another megabyte of RAM. Because the 68K in this example can address a total of 16MB of memory, there's a lot of empty space in the memory map.

I/O Space

The last memory component is the memory-mapped peripheral device. In Figure 4.1, these devices reside in the I/O space area. Unlike some processors, the 68K family doesn't support a separate address space for I/O devices. Instead, they are assumed to live at various addresses in the otherwise empty memory regions between RAM and ROM. Although I've drawn this as a single section, you should not expect to find all memory-mapped devices at contiguous addresses. More likely, they will be scattered across various easy-to-decode addresses.

Detecting Stack Overflow

Notice that in Figure 4.1 on page 71, the arrow to the left of the stack space points into the heap space. It is common for the stack to grow down, gobbling free memory in the heap as it goes. As you know, when the stack goes too far and begins to chew up other read/write variables, or even worse, passes out of RAM into empty space, the system crashes. Crashes in embedded systems that are not deterministic (such as a bug in the code) are extremely difficult to find. In fact, it might be years before this particular defect causes a failure.

In *The Art of Embedded Systems*, Jack Ganssle[1] suggests that during system development and debug, you fill the stack space with a known pattern, such as 0x5555 or 0xAA. Run the program for a while and see how much of this pattern has been overwritten by stack operations. Then, add a safety factor (2X, perhaps) to allow for unintended stack growth. The fact that available RAM memory could be an issue might have an impact on the type of programming methods you use or an influence on the hardware design.

System Startup

Understanding the layout of memory makes it easier to understand the startup sequence. This section assumes the device's program has been loaded into the proper memory space — perhaps by "burning" it into erasable, programmable, read-only memory (EPROM) and then plugging that EPROM into the system board. Other mechanisms for getting the code into the target are discussed later.

The startup sequence has two phases: a hardware phase and a software phase. When the RESET line is activated, the processor executes the hardware phase. The primary responsibility of this part is to force the CPU to begin executing the program or some code that will transfer control to the program. The first few instructions in the program define the software phase of the startup. The software phase is responsible for initializing core elements of the hardware and key structures in memory.

For example, when a 68K microprocessor first comes out of RESET, it does two things before executing any instructions. First, it fetches the address stored in the 4 bytes beginning at location 000000 and copies this address into the stack pointer (SP) register, thus establishing the bottom of the stack. It is common for this value to be initialized to the top of RAM (e.g., 0_XFFFFFFFE) because the stack grows down toward memory location

000000. Next, it fetches the address stored in the four bytes at memory location 000004–000007 and places this 32-bit value in its program counter register. This register always points to the memory location of the next instruction to be executed. Finally, the processor fetches the instruction located at the memory address contained in the program counter register and begins executing the program.

At this point, the CPU has begun the software startup phase. The CPU is under control of the software but is probably not ready to execute the application proper. Instead, it executes a block of code that initializes various hardware resources and the data structures necessary to create a complete run-time environment. This "startup code" is described in more detail later.

Interrupt Response Cycle

Conceptually, interrupts are relatively simple: When an interrupt signal is received, the CPU "sets aside" what it is doing, executes the instructions necessary to take care of the interrupt, and then resumes its previous task. The critical element is that the CPU hardware must take care of transferring control from one task to the other and back. The developer can't code this transfer into the normal instruction stream because there is no way to predict when the interrupt signal will be received. Although this transfer mechanism is almost the same on all architectures, small significant differences exist among how different CPUs handle the details. The key issues to understand are:

- How does the CPU know where to find the interrupt handling code?
- What does it take to save and restore the "context" of the main thread?
- When should interrupts be enabled?

As mentioned previously, a 68K CPU expects the first 1024 bytes of memory to hold a table of exception vectors, that is, addresses. The first of these is the address to load into SP during system RESET. The second is the address to load into the program counter register during RESET. The rest of the 254 long addresses in the exception vector table contain pointers to the starting address of exception routines, one for each kind of exception that the 68K is capable of generating or recognizing. Some of these are connected to the interrupts discussed in this section, while others are associated with other anomalies (such as an attempt to divide by zero) which may occur during normal code execution.

When a device[1] asserts an interrupt signal to the CPU (if the CPU is able to accept the interrupt), the 68K will:

- Push the address of the next instruction (the return address) onto the stack.
- Load the ISR address (vector) from the exception table into the program counter.
- Disable interrupts.
- Resume executing normal fetch–execute cycles. At this point, however, it is fetching instructions that belong to the ISR.

This response is deliberately similar to what happens when the processor executes a call or jump to subroutine (JSR) instruction. (In fact, on some CPUs, it is identical.) You can think of the interrupt response as a hardware-invoked function call in which the address of the target function is pulled from the exception vector. To resume the main program, the programmer must terminate the ISR with a return from subroutine (RTS) instruction, just as one would return from a function. (Some machines require you to use a special return from interrupt [RTE, return from exception on the 68k] instruction.)

ISRs are discussed in more detail in the next chapter. For now, it's enough to think of them as hardware-invoked functions. Function calls, hardware or software, are more complex to implement than indicated here.

Function Calls and Stack Frames

When you write a C function and assemble it, the compiler converts it to an assembly language subroutine. The name of the assembly language subroutine is just the function name preceded by an underscore character. For example, main() becomes _main. Just as the C function main() is terminated by a return statement, the assembly language version is terminated by the assembly language equivalent: RTS.

Figure 4.2 shows two subroutines, FOO and BAR, one nested inside of the other. The main program calls subroutine FOO which then calls subroutine BAR. The compiler translates the call to BAR using the same mechanism as for the call to FOO. The automatic placing and retrieval of addresses from the stack is possible because the stack is set up as a last-in/first-out data structure. You PUSH return addresses onto the stack and then POP them from the stack to return from the function call.

---

1. In the case of a microcontroller, an external device could be internal to the chip but external to the CPU core.

Figure 4.2 Subroutines.

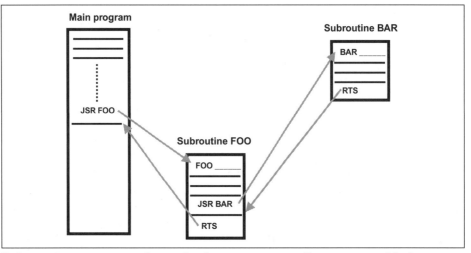

Schematic representation of the structure of an assembly-language subroutine.

The assembly-language subroutine is "called" with a JSR assembly language instruction. The argument of the instruction is the memory address of the start of the subroutine. When the processor executes the JSR instruction, it automatically places the address of the next instruction — that is, the address of the instruction immediately following the JSR instruction — on the processor stack. (Compare this to the interrupt response cycle discussed previously.) First the CPU decrements the SP to point to the next available stack location. (Remember that on the 68K the SP register grows downward in memory.) Then the processor writes the return address to the stack (to the address now in SP).

Hint

A very instructive experiment that you should be able to perform with any embedded C compiler is to write a simple C program and compile it with a "compile only" option. This should cause the compiler to generate an assembly language listing file. If you open this assembly file in an editor, you'll see the various C statements along with the assembly language statements that are generated. The C statements appear as comments in the assembly language source file.

Some argue that generating assembly is obsolete. Many modern compilers skip the assembly language step entirely and go from compiler directly to object code. If you want to see the assembly language output of the compiler, you set a compiler option switch that causes a disassembly of the object file to create an assembly language source file. Thus, assembly language is not part of the process.

The next instruction begins execution at the starting address of the subroutine (function). Program execution continues from this new location until the RTS instruction is encountered. The RTS instruction causes the address stored on the stack to be automatically retrieved from the stack and placed in the program counter register, where program execution now resumes from the instruction following the JSR instruction.

The stack is also used to store all of a function's local variables and arguments. Although return addresses are managed implicitly by the hardware each time a JSR or RTS is executed, the compiler must generate explicit assembly language to manage local variable storage. Here, different compilers can choose different options. Generally, the compiler must generate code to

- Push all arguments onto the stack
- Call the function
- Allocate storage (on the stack) for all local variables
- Perform the work of the function
- Deallocate the local variable storage
- Return from the function
- Deallocate the space used by the arguments

The collection of all space allocated for a single function call (arguments, return addresses, and local variables) is called a stack frame. To simplify access to the arguments and local variables, at each function entry, the compiler generates code that loads a pointer to the current function's stack frame into a processor register — typically called Frame Pointer (FP). Thus, within the assembly language subroutine, a stack frame is nothing more than a local block of RAM that must be addressed via one of the CPU's internal address registers (FP).

A complete description of a stack frame includes more than locals, parameters, and return addresses. To simplify call nesting, the old FP is pushed onto the stack each time a function is called. Also, the "working values" in certain registers might need to be saved (also in the stack) to keep them from being overwritten by the called function. Thus, every time the compiler encounters a function call, it must potentially generate quite a bit of code (called "prolog" and "epilogue") to support creating and destroying a local stack frame. Many CPUs include special instructions designed to improve the efficiency of this process. The 68K processor, for example, includes two instructions, link and unlink (LNK and UNLNK) that were created especially to support the creation of C stack frames.

Run-Time Environment

Just as the execution environment comprises all the hardware facilities that support program execution, the run-time environment consists of all the software structures (not explicitly created by the programmer) that support program execution. Although I've already discussed the stack and stack frames as part of the execution environment, the structure linking stack frames also can be considered a significant part of the run-time environment. For C programmers, two other major components comprise the run-time environment: the startup code and the run-time library.

Startup Code

Startup code is the software that bridges the connection between the hardware startup phase and the program's main(). This bridging software should be executed at each RESET and, at a minimum, should transfer control to main(). Thus, a trivial implementation might consist of an assembly language file containing the single instruction:

```
JMP _main
```

To make this code execute at startup, you also need to find a way to store the address of this JMP into memory locations 000004–000007 (the exception vector for the first instruction to be executed by the processor.) I'll explain how to accomplish that later in the section on linkers.

Typically, however, you wouldn't want the program to jump immediately to main(). A real system, when it first starts up, will probably do some system integrity checks, such as run a ROM checksum test, run a RAM test, relocate code stored in ROM to RAM for faster access, initialize hardware registers, and set up the rest of the C environment before jumping to _main. Whereas in a desktop environment, the startup code never needs to be changed, in an embedded environment, the startup code needs to be customized for every different board. To make it easy to modify the startup behavior, most embedded market C compilers automatically generate code to include a separate assembly language file that contains the startup code. Typically, this file is named crt0 or crt1 (where crt is short for C Run Time). This convention allows the embedded developer to modify the startup code separately (usually as part of building the board support package).

Figure 4.3 shows the flowchart for the crt0 function for the Hewlett-Packard B3640 68K Family C Cross Compiler.

Figure 4.3 crt0 **function.**

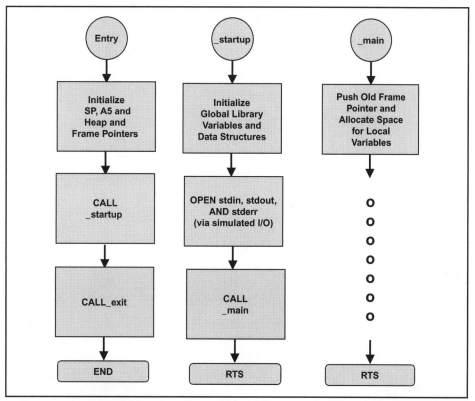

The crt0 **program setup flowchart.[2]**

Why JMP_main Was Used

You might be wondering why I used the instruction JMP_main and not the instruction JSR _main. First of all, JSR_main implies that after it's done running main(), it returns to the calling routine. Where is the calling routine? In this case, main() is the starting and ending point. Once it is running, it runs forever. Thus, function main() might look like this pseudocode representation:

```
main()
{
    Initialize variables and get ready to run;
    While(1)
    {
        Rest of the program here;
    }
    return 0;
}
```

After you enter the `while` loop, you stay there forever. Thus, a `JMP _main` is as good as a `JSR _main`.

However, not all programs run in isolation. Just like a desktop application runs under Windows or UNIX, an embedded application can run under an embedded operating system, for example, a RTOS such as VxWorks. With an RTOS in control of your environment, a C program or task might terminate and control would have to be returned to the operating system. In this case, it is appropriate to enter the function `main()` with a `JSR _main`.

This is just one example of how the startup code might need to be adjusted for a given project.

The Run-Time Library

In the most restrictive definition, the run-time library is a set of otherwise invisible support functions that simplify code generation. For example, on a machine that doesn't have hardware support for floating-point operations, the compiler generates a call to an arithmetic routine in the run-time library for each floating-point operation. On machines with awkward register structures, sometimes the compiler generates a call to a context-saving routine instead of trying to generate code that explicitly saves each register.

For this discussion, consider the routines in the C standard library to be part of the run-time library. (In fact, the compiler run-time support might be packaged in the same library module with the core standard library functions.)

The run-time library becomes an issue in embedded systems development primarily because of resource constraints. By eliminating unneeded or seldom used functions from the run-time library, you can reduce the load size of the program. You can get similar reductions by replacing complex implementations with simple ones.

These kinds of optimizations usually affect three facilities that application programmers tend to take for granted: floating-point support, formatted output (`printf()`), and dynamic allocation support (`malloc()` and C++'s `new`). Typically, if one of these features has been omitted, the embedded development environment supplies some simpler, less code-intensive alternative. For example, if no floating-point support exists, the compiler vendor might supply a fixed-point library that you can call explicitly. Instead of full `printf()` support, the vendor might supply functions to format specific types (for example, `printIntAsHex()`, `printStr()`, and so on).

Dynamic allocation, however, is a little different. How, or even if, you implement dynamic allocation depends on many factors other than available code space and hardware support. If the system is running under an

RTOS, the allocation system will likely be controlled by the RTOS. The developer will usually need to customize the lower level functions (such as the getmem() function discussed in the following) to adapt the RTOS to the particular memory configuration of the target system. If the system is safety critical, the allocation system must be very robust. Because allocation routines can impose significant execution overhead, processor-bound systems might need to employ special, fast algorithms.

Many systems won't have enough RAM to support dynamic allocation. Even those that do might be better off without it. Dynamic memory allocation is not commonly used in embedded systems because of the dangers inherent in unexpectedly running out of memory due to using it up or to fragmentation issues. Moreover, algorithms based on dynamically allocated structures tend to be more difficult to test and debug than algorithms based on static structures.

Most RTOSs supply memory-management functions. However, unless your target system is a standard platform, you should plan on rewriting some of the malloc() function to customize it for your environment. At a minimum, the cross-compiler that might be used with an embedded system needs to know about the system's memory model.

For example, the HP compiler discussed earlier isolates the system-specific information in an assembly language function called _getmem(). In the HP implementation, _getmem() returns the address of a block of memory and the size of that block. If the size of the returned block cannot meet the requested size, the biggest available block is returned. The user is responsible for modifying this getmem() according to the requirements of the particular target system. Although HP supplies a generic implementation for getmem(), you are expected to rewrite it to fit the needs and capabilities of your system.

Note

You can find more information about dynamic allocation in embedded system projects in these articles:

- Dailey, Aaron. "Effective C++ Memory Allocation." *Embedded Systems Programming*, January 1999, 44.
- Hogaboom, Richard. "Flexible Dynamic Array Allocation." *Embedded Systems Programming*, December 2000, 152.
- Ivanovic, Vladimir G. "Java and C++: A Language Comparison." *Real Time Computing*, March 1998, 75.
- Lafreniere, David. "An Efficient Dynamic Storage Allocator." *Embedded Systems Programming*, September 1998, 72.
- Murphy, Niall. "Safe Memory Utilization." *Embedded Systems Programming*, April 2000, 110.
- Shaw, Kent. "Run-Time Error Checking," *Embedded Developers Journal*, May 2000, 8.

- Stewart, David B. "More Pitfalls for Real-Time Software Developers." *Embedded Systems Programming*, November 1999, 74.

Object Placement

It should be clear by now that an embedded systems programmer needs to be able to control the physical position of code and data in memory. To create a table of exception vectors, for example, you must be able to create an array of ISR addresses and force it to reside at location zero. Similarly, embedded systems programmers must be able to force program instructions to reside at an address corresponding to EPROM and to force global data to reside at addresses corresponding to RAM. Startup code and ISRs pose similar challenges.

The linker is the primary tool for controlling code placement. Generally, the assembler creates relocatable modules that the linker "fixes" at specific physical addresses. The following sections explain relocatable modules and how the embedded systems programmer can exercise control over the physical placement of objects.

Relocatable Objects

Figure 4.4 represents the classical development model. The C or C++ source file and include files are compiled into an assembly language source file and then the assembler creates a relocatable object file.

Figure 4.4   Embedded software development process.

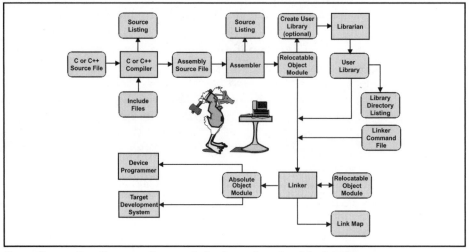

A road map for the creation and design of embedded software.

As the assembler translates the source modules, it maintains an internal counter — the location counter — to keep track of the instruction boundaries, relative to the starting address of the block.

Figure 4.5 is a snippet of 68K assembly language code. The byte count corresponding to the current value of the location counter is highlighted in Figure 4.5. The counter shows the address of the instructions in this block of code, although it could just as easily show the relative byte counts (offsets) for data blocks. In the simplest development environments, the developer uses special assembly language pseudo-instructions to place objects at particular locations (such as ORG 200H to start a module at address 512.) When working in a higher-level language, you need some other mechanism for controlling placement.

Figure 4.5   Assembly language snippet.

```
            Source file: EXAMW00.X68
            Assembled on: 00-12-30 at: 12:27:47
            by: X68K PC-2.2 Copyright (c) University of Teesside 1989,97
            Defaults: ORG $0/FORMAT/OPT A,BRL,CEX,CL,FRL,MC,MD,NOMEX,NOPCO

        1
        2    00000000 1803              MOVE.B      D3,D4
        3    00000002 267C00008000      MOVEA.L     #$00008000,A3
        4    00000008 DE43              ADD.W       D3,D7
        5    0000000A 0245F7A3          ANDI.W      #$F7A3,D5
        6             00000000          END         0

     Lines: 6, Errors: 0, Warnings: 0.
```

In this snippet of 68K assembly-language code, the location counter is highlighted.

The solution is to have the assembler generate relocatable modules. Each relocatable module is translated as if it will reside at location zero. When the assembler prepares the module, it also prepares a symbol table showing which values in the module will need to change if the module is moved to some location other than zero. Before loading these modules for execution, the linker relocates them, that is, it adjusts all the position-sensitive values to be appropriate for where the module actually will reside. Modern instruction sets often include instructions specifically designed to simplify the linker's job (for example, "jump-relative" instructions, which do not need adjusting). Often, the compilers and linkers for such machines can be instructed to generate position-independent code (PIC), which requires no adjustments, regardless of where the code will ultimately reside in memory.

The relocatable modules (or files) typically reference functions in other modules, so, at first glance, you have a Pandora's box of interconnected function calls and memory references. In addition to adjusting internal references for actual location, the linker is also responsible for resolving these inter-module references and creating a block of code that can be loaded into a specific location in the system.

Advantages of Relocatable Modules

Relocatable modules are important for many reasons. For the embedded systems programmer, relocatable modules simplify the physical placement of code generated from a high-level language and allow individual modules to be independently updated and recompiled.

In general-purpose systems, relocatable modules have the added benefits of simplifying memory management (by allowing individual programs to be loaded into any available section of memory without recompilation) and facilitating the use of shared, precompiled libraries.

Using the Linker

The inputs to the linker are the relocatable object modules and the linker command file. The linker command file gives the software engineer complete control of how the code modules are linked together to create the final image. The linker command file is a key element in this process and is an important differentiator between writing code for an embedded system and a desktop PC.

The linker command file is a user-created text file that tells the linker how the relocatable object modules are to be linked together. Linkers use *program sections*. A program section is a block of code or data that is logically distinct from other sections and can be described by its own location counter.

Sections have various attributes that tell the linker how they are to be used. For example, a section might be:

- Program code
- Program data
- Mixed code and data
- ROMable data

Listing 4.1 shows a typical Motorola 68K family linker command file. The meanings of the linker commands are explained in Table 4.1.

Note

ROM Code Space as a Placeholder

Another reasonable design practice is to use the ROM code space simply as a placeholder. When the system starts up the first set of instructions, it actually moves the rest of the operational code out of ROM and relocates it into RAM. This is usually done for performance reasons because RAM is generally faster than ROM. Thus, the system might contain a single 8-bit wide ROM, which it relocates into a 32-bit wide RAM space on bootup. Thus, aside from the boot-loader code, the remainder of the code is designed and linked to execute out of the RAM space at another address range in memory.

Listing 4.1 Example of a linker command file.

(from Microtec Research, Inc.).[2]

```
CHIP 68000
LISTMAP INTERNALS,PUBLICS,CROSSREF
COMMON COMSEC=$1000
ORDER SECT2,SECT3,COMSEC
PUBLIC EXTRANEOUS=$2000
NAME TESTCASE
PAGE SECT2
FORMAT IEEE
*Load first two modules
LOAD Lnk68ka.obj, lnk68kb.obj
*Load last module
LOAD lnk68kc.obj
END
```

2. Microtec Research, Inc., is now part of Mentor Graphics, Inc.

Table 4.1 Linker commands.

CHIP	specifies the target microprocessor. It also determines how sections are aligned on memory address boundaries and, depending upon the microprocessor specified, how much memory space is available. Finally, it determines the behavior of certain processor-specific addressing modes.
LISTMAP	generates a symbol table listing both local and external definition symbols. It also causes these symbols to be placed in the output object module so that a debugger can associate symbols with memory addresses later on. The symbol table displays the symbols along with their final absolute address locations. You can look at the link map output and determine whether all the modules were linked properly and will reside in memory where you think they should be. If the linker was successful, all addresses are adjusted to their proper final values and all links between modules are resolved.
COMMON; named COMSEC	is placed at hexadecimal starting address 1000 ($ means hexadecimal). The linker places all COMMON sections from different modules with the same name in the same place in memory. COMMON sections are generally used for program variables that will reside in RAM, such as global variables.
ORDER	specifies the order that the sections are linked together into the executable image.
PUBLIC	specifies an absolute address, hexadecimal 2000, for the variable EXTRANEOUS. This is an interesting command, and I'll return to it in Chapter 5, when I discuss using "casting" to assign absolute addresses to variables, as you might do for memory-mapped hardware peripheral devices.
NAME TESTCASE	specifies the filename of the final output module.
PAGE	specifies that the next section begins on a page (256-byte) boundary. After the PAGE command is read, each subsection, or module, of the specified section is aligned on page boundaries. In this example, SECT2 will be started on the next available page boundary.

FORMAT	specifies the output file format. In this case, it is IEEE-695, an industry-standard file format. Another file format could be Motorola S-Record files. S-Records are ASCII-based files and human readable. S-Records are typically used for loading the code into a ROM programming device.
LOAD	loads the next three specified object files.
END	signifies the end of the file.

Additional Reading

- Ganssle, Jack G. "Wandering Pointers, Wandering Code." *Embedded Systems Programming*, November 1999, 21.
- Jones, Nigel. "A 'C' Test: The 0x10 Best Questions for Would-be Embedded Programmers." *Embedded Systems Programming*, May 2000, 119.
- Kernighan, Brian W. and Dennis M. Ritchie. *The C Programming Language*, 2nd ed. Englewood Clifs, NJ: Prentice-Hall, 1988.
- Madau, Dinu. "Rules for Defensive Programming." *Embedded Systems Programming*, December 1999, 24.
- Murphy, Niall. "Watchdog Timers." *Embedded Systems Programming*, November 2000, 112.
- Saks, Dan. "Volatile Objects." *Embedded Systems Programming*, September 1998, 101.
- Saks, Dan. "Using const and volatile in Parameter Types." *Embedded Systems Programming*, September 1999, 77.
- Silberschatz, Abraham, and Peter Baer Galvin. *Operating System Concepts*, 5th ed. Reading, MA: Addison Wesley Longman, 1998.
- Simon, David E. *An Embedded Software Primer.* Reading, MA: Addison-Wesley, 1999, 149.
- Stewart, Dave. "The Twenty-Five Most Common Mistakes with Real-Time Software Development." A paper presented at the Embedded Systems Conference, San Jose, 26 September 2000.
- Sumner, Scott A. "From PROM to Flash." *Embedded Systems Programming*, July 2000, 75.

Summary

Because embedded systems developers must explicitly control the physical placement of code and data, they must have a more detailed understanding of the execution environment and their development tools. Developers whose prior work has been limited to the desktop-application domain need to pay special attention to the capabilities of their linker.

Embedded systems developers also need a more detailed understanding of many system-level issues. The typical application developer can usually ignore the internal mechanisms of `malloc()` and `free()`, for example. Because embedded systems developers might need to write replacements for these services, they should become familiar with several allocation algorithms and their relative trade-offs. Similarly, the embedded systems developer might need to understand the implications of using fixed-point arithmetic instead of floating-point arithmetic.

Finally, embedded systems developers should expect to become intimately familiar with the details of their system's hardware and run-time initialization needs. It is impossible to write reliable startup code without understanding the proper initialization of the relevant hardware.

Although I can't hope to explain how every kind of hardware works, I can show some of the tricks used to manipulate the hardware from C instead of assembly. The next chapter addresses this and other special techniques commonly used by embedded systems programmers.

Works Cited

1. Ganssle, Jack. *The Art of Designing Embedded Systems*. Boston, MA: Newnes, 2000, 61.
2. Microtec Research. *Assembler/Linker/Librarian User's Guide*, from the Software Development Tools Documentation Set for the 68000 Family, Document #100113-011. Santa Clara, CA: Microtec Research, Inc., 1995, 4-1.

Chapter 5

Special Software Techniques

Chapter 4 looked at how the embedded systems software-development process differs from typical application development. This chapter introduces several programming techniques that belong in every embedded systems programmer's toolset. The chapter begins with a discussion of how to manipulate hardware directly from C, then discusses some algorithms that aren't seen outside the embedded domain, and closes with a pointer toward a portion of the Unified Modeling Language (UML) that has special significance for embedded systems programmers.

Manipulating the Hardware

Embedded systems programmers often need to write code that directly manipulates some peripheral device. Depending on your architecture, the device might be either port mapped or memory mapped. If your architecture supports a separate I/O address space and the device is port mapped, you have no choice but to "drop down" to assembly to perform the actual manipulation; this is because C has no intrinsic notion of "ports." Some C compilers provide special CPU-specific intrinsic functions, which are replaced at translation time by CPU-specific assembly language operations. While still machine-specific, intrinsic functions do allow the programmer to avoid in-line assembly. Things are much simpler if the device is memory mapped.

In-line Assembly

If you only need to read or write from a particular port, in-line assembly is probably the easiest solution. In-line assembly is always extremely compiler dependent. Some vendors use a #pragma directive to escape the assembly instructions, some use special symbols such as _asm/_endasm, and some wrap the assembly in what looks like a function call.

```
asm( "assembly language statements go here" );
```

The only way to know what a particular compiler expects (or if it even allows in-line assembly) is to check the compiler documentation.

Because in-line assembly is so compiler dependent, it's a good idea to wrap all your assembly operations in separate functions and place them in a separate support file. Then, if you need to change compilers, you only need to change the assembly in one place. For example, if you needed to read and write from a device register located at port address 0x42, you would create access functions like these:

```
int read_reg( )
{
    asm( "in acc,0x42");
}


void write_reg(int newval)
{
    asm( "
        mov acc,newval
        out 0x42
    ");
}
```

In this example, the instructions in and out are I/O access instructions and not memory access (read/write) instructions.

Please note that these functions involve some hidden assumptions that might not be true for your compiler. First, read_reg() assumes that the function return value should be placed in the accumulator. Different compilers observe different conventions (sometimes dependent on the data size) about where the return value should be placed. Second, write_reg() assumes that the compiler will translate the reference to newval into an appropriate stack reference. (Remember, arguments to functions are passed on the stack.) Not all compilers are so nice!

If your compiler doesn't support in-line assembly, you'll have to write similar read/write functions entirely in assembly and link them to the rest of your program. Writing the entire function in assembly is more complex, because it must conform to the compiler's conventions regarding stack frames. You can get a "template" for the assembly by compiling a trivial C function that manipulates the right number of arguments directly to assembly

```
int read_reg_fake( )
{
    return 0x7531;
}
```

Substituting the desired port read in place of the literal load instruction and changing the function name converts the generated assembly directly into a complete port read function.

Memory-Mapped Access

Manipulating a memory-mapped device is far simpler. Most environments support two methods, linker-based and pointer-based. The linker-based method uses the `extern` qualifier to inform the compiler that the program will be using a resource defined outside the program. The line

```
extern volatile int device_register;
```

tells the compiler that an integer-sized resource named `device_register` exists outside the program, in a place known to the linker. With this declaration available, the rest of the program can read and write from the device just as if it were a global variable. (The importance of `volatile` is explained later in this chapter.)

Of course, this solution begs the question because it doesn't explain how the linker knows about the device. To successfully link a program with this kind of external declaration, you must use a linker command to associate the "variable" name with the appropriate address. If the register in question was located at $40000000, the command might be something like

```
PUBLIC _device_register = $40000000
```

Be forewarned, the linker might not recognize long, lowercase names such as `device_register`. (Linkers are usually brain-dead compared to compilers.) One way to find out what name the linker is expecting is to compile the module before you add the `PUBLIC` linker command and see what name the linker reports as unresolvable.

Those who prefer this method argue that you should use the linker to associate symbols with physical addresses. They also argue that declaring the device register as extern keeps all the information about the system's memory map in one place: in the linker command file, where it belongs.

The alternative is to access memory-mapped hardware through a C pointer. A simple cast can force a pointer to address any specific memory address. For example, a program can manipulate an Application-Specific Integrated Circuit (ASIC) device that appears to the software as 64, 16-bit, memory-mapped registers beginning at memory address 0x40000000 with code like this

```
unsigned short x;                          /* Local variable   */
    volatile unsigned short *io_regs;      /* Pointer to ASIC */
    io_regs = (unsigned short* ) 0x40000000;   /* Point to ASIC    */
    x = io_regs[10];                       /* Read register 10 */
```

This example declares io_regs to be a pointer to an unsigned, 16-bit (short) variable. The third assignment statement uses a cast to force io_regs to point to memory location 0x40000000. The cast operator directs the compiler to ignore everything it knows about type checking and do exactly what you say because you are the programmer and, best of all, you do know exactly what you are doing.

Bitwise Operations

Embedded programs often need to manipulate individual bits within hardware registers. In most situations, the best practice is to read the entire register, change the bit, and then write the entire register back to the device. For example, to change the third bit from the right

```
const char status_mask=0x04;
extern volatile char device_register;


device_register = device_register | status_mask;
        // force the third from the right bit to a one.
device_register = device_register & (~status_mask);
        // force the third from the right bit to a zero
device_register = device_register ^ status_mask;
        // change the state of the third from the right bit.
```

You get the exact same result using the shorthand assignment operators:

```
device_register |= status_mask;
device_register &= (~status_mask);
device_register ^= status_mask;
```

The literal that corresponds to the bit to be changed is called a *mask*. Defining the constant to represent the mask (status_mask) insulates the rest of your code from unanticipated changes in the hardware (or in your understanding of the hardware). The constant also can greatly improve the readability of this kind of code. Not all embedded compilers support ANSI C's const. If your compiler doesn't support const, you can use the preprocessor to give the status mask a symbolic name, as in the following listing. The const form is preferred because it supports static type checking.

```
#define STATUS_MASK 0x04
device_register = device_register | STATUS_MASK;
```

Although this read/modify/write method works in most cases, with some devices, the read can cause unwanted side-effects (such as clearing a pending interrupt). If the register can't be read without causing a problem, the program must maintain a shadow register. A shadow register is a variable that the program uses to keep track of the register's contents. To change a bit in this case, the program should:

- Read the shadow register
- Modify the shadow register
- Save the shadow register
- Write the new value to the device

In its most compact form, the code would look something like this

```
#define STATUS_MASK 0x04
int shadow;
device_register = (shadow |= STATUS_MASK;)
```

Using the Storage Class Modifier Volatile

Another important data modifying attribute is sometimes missed when interfacing C or C++ code to hardware peripheral devices: the storage class modifier, volatile. Most compilers assume that memory is memory and, for the purpose of code optimization, can make certain assumptions about that memory. The key assumption is that a value stored in memory is not going to change unless you write to it. However, hardware peripheral registers change all the time. Consider the case of a simple universal asynchronous receiver/transmitter (UART). The UART receives serial data from the outside world, strips away the extraneous bits, and presents a byte of data for reading. At 50 kilobaud, it takes 0.2 milliseconds to transmit one character. In 0.2 milliseconds, a processor with a 100MHz memory bus, assuming four clock cycles per memory write, can write to the UART output data register about 5,000 times. Clearly, a mechanism is needed to control the rate that the transmitted data is presented to the UART.

The UART paces the data rate by having a status bit, typically called Transmitter Buffer Empty (TBMT). Thus, in the example case, the TBMT bit might go low when the first byte of data to be transmitted is sent to the UART and then stay low until the serial data has been sent and the UART is ready to receive the next character from the processor. The C code for this example is shown in Listing 5.1.

Listing 5.1 UART code.

```
/* Suppose that an I/0 port is located at 0x4000
I/0 port status is located at 0x4001
Transmitter buffer empty = DB0; DB0 = 1 when character may be sent */


void main(void)
    {
    int *p_status;              /* Pointer to the status port */
    int *p_data;                /* Pointer to the data port */
    p_status = (int*) 0x4001 ;    /* Assign pointer to status port */
    p_data = ( int* ) 0x4000 ;    /* Assign pointer to data port */
      do { } while (( *p_status & 0x01) == 0 );        /* Wait */
      .....
      .....
    }
```

C code for a UART polling loop.

Suppose your C compiler sees that you've written a polling loop to continuously read the TBMT status bit. It says, "Aha! I can make that more efficient by keeping that memory data in a local CPU register (or the internal data cache)." Thus, the code will be absolutely correct, but it won't run properly because the new data in the memory location representing the UART is never updated.

The keyword volatile[7,8] is used to tell the compiler not to make any assumptions about this particular memory location. The contents of the memory location might change spontaneously, so always read and write to it directly. The compiler will not try to optimize it in any way nor allow it to be assigned to the data cache.

Some compilers can go even further and have special keywords that allow you to specify that this is noncachable data. This forces the compiler to turn off caching in the processor.

Speed and Code Density

In many cases, the compiler generates much more efficient code, both in terms of space and speed, if an operation is performed through a pointer rather than through a normal variable reference. If a function manipulates the same variable several times or steps through the members of an array, forming the reference through a pointer might produce better code.

Both time and RAM are usually in short supply in most embedded systems, so efficiency is key. For example, this snippet of C code

```
void strcpy2(char dst[], char const src[])
}
        int i;
        for (i=0; src[i]; i+=1)
        {
                dst[i] = src[i];
        }
}
```

translates to the following sequence of assembly language instructions.

```
void strcpy2(char dst[], char const src[])
{
        int i;
00000000: 4E56 0000            link        a6,#0
00000004: 226E 0008            movea.l     8(a6),a1
00000008: 206E 000C            movea.l     12(a6),a0
        for (i=0; src[i]; i+=1)
        {
0000000C: 7000                 moveq       #0,d0
0000000E: 6008                 bra.s       *+10            ; 0x00000018
                dst[i] = src[i];
00000010: 13B0 0800 0800       move.b      (a0,d0.1),(a1,d0.1)
        }
```

```
00000016: 5280                    addq.l    #1,d0
00000018: 4A30 0800               tst.b     (a0,d0.1)
0000001C: 66F2                    bne.s     *-12           ; 0x00000010

0000001E: 4E5E                    unlk      a6
00000020: 4E75                    rts
00000022: 8773 7472 6370          dc.b      0x87,'strcpy2'
          7932
0000002A: 0000
}
```

When written with subscript references, the function requires 34 bytes. Notice that the repeatedly executed body of the loop (from move.b to bne.s) spans four instructions.

Like many array operations, this loop can be written in terms of pointers instead of subscripted references:

```
void strcpy(char *dst, char const *src)
{
    while (( *dst++ = *src++ )){;}
}
```

(The double parentheses quiet a compiler warning about the assignment. The curly braces around the semi-colon quiet a compiler warning about the empty statement.) On the same compiler, this version translates to the following assembly:

```
void strcpy(char *dst, char const *src)
{
00000000: 4E56 0000               link      a6,#0
00000004: 226E 0008               movea.l   8(a6),a1
00000008: 206E 000C               movea.l   12(a6),a0
          while (( *dst++ = *src++ )){;}
0000000C: 12D8                    move.b    (a0)+,(a1)+
0000000E: 66FC                    bne.s     *-2            ; 0x0000000c

00000010: 4E5E                    unlk      a6
00000012: 4E75                    rts
00000014: 8673 7472 6370          dc.b      0x86,'strcpy',0x00
          7900
0000001C: 0000
}
```

In this case, the compiled code occupies only 20 bytes and the loop body reduces to only two instructions: move.b, bne.s.

Anyway, if the example $69 embedded system had 256Mb of RAM and a 700MHz Pentium-class processor, you could probably ignore the overhead issues and not use pointers. However, reality sometimes rears its ugly head and forces you to program in C with the same care that you would use if programming directly in assembly language.

Interrupts and Interrupt Service Routines (ISRs)

Interrupts are a fact of life in all computer systems. Clearly, many embedded systems would be severely hampered if they spent the bulk of the CPU cycles checking the state of a single status bit in a polling loop.

Interrupts need to be prioritized in order of importance (or criticality) to the system. Taking care of a key being pressed on the keyboard is not as time critical as saving data when an impending power failure is detected.

Conceptually, an ISR is a simple piece of code to write. An external device (for a microcontroller, an external device could be internal to the chip but external to the CPU core) asserts an interrupt signal to the interrupt input of the CPU. If the CPU is able to accept the interrupt, it goes through a hardwired ISR response cycle and typically:

- Pushes the return address of the next instruction onto the stack
- Picks up the address of the ISR (vector) from the exception table and goes to that address in memory to execute the next instruction

After it has begun, the ISR should:

- Decide when to disable and re-enable further interrupts (more about this later)
- Save the state of any internal resources (registers) used in the ISR
- Determine which device is causing the interrupt (especially with shared interrupts)
- Execute the ISR code
- Reset the external interrupting devices, if necessary
- Restore the state of the system
- Enable interrupts
- Return from the interrupt

From Polling Loop to Interrupt-Driven

An example of an embedded application that doesn't require any interrupts is a home burglar alarm. Figure 5.1 is a flow chart for a burglar alarm algorithm. Note that after the system has initialized itself, the processor continuously cycles through every sensor checking to see whether it has been triggered. Because it's highly likely that the time required to check every sensor is extremely brief, the potential time delay from the time a sensor has been triggered to the time that the processor checks it would be short, perhaps a few milliseconds or less. Thus, the worst-case latency in servicing the hardware is just the transit time through the loop.

Figure 5.1 Burglar alarm flowchart.

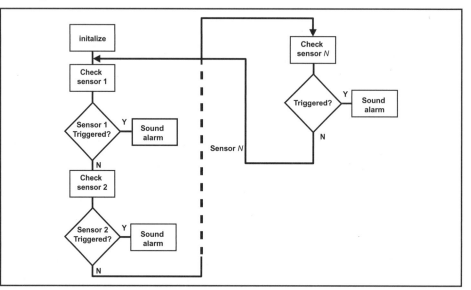

Flowchart for a simple burglar alarm.

Note

Flowcharts may be out of vogue in today's world of object-oriented design, but they are still useful design tools to describe algorithms that require the control of systems rather than the manipulation of data within a system.

Now, add some complexity. Perhaps the system includes a real-time clock and display panel. Add an automatic phone dialer for good measure, and you are beginning to reach a decision point in your design. Is it the system not behaving properly because the time required to poll each hardware device is a significant fraction of the available processing time? Is a delay between a hardware device needing servicing and the processor finally checking the device resulting in system failure? As soon as these issues require attention, your system probably needs to become interrupt driven.

Nested Interrupts and Reentrancy

If a higher-priority interrupt can preempt and interrupt a lower-priority interrupt, things get more complicated. For that reason, simple systems disable all other interrupts as soon as the program responds to the current interrupt. When the interrupt routine is finished, it re-enables interrupts. If instead interrupts are allowed to "nest," the programmer must take special care to insure that all functions called during the interrupt service time are *reentrant*. A function that can be called asynchronously from multiple threads without concern for synchronization or mutual access is said to be reentrant.

In *An Embedded Software Primer*, David Simon[10] gives three rules to apply to decide whether a function is reentrant:

1. A reentrant function *cannot* use variables in a non-atomic way unless they are stored on the stack of the task that called the function or are otherwise the private variables of the task. (A section of code is *atomic* if it cannot be interrupted.)

2. A reentrant function *cannot* call any other functions that are not themselves reentrant.

3. A reentrant function *cannot* use the hardware in a non-atomic way.

If an ISR were to call a function that was not reentrant, the program would eventually exhibit a mutual access or synchronization bug. Generally, this situation arises when an interrupt asynchronously modifies code that is being used by another task. Suppose that a real-time clock in the system wakes up every second and generates an interrupt, and the ISR updates a clock data structure in memory. If a task is in the middle of reading the clock when the clock interrupts and changes the value so that the task reads half of the old time and half of the new time, the time reported could easily be off by days, weeks, months, or years, depending on what counter was rolling over when the time was read.

Simon gives this example of a non-reentrant function shown in Listing 5.2.

Listing 5.2 Non-reentrant function.

```
Bool fError;                         /* Someone else sets this */

void display( int j )
{
   if ( !fError )
   {
      printf ( "\nValue:  %d", j );
      j = 0;
      fError = TRUE;
   }
   else
   {
      printf ("\nCould not display value");
      fError = FALSE;
   }
}
```

A non-reentrant function from Simon[10] (courtesy of Addison-Wesley).

In Listing 5.2, the function is non-reentrant for two reasons. The Boolean variable fError is outside the function display() in a fixed location in memory. It can be modified by any task that calls display(). The use of fError is not atomic because a task switch can occur between the time that fError is tested and fError is set. Thus, it violates rule 1. The variable "j" is okay because it is private to display(). The next problem is that display() might violate rule 2 if the printf() function is non-reentrant. Determining whether printf() is reentrant requires some research in the compiler's documentation.

If you've written all your own functions, you can make sure they meet the requirements for a reentrant function. If you are using library functions supplied by the compiler vendor, or other third-party sources, you must do some digging.

Measuring Execution Time

Although the trend is to insist that everything possible should be written in a high-level language, in "The Art of Designing Embedded Systems," Jack Ganssle[4] argues that ISRs and other tight timing routines should be written in assembly because it is straightforward — although somewhat tedious — to calculate the exact execution time for each instruction. Conversely, there is no easy way to tell what the eventual execution time will be for a routine that is coded in C. Of course, you could have the compiler produce the assembly language output file and then do a hand calculation with that code, but it defeats the purpose of coding in C in the first place.

In many embedded applications, it is essential that the programmer knows exactly how long the routine will take. A time-critical ISR can be logically correct but fail because the execution time is too long. Assembly language routines can, theoretically, account for every machine cycle, though the accounting becomes more and more complex as architectures become more sophisticated.

Modern tools, such as Instruction Set Simulators and Architectural Simulators, allow the designer to compile and run embedded code on the workstation and keep track of the actual machine cycle counts. The good tools also keep track of cache hits and miss penalties, Dynamic RAM(DRAM) access times, and wait cycles. So, even though you might not write your ISR in assembly language, you can certainly determine to high precision how much time it will take the ISR to execute. Of course, if you don't have access to these tools or choose not to use them, you have only yourself, the hardware designer, or the intern to blame.

An old software adage recommends coding for functionality first and speed second. Since 80 percent of the speed problems are in 20 percent of the code, it makes sense to get the system working and then determine where the bottlenecks are. Unfortunately, real-time systems by their nature don't work at all if things are slow.

Note

Having spent my productive years[1] designing hardware and firmware, writing ISRs always seemed straightforward to me. However, I was surprised to see how much trouble many of my students seemed to have getting their ISRs to work properly in lab experiments. The problem stems from a number of contributing factors, but the root cause is that it's difficult to incrementally debug an ISR. It either works, or it doesn't.

My students also had problems with the chip manufacturer's data book. Trying to decipher and dig through the various levels of indirection in the documentation to figure out how to set the appropriate bits in various registers has proven to be the defining task of writing an ISR. Having gone through it with several classes, I now provide a cookbook-like flow chart to explain how to set up the various registers so they can proceed with their experiments. In general, this is the student's first experience with a microprocessor documentation, and it isn't pretty. If the experience of my students is any indication of the state of affairs in the industry in general for new engineers, companies should seriously look at tools that automatically and painlessly generate device driver code (such as Driveway from Aisys Ltd).

---

1. Defined as "prior to being promoted to management."

Real-Time Operating Systems (RTOS)

Discussing real-time, interrupt-driven environments naturally leads to the topic of RTOSs. Managing a system of hardware resources with tight timing restrictions is a complex process, and commercially available RTOSs do an excellent job of easing the pain (for a price).

This book doesn't explain how to use and program for RTOSs. If you are interested in this subject, read *An Embedded Software Primer* by David E. Simon.[10] I use Simon's book as the textbook for my *Introduction to Embedded Systems* class at the University of Washington–Bothell. Simon's book is especially strong in describing writing software to be used under RTOSs.

An RTOS isolates tasks from one another, allowing each developer on the team to write code as if they had exclusive use of the target system and its resources. While this is a big plus, the overall design must still properly address the issues of shared data and concurrency. Similarly, the programmers implementing that design must fully understand those issues and the use of correct use of critical sections, semaphores, interprocess communication, and more.

Moreover, any RTOS must be customized, to some degree, for the target environment that it will be supervising. Typically, this involves developing the board support package (BSP) for the operating system and the target. This could be a minor task of several weeks or a major effort that is so complex it is contracted back to the RTOS vendor to create.

At any rate, any software developer responsible for real-time code should have already taken a class in operating systems as part of their undergraduate education. I use *Operating Systems Concepts* by Abraham Silberschatz and Peter Baer Galvin[9] in my class on operating systems.

Watchdog Timers

Particular to embedded system software, the *watchdog timer* is literally, a "watchdog." If a fault occurs in the system and sends the system "into the weeds," it's the watchdog timer's job bring the system back on line. The watchdog timer is a must in any high-reliability application.

The basic idea is simple. Suppose the main loop of the software takes, on average, 25 milliseconds to execute, and worst-case, 35 milliseconds to execute. Suppose you have a device (the watchdog timer) connected to a high-priority interrupt on your system, such as RESET or the non-maskable interrupt (NMI). Also, suppose after it's triggered, the device waits 50 milliseconds and then yanks on the RESET pin, causing the processor to start over from RESET. The only way to prevent it from yanking on RESET is to send it a pulse causing it to start the 50-millisecond delay all over again. In technical terms, it is a *retriggerable, one-shot multivibrator*, but watchdog timer works just fine.

In the example application, the code usually is cycled completely through the main loop in at least 35 milliseconds. Therefore, the last operation to perform in the main loop is to retrigger the watchdog timer for another 50-millisecond interval. If anything goes wrong with the software or hardware that can be recovered from — such as a power glitch — the software won't execute properly, and the watchdog timer won't be retriggered within the appropriate time window. Under these conditions, the timer times out and causes the system to restart itself.

In his "Watchdog Timers" article, Niall Murphy[6] suggests that before resetting the timer, the system should perform some sanity checks. For example, he suggests checking stack depth, number of buffers allocated, and the state of mechanical components in the system before resetting the watchdog timer. He also suggests that a flag should be set at various points in the code indicating successful completion of that block of code. Just before the timer is reset (Murphy calls it "kicking the dog"), all flags are checked. If all flags have been set, the timer can be retriggered for another interval. If not, the failure mode is recorded, and the timer is allowed to time out as shown in Figure 5.2.

Figure 5.2   Watchdog timer.

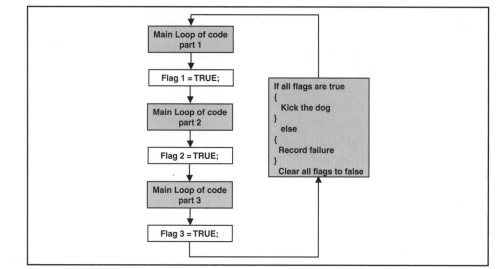

Watchdog timer flow diagram (from Murphy[6]).

Watchdog Timer: Debugging the Target System

The next problem you face with a watchdog timer is debugging the target system. Because the watchdog timer runs independently of the rest of the system, if you suspend program execution, as you might do with a debugger, you're done for. The watchdog timer times out and resets the system. Therefore, if your target system has a watchdog timer, and most embedded systems do, build an easy way to enable or disable the timer into your software and hardware, if possible. If the timer is external to the CPU, a simple solution is to put a jumper on the board that can break the connection between the timer and the CPU. In software, isolate the timer routines so that you can use conditional compilation (`#if DEBUG`) to remove the timer code.

If the watchdog timer is to be used in the context of an RTOS, you must consider the control of the timer with respect to the rest of the system. Murphy suggests that one of the RTOS tasks be dedicated to operating the watchdog timer. This task has a higher priority than the other tasks it is monitoring. The RTOS task wakes up at regular intervals and checks the sanity of the other tasks. If all the checks pass, it retriggers the watchdog timer.

Flash Memory

If you have a digital camera or an MPEG music player, you're already familiar with *flash memory*. Flash memory is rapidly replacing other nonvolatile memory technologies as the method of choice for storing firmware in embedded systems. At this writing, the demand for flash-memory devices has outpaced the silicon manufacturer's production capacity, and the parts have been on allocation for several years.

From the point of view of embedded systems, flash memories are attractive because they can be reprogrammed in the field. The most convenient versions feature *in-circuit programmability*, meaning they can be reprogrammed while in service, without the need for special power supplies. If you've ever "flashed the BIOS" in your PC or laptop, you've already gone through the drill. This has not only impacted how a customer takes advantage of field upgradability, it has also impacted the cost of development tools that an embedded design team needs.

Upgradability isn't the only use for flash, however. Using flash memory in an embedded design enables that design to have its performance parameters modified while the device is in service, allowing it to be optimized (tuned) for the current state of its operational environment. In all probability, your car uses flash memory in this way to adjust for wear on spark plugs, injectors, and other factors affecting combustion.

The complicating factor in implementing a flash-based software architecture is that the code must be capable of self-modifying, and, perhaps even more restrictive, it must be able to recover from a fault in a way that doesn't render the product inoperable. In "The How-To's of Flash: Implementing Downloadable Firmware" presented at the Embedded Systems Conference in 2000, Bill Gatliff[5] discussed two possible strategies, the *embedded programmer* and the *microprogrammer.*

The embedded programmer is code that is part of the firmware shipped with the product. The advantages of this approach are that it is straightforward to implement and doesn't require sophisticated supporting programs. The disadvantages are that it must be right in the first release of the product, it might use RAM and ROM resources to the exclusion of the operational code of the device, and it generally lacks flexibility.

The microprogrammer approach is to have only the absolute minimum code necessary on the chip (boot loader) to download the flash programming algorithm (the microprogrammer) and the new software image. The microprogrammer has the advantages that it's flexible and requires minimal ROM overhead. The disadvantages are that it is more difficult to implement than the target-resident programming algorithm and that the supporting programs need to have more intelligence.

In "From PROM to Flash," Scott Sumner[11] discusses the design of his flash-programming algorithm and stresses the need for protection against code corruption due to power interruption during the reprogramming phase. He suggests the system designer should reserve some sectors in the flash for a permanent recovery program capable of booting the system and restarting the programs should a programming cycle be interrupted.

Sumner actually suggests placing three independent programs in the memory space of the flash chip. These programs each have a different memory map for code and data:

- A boot loader program that executes on power-up and initializes the system in a rudimentary way, so that RAM and some I/O support is available. The boot loader then prompts the user to decide whether the normal application should be run or whether the flash reprogramming algorithm should be implemented. Because most people don't want to answer this question each time a system is powered-up, this prompt also could be a switch on the back of the device or a jumper on the motherboard that is tested during the boot process.
- The real application code that can be reprogrammed by the flash reprogramming algorithm.
- A RAM resident reprogramming algorithm that does the actual reprogramming of the device. The code is located in a protected region of the flash and moved into RAM when the reprogramming option is chosen. Thus, Sumner has implemented the embedded programmer model, described by Gatliff.

Design Methodology

In the early '90s, Dataquest (an industry-research company) studied the size of software projects over a period of several years. Each year, Dataquest surveyed a number of software projects and asked the managers to estimate the size of the code base for the last project they completed, the project on which they were currently working, and the next project they would do. Thus, the Dataquest researchers were able to compare the manager's estimate of the size of the next project with the actual size of the same code base, because Dataquest came back a year or so later. Dataquest found that the growth of the size of the code image plotted nicely on a semi-log graph, indicating that the code base was growing exponentially each year. Also, the manager's estimate of the size of the code versus the actual size of the code was consistently low by at least a factor of two.

The message here is that developers can't keep building systems with the same methods and processes they've used in the past. There just aren't enough software developers in the world to keep staffing the design teams. Developers need a new way to build systems.

That's why you hear so much about various design methodologies. Even run-of-the-mill projects have become so complex that you can't hope to get predictable results without following some disciplined design practices. Interestingly enough, the exact practice might not be as important as the discipline. (See the "One Success Story" sidebar coming up.)

Graphical descriptions of the system are a big part of nearly every design methodology. In the early 1990s, as many as 50 object-oriented methods were in use according to Carolyn Duby in her presentation of "Getting Started with the Unified Modeling Language."[3] These methods had similar concepts but, as you might expect, used different notations for their graphical representations. Having different notations complicated communications and made the adoption process difficult because companies and developers did not want to adopt a design methodology that lacked industry-wide support. Work continued to make progress to unify the different methods, and, in 1996, the UML Consortium was formed. A year later, UML was standardized by the Object Management Group (OMG), thus giving UML the legitimacy it needed to be adopted across the industry. Today, UML has wide support across the industry with many tool vendors providing UML-based system-design tools.

If you are familiar with C++ and object-oriented design, you are probably familiar with class and object diagrams from the UML. Class and object diagrams are powerful tools for describing relationships between data and types. However, another less known portion of the UML — statecharts — is probably more relevant to embedded systems design.

One Success Story

About 10 years ago, I was leading a large project with 15 hardware and software developers. We made the decision to follow the latest design methods of structured analysis and structured design. Two books by Tom DeMarco[1,2] — *Structured Analysis and System Design* and *Controlling Software Projects* — became required reading, and we were all anxious to see whether we could do it better this time. We even purchased the latest in Computer-Aided Software Engineering tools (CASE) to help us structure our design and documentation process.

The design process we followed was by the book and rigorous. We developed volumes and volumes of data flow diagrams and system specifications. APIs were defined for all the functions and system abstraction layers. Then, when the design phase was completed, we put the books away and wrote code like we always did before. Gradually, as changes and corrections began to appear, the original design specification became out of synch with the current state of the design.

Although we had the latest tools at our disposal, we lacked a way to "back annotate" our design so that corrections made downstream would be reflected in the higher-level design documents. Back annotation is a common practice in Electronic Design Automation (EDA) circles. Hardware designers, both IC and board-level, routinely back annotate their designs to reflect lower-level changes at the higher design layers. This capability, at least in an automated form, is still relatively rare in software engineering processes.

Also, a major shortcoming of this method is that the CASE tool we used didn't allow the designer to continue to drill down into the coding phase and stay in the design environment. Design and coding were separated from each other. Fortunately, today's tools enable the designer to go to any level in the design and rapidly move between abstraction layers.

Back in the example, because the software designers couldn't stay in the CASE design environment as they progressed from design to coding, they just wrote code as usual. We took a lot of heat from management because progress was viewed as code being written, not time spent in design and specification. The big payback came when we integrated the hardware and the software. The process went incredibly well. Similar projects had spent two to six months in the HW/SW integration phase. We were essentially done in two weeks.

Hardware designers are well-versed in *finite state machines* (FSMs); programmers familiar with compiler design have probably also seen FSMs but might have called them automata. Most digital logic systems can be described and designed using these tools. FSMs are powerful tools for representing systems that exhibit complex functional behavior, that is, exhibit a complex relationship between their inputs and outputs.

Statecharts are a hierarchical extension of FSMs. Statecharts aren't just nested FSMs. Statecharts allow the programmer to treat certain inputs as causing an immediate "shift in context" from the current statechart to its "parent." This gives statecharts much of the same power as other object-oriented paradigms.

From the Trenches

During a customer research/sales visit to a large telecommunications customer, we were pitching a new simulation tool for software design-ers and were demonstrating how you could run your favorite debug-ger in one window and our simulation representation of the hardware in a second window. The customers were obviously interested because they stayed awake (always a good sign) even after our free pizza was gone. However, when we started our question-and-answer session at the tail end of the visit, their manager spoke up and told us they rarely use software debuggers any more. Almost all their design and debug-ging is done using a modern statechart design tool, and they do all their designs graphically. The tool itself creates the C++ code directly from the statecharts. His comments were surprising and indicative that the new paradigm shift is coming and that designers will be fol-lowing a variant of the old axiom that "One picture is worth a thou-sand lines of code." His team was designing a complex embedded system. Clearly they realized that they would not be able to compete in the market unless they could bring a better product to market in time. They opted to develop their software by the most modern method available, namely statechart design.

Another reason for considering statechart-based methods is that many of today's embedded systems designs can be expressed as message-passing architectures. In a message-passing architecture, the various elements of the system can be represented as loosely coupled, autonomous entities that interact by passing messages back and forth. These messages, or events, rep-resent the transfer of data, such as a high-speed direct memory access (DMA) data transfer between two processors on a bus. Similarly, an event might be the receipt of an external interrupt. In each of these situations, it is the event, DMA, or interrupt that triggers the system to move to a new state in response to the event. Today, as you contemplate the future, which con-sists of great arrays of distributed embedded systems connected to each other and the users over the Internet spinal cord, the idea of system designs based upon loosely coupled autonomous entities is not only a convenient way to describe an embedded system design, it's the correct way.

This way of thinking about the system is natural for hardware designers; they've been doing state machine-based hardware designs for many years. However, it is a rather new way for the software designers to think about their designs, and it tends to lend itself to embedded systems due to the real-time, interrupt-driven nature of the environments inwhich they operate. Considering that embedded systems typically involve complex relationships among many inputs and various outputs, statecharts are an important embedded systems design tool for both hardware and software designers.

Additional Reading

- Douglass, Bruce Powel. "Designing Real-Time Systems with the Unified Modeling Language." *Supplement to Electronic Design*, 9 March 1998, 25.
- Douglass, Bruce Powel. "UML for Systems Engineering." *Computer Design*, November 1998, 44.
- Douglass, Bruce Powel. "UML Statecharts." *Embedded Systems Programming*, January 1999, 22.
- Grehan, Rick. "Real-Time Design Goes Object-Oriented." *Computer Design,* December 1997, 57.
- McElroy, Jim. "The ABCs of Visual Programming." *Embedded Developers Journal*, May 2000, 16.
- Mellor, Stephen J. "UML Point/Counterpoint: Modeling Complex Behavior Simply." *Embedded Systems Programming*, March 2000, 38.
- Moore, Alan. "UML's Shortfalls in Modeling Complex Real-Time Systems." *Computer Design*, November 1998, 53.
- Pacheco, Sylvia. "UML Delivers Real-Time Software Standardization." *Real Time Computing*, March 2000, 87.
- Varhol, Peter. "Front-End Design Automation for Building Complex Systems." *Computer Design*, July 1998, 87.
- Varhol, Peter. "New Designs Model Complex Behavior." *Electronic Design*, 21 February 2000, 79.

Summary

More than anything else, the need to "work on the metal" differentiates embedded systems programming from other kinds of programming. Although many "big picture" programmers find direct interaction with the hardware distasteful at best, most embedded systems programmers take a certain amount of pride in getting their hands dirty.

A willingness to get your hands dirty, however, shouldn't translate into sloppy practice. Little things, like declaring a variable extern or packaging in-line assembly in a function wrapper, mark the difference between professionally written, *maintainable* code and sloppy work. The lessons of software engineering and good coding practice apply here just as much as anywhere else — they just have to be interpreted within the context.

Although I have tried to mention some key factors that I think contribute to getting started with interrupts, I want to stress that this chapter does *not* teach how to write real-time code. Real-time programming requires a precise and complete understanding of the issues of mutual exclusion, synchronization, deadlock, and scheduling. On these issues, there can be no compromise. Errors are subtle and *impossible* to fix through standard debugging techniques. If you are not well-versed in these topics, don't write real-time code.

Works Cited

1. DeMarco, Tom. *Structured Analysis and System Specifications.* New York: Yourdon, 1978.

2. DeMarco, Tom. *Controlling Software Projects* (New York: Yourdon, 1982).

3. Duby, Carolyn. "Getting Started with the Unified Modeling Language." A paper presented at the Embedded Systems Conference, San Jose, 26 September 2000.

4. Ganssle, Jack. "The Art of Designing Embedded Systems." Boston, MA: Newnes, 2000, 61.

5. Gatliff, Bill. "The How-To's of Flash: Implementing Downloadable Firmware." A paper presented at the Embedded Systems Conference, San Jose, 25 September 2000.

6. Murphy, Niall. "Watchdog Timers." *Embedded Systems Programming*, November 2000, 112.

7. Saks, Dan. "Volatile Objects." *Embedded Systems Programming*, September 1998, 101.

8. Saks, Dan. "Using `const` and `volatile` in Parameter Types." *Embedded Systems Programming*, September 1999, 77.

9. Silberschatz, Abraham, and Peter Baer Galvin. *Operating System Concepts*, 5th ed. Reading, MA: Addison Wesley Longman, 1998.

10. Simon, David E. *An Embedded Software Primer.* Reading, MA: Addison-Wesley, 1999, 149.

11. Sumner, Scott A. "From PROM to Flash." *Embedded Systems Programming*, July 2000, 75.

Chapter 6

A Basic Toolset

Unlike host-based application developers, embedded systems developers seldom program and test on the same machine. Of necessity, the embedded system code must eventually run on the target hardware. Thus, at least some of the testing and debugging must happen while the system is running in the target. The target system seldom includes the file system storage or processor throughput necessary to support a typical development environment, and even when it does, it's likely to be running a minimal (or even custom) operating system supported by few, if any, tool vendors.

Thus, system integration requires special tools: tools that (mostly) reside on the development platform but that allow the programmer to debug a program running on the target system. At a minimum these tools must:

- Provide convenient run control for the target
- Support a convenient means to replace the code image on the target
- Provide non-intrusive, real-time monitoring of execution on the target

The lowest cost tool set that adequately addresses these needs is comprised of a debug kernel (usually in connection with a remote debugger) and a logic analyzer. Some targets also require a ROM emulator to allow quick code changes on the target. This chapter explains why these tools are necessary, how they work, and what they do.

Host-Based Debugging

Although you can do a certain amount of testing on your desktop PC, unless you are lucky enough to be programming for an embedded PC, eventually differences between the desktop hardware and the target hardware will force you to move the testing to the target.

If you write your applications in C or C++, you should be able to debug an algorithm on the host (as long as you watch out for a few minor differences that tend to cause major bugs that I'll discuss shortly). Even if you write in assembly (or have inherited a library of legacy code in assembly), you can execute the code on your desktop system using an Instruction Set Simulator (ISS) until you need to test the real-time interaction of the code and the target system's special hardware.

Aside from the availability of real working peripherals, the greatest source of problems for host-based debugging derives from two architectural characteristics: word size and byte order.

Word Size

Obviously, if your embedded processor has a 16-bit wide architecture and your host-based compiler is expecting a 32-bit data path, you can have problems. An integer data type on a PC can have a range of approximately ± 2 billion, whereas an integer in your target might have a range of approximately ± 32 thousand. Numbers bigger than the targeted range will cause bugs that you'll never see on the PC.

Byte Order

Another problem is the "Little Endian, Big Endian" problem, which is legendary for the amount of money that's been spent over the years finding and fixing this particular bug. Consider Figure 6.1.

Figure 6.1 is a simple example of storing a C string data type in an 8-bit wide memory. Because a char is also eight bits wide, there's no problem. Each character of the string occupies exactly one memory location. Now suppose that the processor has a 16-bit wide data bus, such as Motorola's original 68000-based family of devices or Intel's 80186-based family. Storing only eight bits of data (a char) in a memory location that is capable of holding 16 bits of data would be wasteful, so give the processors the capability of addressing individual bytes within the 16-bit word. Usually, the least significant bit (LSB) is used to designate which byte (odd or even) you are addressing. It's not obvious that byte addressability causes a problem until you have a choice as to how the bytes are packed into memory.

Figure 6.1   Storing a `char` type.

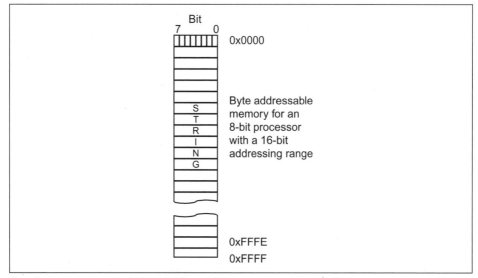

Storing a type `char` in an 8-bit wide memory.

Figure 6.2 shows the two different ways one can store a string of characters in a 16-bit wide memory. You can align the even byte address with the high-order end of the 16-bit data word (Big Endian), or you can align it with the low-order end of the 16-bit data word (Little Endian).

Figure 6.2   16-bit wide memory storing the string.

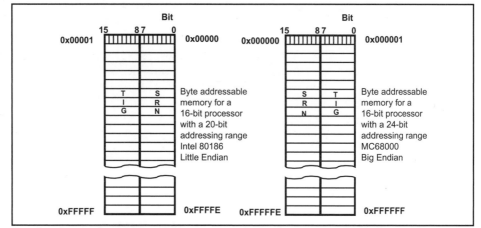

Storing bytes in 16-bit wide memory introduces an ambiguity with respect to the order in which these bytes are stored.

This ambiguity can cause mischief. Fresh engineers trained on Little Endian systems, such as PCs, are suddenly reading the wrong half of memory words.

The problem also extends to 32-bit data paths. Figure 6.3 shows the Big and Little Endians ordering for a 32-bit machine. In a 32-bit data word, the two least significant address bits — A0 and A1 — become the byte-selector bits, but the same ambiguity exists: "From which end of the 32-bit word do you count the address?"

Figure 6.3   Big and Little Endians.

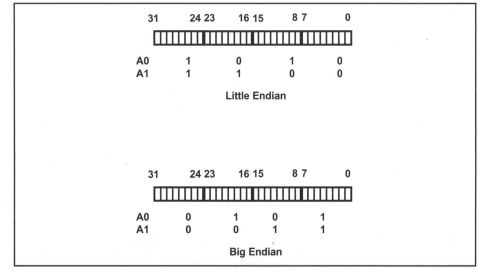

Big and Little Endian organization in a 32-bit data word.

Debug with ISS

Another possible solution is for the software team to use Instruction Set Simulators (ISS) to allow them to compile their target code for their chosen microprocessor but execute the code on their workstations. The ISS is a program that creates a virtual version of the microprocessor. Some ISS's are very elaborate and maintain cycle-by-cycle accuracy of the target microprocessor, including cache behavior, pipeline behavior, and memory interface behavior. My hardware architecture class at UWB uses an ISS for the Motorola MC68000 microprocessor, developed by Paul Lambert, Professor Alan Clements and his group at the University of Teeside, in Great Britain.

Instruction set simulators can be very complex simulation programs. At AMD, we drew a distinction between the architectural simulator, which accurately modeled the processor and memory interface behavior, and the instruction set simulator, which was fast enough for code development but could not be used to accurately predict software execution times for given memory configurations. Today, you can purchase ISS's that are both fast and cycle-accurate. Given the power of today's workstations and PC's, it is reasonable to expect an ISS to be able to have a throughput in the range of 1 to 25 million instructions per second, certainly fast enough to meet the needs of most software developers.

Software developers can also build virtual representations of the target hardware (not just the processor) prior to the general availability of the real hardware. Ledin[3,4] describes a method based upon representing the hardware as a set of non-linear differential equations. Clearly, there is a considerable investment of time required to build these hardware models; however, the investment may well be worth it because they can provide an early indicator of relative task-timing requirements. If the embedded system is to be run under an RTOS, then it is important to know whether a task will be able to run to completion in its allotted time slot. It is better to know this sooner than later.

Smith[5] describes another method of hardware simulation that uses the ability of some processors to execute an exception if an attempt is made to access illegal or non-existent memory. In Smith's example, a single-board computer is used, and the simulated I/O is accessed through a memory fault exception handler. The vector transfers the application to the user's simulation code. The assembly language code example, shown below (from Smith), is written for the Motorola 68332 microcontroller.

As I've discussed earlier, being able to integrate hardware and software sooner in the design process generates big advantages. Clearly, bugs found in the hardware before the hardware is "real" should be much less costly to repair, and design issues uncovered in the software will be simpler to analyze and correct because the hardware is still virtual.

Remote Debuggers and Debug Kernels

Typically, embedded platforms are too resource limited and specialized to support a full-featured debugger. Debuggers for embedded systems address this limitation by distributing the debugger; a portion of the debugger resides on the host computer, and a portion resides in the target system. The two elements of the debugger communicate with each other over a communications channel, such as a serial port or Ethernet port. The portion of the debugger that resides in the target is called the target agent or the debug kernel. The portion of the debugger that resides in the host computer is sometimes called the debugger front end or GUI. The same functionality that you expect from your host debugger is generally available in an embedded debugger, assuming that you have a spare communications channel available. Figure 6.4 shows a typical architectural block diagram for an embedded debugger. (The Wind River debug kernel is a bit more complex than most because it is integrated with VxWorks, Wind River's RTOS.)

Figure 6.4   Typical architectural block diagram.

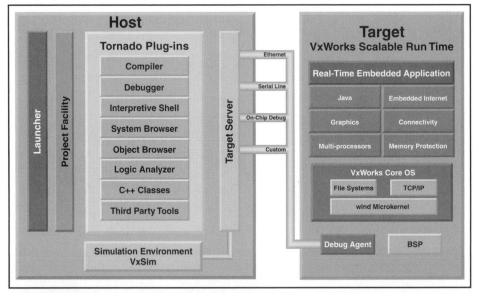

Schematic representation of the Wind River Systems debugger (courtesy of Wind River Systems).

The debugger generally provides a range of run control services. Run control services encompass debugging tasks such as:

- Setting breakpoints
- Loading programs from the host
- Viewing or modifying memory and registers
- Running from an address
- Single-stepping the processor

The debugging features encompassed by run control are certainly the most fundamental debugging tools available. The combination of the functionality of the remote debug kernel with the capabilities of the user interface portion of the tool is the most important debugging requirement.

The debug kernel requires two resources from the target. One is an interrupt vector, and the other is a software interrupt, which is discussed later. Figure 6.5 shows how the debugger is integrated with the target system code. The interrupt vector for the serial port (assuming that this is the communications link to the host) forces the processor into the serial port ISR, which also becomes the entry point into the debugger. Again, this assumes that the serial port's interrupt request will be taken by the target processor most, if not all, of the time. After the debug kernel is entered, the designer is in control of the system. The debug kernel controls whether other lower-priority interrupts are accepted while the debugger is in active control. In many situations, the target system crash as if the debugger does not re-enable interrupts. Obviously, this major compromise must be dealt with.

Figure 6.5   Debug kernel in a target system.

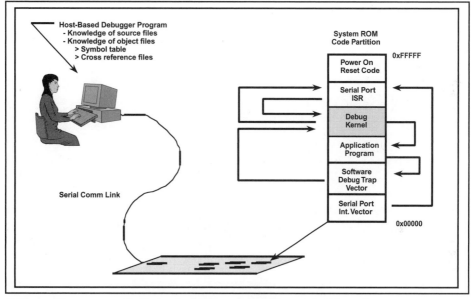

Schematic representation of a debug kernel in a target system.

The debug kernel is similar to an ISR in many ways. An interrupt is received from a device, such as the serial port, which happens to be connected to the designer's host computer. The interrupt is usually set at a high enough priority level — sometimes as high as the non-maskable interrupt (NMI) — that a debugger access interrupt is always serviced. If this were not the case, an errant ISR could disable any other interrupt and you wouldn't be able to regain control of the system. Just like an ISR, the arrival of a command from the host computer stops the execution of the application code and can cause the processor to enter the debug kernel ISR. The machine context is saved, and the debugger is now in control of the target. You can see this schematically in Figure 6.5.

Implementing Breakpoints

To understand how you set a breakpoint in the first place, consider Figure 6.6.

Let's consider the assembly case because it's the most straightforward. The user wants to set a breakpoint at a certain instruction location in RAM. The breakpoint request is acted on by the host-based part of the debugger, and the address of that instruction's memory location is sent to the debug kernel in the target. The debug kernel copies the instruction at that location into a safe place and replaces it with a software breakpoint or trap instruction, which forces control back into the debugger when the breakpoint is accessed. This way, you can single step, run to a breakpoint, and exercise the software while continually transitioning in and out of the debugger.

However, most developers want to debug in C or C++, not assembly. Most likely, in these instances, you will need to enable debugging as a compiler switch so that the debugger and debug kernel can figure out where the breakpoint should be set in memory.

Another obvious problem with this mechanism is that you need to be able to replace the user's instruction code with the trap code, thus implying that you can read and write to this memory region. If the code you're trying to debug is in true ROM or EPROM, you can't get there from here. You'll need to use a RAM-based ROM emulation device to give you the ability to replace user code with breakpoint traps. Several companies manufacture ROM emulators, which are devices that plug into a ROM socket on the target system and contain RAM rather than ROM. Thus your code couldn't be in the traditional ROM (It's possible to set trap codes in EPROM or flash memory). Depending on the architecture of the actual device, flash might not be so difficult with which to work. The debugger might have to erase an entire sector on the device (perhaps 16KB) and then reprogram the sector, but it's possible. Response wouldn't be instantaneous because programming these devices takes much longer than simply writing to a RAM device.

If a software-only breakpoint mechanism isn't possible, you must turn to the additional features that hardware has to offer. Many processors contain special breakpoint registers that can be programmed directly under software control or through the JTAG or BDM ports (See Chapter 7 for more details on these standards.). These registers provide a simple, yet extremely powerful, capability for the debugger. By placing the appropriate address into the breakpoint register, when the processor fetches an instruction from that address, the breakpoint is asserted, and the mechanism for entering the debugger becomes active.

Having the breakpoint register mechanism on the processor itself yields another advantage. In a processor with an on-chip instruction cache, a potential problem exists with coherency between the instruction memory and cache memory. Usually, you don't expect people to write self-modifying code, so you might not be able to detect that an instruction in external memory and an instruction in the cache are different. In that case, you are setting a breakpoint, but it's not detected because the breakpoint in the cache was never changed. Thus, you might have to run the debug session with the caches turned off. An on-chip debug register doesn't have this problem because it looks at the output of the program counter and not the physical memory location.

Figure 6.6   Breakpoints.

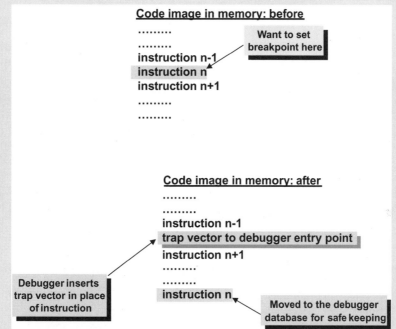

How a debugger sets a breakpoint in read/write memory.

Setting a breakpoint on a data value or range of values is also a necessary debugging capability. You might be able to break into the debugger on a data value that's out of range by running the debugger in a virtual single-step mode. After every instruction executes, break in to the debugger and examine registers and memory for this data value. This will be extremely intrusive (read this as slow) but it would work. In this mode, your target system might not tolerate running this slowly because it's closer to running as an instruction set simulator than to a processor running at speed.

The venerable old 68000 microprocessor was among the first processors to include on-chip debug facilities. It includes a trace bit in the status register that, when set, forces a trap instruction to occur after every real instruction is processed. Using this mechanism, it's not necessary to replace the actual instructions in memory with exception traps or software interrupts, but it is a hardware assist.

The debugger and debug kernel must always remain synchronized with each other. Unexpected events in the target system, such as overwriting the debugger with an errant pointer, causes the whole debugging session to be lost, which forces you to RESET the system and reload the code. Sometimes, the debugger can be isolated from target mishaps by placing it in a protected region of memory (for example, in flash memory); generally, however, it has the same level of fragility as any other piece of software.

Note

Debug kernels are extremely useful in field service applications, enabling a technician to plug into a target and learn something about what is going on inside. If you've ever seen a target system with a RESERVED switch on the back, there's a good chance that switch can kick you into an embedded debug kernel when the target is powered up.

Most embedded systems place their code into some kind of non-volatile memory, such as flash or EPROM. The debug kernel, however, needs to be able to modify the program, set breakpoints, and update the code image. These systems require some means of substituting RAM for the normal code memory, usually via some form of ROM emulator. As the next section explains, a ROM emulator offers many other advantages as well.

The advantages and disadvantages of the debug kernel are summarized in Table 6.1.

Table 6.1 Advantages/disadvantages of the debug kernel.

Advantages of the debug kernel	Disadvantages of the debug kernel
• Low cost: $0 to < $1,000 • Same debugger can be used with remote kernel or on host • Provides most of the services that software designer needs • Simple serial link is all that is required • Can be used with "virtual" serial port • Can be linked with user's code for ISRs and field service • Good choice for code development when hardware is stable • Can easily be integrated into a design team environmen	• Depends on a stable memory subsystem in the target and is not suitable for initial hardware/software integration • Not real time, so system performance will differ with a debugger present • Difficulty in running out of ROM-based memory because you can't single step or insert breakpoints • Requires that the target has additional services, which, for many target systems, is not possible to implement • Debugger might not always have control of the system and depends on code being "well behaved"

ROM Emulator

The ROM emulator contains the following system elements:
- Cabling device(s) to match the target system mechanical footprint of the target system ROM devices
- Fast RAM to substitute for the ROM in the target system
- Local control processor
- Communications port(s) to the host
- Additional features, such as trace memory and flash programming algorithms

At the minimum, a ROM emulator allows you the luxury of quickly downloading new object code images to run in your target system. An important metric for any developer to consider is the change cycle time. The cycle time is the time duration from the point that you discover a bug with the debugger to going back through the edit–compile–assemble–link–download process until you can be debugging again. For a large code image, this can be hours (no kidding!). A ROM emulator with a TBase100 Ethernet channel to the host is an almost ideal method to quickly load large code images into target memory and decrease the cycle time to manageable proportions. Even if your target system uses flash memory, not having to reprogram the flash can be a major time-saver.

Figure 6.7 ROM emulator.

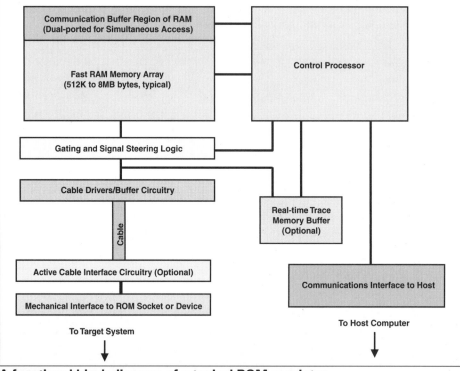

Communication Buffer Region of RAM
(Dual-ported for Simultaneous Access)

Fast RAM Memory Array
(512K to 8MB bytes, typical)

Control Processor

Gating and Signal Steering Logic

Cable Drivers/Buffer Circuitry

Cable

Real-time Trace
Memory Buffer
(Optional)

Active Cable Interface Circuitry (Optional)

Mechanical Interface to ROM Socket or Device

Communications Interface to Host

To Target System

To Host Computer

A functional block diagram of a typical ROM emulator.

A ROM emulator is really RAM, so you'll have no problem setting breakpoints in memory. Also, breakpoints can be set in two ways. If the debugger has been ported to work with the ROM emulator, the code substitution can be accomplished via the emulator control processor instead of by the target processor running in the debug kernel. This offers a distinct advantage because a breakpoint can be inserted into the emulation memory while the processor is still running the user code. It can be difficult to interface to the ROM emulator if the hardware designer didn't connect a `write` signal to the ROM socket (After all, one doesn't usually write to the ROM). Most ROM emulators have a method of writing to ROM by executing a sequence of ROM `read` operations. It's an involved process, but it gets around the problem of needing a `write` signal.

Although a ROM emulator is essential to get around the "write to ROM" problem, in many cases, the ROM emulator does much more than substitute RAM for ROM. For example, suppose your target system doesn't have a communications port, or the communications port is already used by the embedded application and is not available to the debugger as communications channel to the host (The last 3.5-inch hard disk drive I looked at didn't have an RS232 port on it). The ROM emulator can deal with this shortcoming by creating a virtual UART port to the host computer.

Some ROM emulators (see Figure 6.8) can emulate a virtual UART by replacing the communications driver in the debug kernel with a data write operation to a reserved area of the emulation memory. Writing to this region wakes up the control processor in the ROM emulator to send the data to the host, mimicking the behavior of the serial port. Of course, your debugger must be ported to the ROM emulator to take advantage of this feature, but many of the popular debuggers have been ported to the popular ROM emulators, so it's not usually an issue. A little later, you'll read about the advantages of real-time trace as a way to view code flow. Some ROM emulators also offer this feature so that you can take a snapshot of real-time code flow within your ROM.

Figure 6.8   ROM emulators.

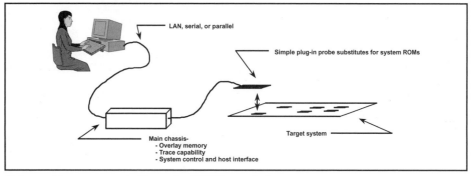

Schematic representation of a ROM emulator.

Limitations

The ROM emulator also has some limitations. If your code is supposed to be transferred from ROM into RAM as part of the boot-up process, you might not need the features the ROM emulator provides. Also, like the debug kernel itself, the ROM emulator is not suitable for the earliest stages of hardware/software integration, when the target system's memory interface might be suspect. The advantages and disadvantages of the ROM emulator are listed in Table 6.2.

Table 6.2   Advantages/disadvantages of ROM emulator.

Advantages of the ROM emulator	Disadvantages of the ROM emulator
• Very cost-effective ($1,000–$5,000) • Generic tool, compatible with many different memory configurations • Can download large blocks of code to the target system at high-speed • Most cost-effective way to support large amounts of RAM substitution memory • Can trace ROM code activity in real time • Provides virtual UART function, eliminating need for additional services in target system • Can be integrated with other hardware and software tools, such as commercially available debuggers • Can set breakpoints in ROM	• Requires that the target system memory is in a stable condition • Feasible only if embedded code is contained in standard ROMs, rather than custom ASICs or microcontrollers with on-chip ROM • Real-time trace is possible only if program executes directly out of ROM • Many targets transfer code to RAM for performance reasons

Intrusiveness and Real-Time Debugging

Although the debug kernel is an important part of the embedded system designer's debugging tool kit, it clearly has shortcomings with respect to debugging embedded systems whose problems are related to real-time events. It's easy to see why these shortcomings exist when you consider that the debug kernel is highly *intrusive*. Intrusion — the modification of behavior as a result of the presence of the tool — is a quantitative issue, a subjective issue, and all shades of gray in between. If your target system fails to work with a debug tool connected to it, the tool is too intrusive. If it does work, sort of, will you have to debug the debugger, and debug your target system at the same time?

Generally, intrusiveness encompasses all the aspects of embedded systems design and debug. The mechanical compatibility issue exists between external tools and a target system, with parametric (electrical) compatibility, with software compatibility, and finally with the realities imposed by real-time systems.

Signal Intrusion

Anytime the testing tool has a hardware component, signal intrusion can become a problem. For example, a design team unable to use a particular ROM emulator in its target system complained long and hard to the vendor's tech-support person. The target worked perfectly with the EPROMs inserted in the ROM sockets but failed intermittently with the ROM emulator installed. Eventually, after all the phone remedies failed, the vendor sent the target system to the factory for analysis. The application was a cost-sensitive product that used a two-sided printed circuit board with wide power and ground bus traces but without the power and ground planes of a more costly four-layer PC board.

The ROM emulator contains high-current signal driver circuits to send the signals up and down the cables while preserving the fidelity of the signal edges. These buffer circuits were capable of putting into the target system large current pulses that the ground bus trace on the target couldn't handle properly. The result was a "ground bounce" transient signal that was strong enough to cause a real signal to be misinterpreted by the CPU.

The problem was solved by inserting some series termination resistors in the data lines to smooth out the effect of the current spike. The customer was happy, but this example makes a real point. Plugging any tool into a user's target system implies that the target system has been designed to accommodate that tool. ("Designed" is probably too strong a term. In reality, most hardware designers don't consider tool-compatibility issues at all when the hardware is designed, forcing some amazing kludges to the target system and/or tool to force them to work together.) For more information on this problem, see my article, in *EDN*.[2]

Physical Intrusion

Modern high-density packages make physical intrusion a serious design issue. Suppose your target system is one of several tightly packed PC boards in a chassis, such as a PC104 or VXI card cage. The hardware designer placed the ROM sockets near the card-edge connector, so when the card is inserted into the card cage, the ROM is far from sight inside the card cage. The software team wants to use a ROM emulator as its development tool but never communicates any particular requirements to the hardware designers. The ROM emulator cable is about one foot long, and the cables are standard 100-signal wide flat ribbon cable. The cards are spaced on three-quarter-inch centers in the card cage. For good measure, the socket is oriented so that the cable must go through two folds to orient the plug with the socket, leaving about four inches of available cable length.

The obvious solution is to place the PC board on an extender card and move it out of the chassis, but the extender card is too intrusive and causes the system to fail. The problem was ultimately solved when the PC board was redesigned to accommodate the ROM emulator. The ultimate cost was two weeks of additional time to the project schedule and a large premium paid to the PC fabricator to facilitate a "rocket run" of the board.

The tool was so intrusive that it was unusable, but it was unusable because the designers did not consider the tool requirements as part of their overall system design specification. They designed the tool out of their development process.

Designing for Test

Figure 6.9 shows the Motorola ColdFIRE MF5206eLITE Evaluation Board, which I use in the lab portion of my Embedded Systems class. By anticipating the connection to a logic analyzer during the project design phase, I was able to easily provide mechanical access points for connecting to the processor's I/O pins.

Figure 6.9   Evaluation board.

Motorola ColdFIRE MF5206eLITE Evaluation Board. The I/O pins on the processor (large black square with three dots) are spaced 0.1mm apart, and the package has a total of 160 pins.

The large chip with the three black dots in the lower portion of the figure is the Motorola ColdFIRE MF5206e microcontroller, which comes in a 160-pin package that is surface-mounted to the printed circuit board. The I/O pins are spaced approximately every 0.25 mm around the sides of the package. The spacing between the pins is 0.10 mm, or 0.004 inches. Obviously, without help, it will be impossible to connect 160 probes to this circuit. The help needed is located on the right side of the board. Two high-density connectors that connect to all the pins of the processor enable you to design a mechanical interface to the board so that you can use a logic analyzer.

These connectors, however, won't mate directly with our logic analyzers. To bridge the gap, I designed a "transition board" (see Figure 6.10), which interfaces to the ColdFIRE evaluation board through the two connectors shown in Figure 6.9.

Figure 6.10 Transition board.

Transition board for use with the ColdFIRE evaluation board. Eight 20-pin connectors along the top and bottom edges of the board provide direct connection to a logic analyzer.

The transition board has two purposes:
• Provide a convenient connection point for a logic analyzer
• Provide a simple way to bring the ColdFIRE I/O signals to other boards for lab experiments

The transition board contains two mating connectors on the underside of the board that directly connect to the two expansion connectors on the evaluation board. The transition board's eight 20-pin connectors were designed to match directly the cable specifications for the logic analyzers used. Thus, interconnecting the target system and the tool was relatively straightforward. The circuitry on the transition board also provides some signal-isolation and bus-driving capabilities so that the processor signals can be transmitted at high speed and fidelity to experimental boards through the five 60-pin connectors shown in the center of the photograph (labeled CONNECTOR 1 through CONNECTOR 5).

To minimize intrusion, the tool must somehow be able to live outside of the direct relationship that exists between the processor, memory, application software, and real-time requirements. You can imagine that together these elements form the heart of your embedded system. To debug this system, you must somehow break the bonds of these dependencies and insert your tool. In the case of a debugger, inserting it between the processor and the real-time requirements will often mean that the system cannot be debugged because the tool itself breaks the part of the system that you are trying to debug. Therefore, we need to move up a level in debugging sophistication. Traditionally, this has meant applying specialized hardware to the problem.

Other Kinds of Intrusion

The issue of intrusion is one of the key reasons that the target system hardware, its operational software, and the tools that will be used as part of the design and debug process must be considered as a complete system, in other words, holistically. If you've ever thumbed through *Embedded Systems Programming* or *Real Time Computing* magazines, you've seen advertisements for tools that show some sort of tool plugged into a target system that consists of a single PC board sitting alone on a desktop, with not even a power supply in sight to spoil the view. The real situation is far less ideal. For example, a customer once hung our first generation in-circuit emulators (ICEs) by chains from the ceiling to get them close to the highest boards in a floor-to-ceiling equipment rack. These emulators weighed about 75 pounds each and were not designed for skyhook applications.

Make your tool selection part of your system-planning exercise. Bring the software team into the discussion and make certain the overall system design is compatible with the team's tool requirements. If a conflict arises, you'll know about it sooner. It can be as simple as locating the ROM socket at the other end of the board, but, if this isn't specified at the beginning of the project, you'll end up having to live with what you get.

Logic Analyzer

If you need to see what the processor is doing in real time, without "significantly" perturbing the system, you need to move to the next level of embedded systems debugging power, the logic analyzer. The logic analyzer is an extremely powerful tool for examining digital systems. Even so, there are problems with using logic analyzers with today's modern processors, which are discussed shortly. For now, let's focus on how you might use a logic analyzer to debug the real-time problems you encounter with an embedded system.

The logic analyzer has two basic modes of operation: timing and state. In timing mode, an internal high-speed clock determines when the memory of the logic analyzer takes a snapshot of the state of the processor, or processor and other digital signals in the system. A snapshot is just the voltage, or logic level, on every pin of the processor, taken at a sufficiently high capture rate so that you can see the timing relationships between the various processor bus signals.

Note

In the previous paragraph, "every pin" really means "every pin of interest." You would have no reason to probe the power supply voltage unless you thought it was noisy and causing problems.

Timing Mode

In Figure 6.11, the logic analyzer is driven by a high frequency internal clock, perhaps 400MHz or faster. The processor clock in this example is 100MHz. Thus, for each cycle of the processor clock, you can record four samples of each pin of interest of the microprocessor. Also, the logic analyzer clock allows you to measure the transition times of the various digital signals to ±2.5 nanoseconds (1/400MHz). To make this recording, you just assign each logic analyzer probe to one of the pins of the processor. Thus, probe0 is assigned to address line 0, probe1 to address line 1, and so on. It's easy to see why a complex processor might require 200 or more logic analyzer probes — each probe connected to a physical pin of the microprocessor — to completely determine what the processor is doing. Each logic analyzer probe can only measure if the corresponding digital signal is a "1" or a "0".

Figure 6.11 Logic analyzer display.

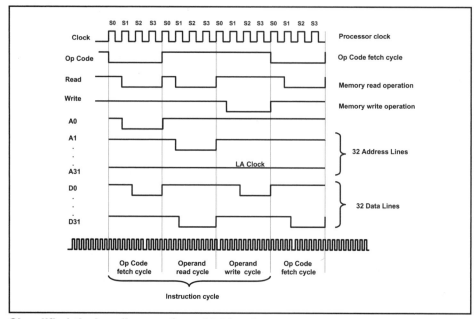

Simplified timing diagram for a 32-bit microprocessor.

If the logic analyzer has a memory that can store one sample every 2.5ns and the memory is 200 bits wide and 1 million states deep, you can capture 250,000 processor bus cycles. Then, you can play this information back on the logic analyzer display as if it were a strip chart recorder.

This information is invaluable for a hardware designer because the greater the logic analyzer clock speed, the finer the resolution with which the designer can measure the relative timing relationships between the system signals. Thus, given a memory with a maximum access time of 25ns, if the logic analyzer display shows that the processor expects the memory data to be ready in 20ns, it would clearly signal a very real timing problem.

However, the information provided by the timing diagram is not particularly useful to the software developer. The software designer needs to see the instruction flow of the program, not the timing relationships between the various binary signals. The timing analysis point of view provides too much information (precise time durations) and too little information (processor instruction execution) at the same time. Also, the data presented in a timing diagram is useless for debugging software.

State Mode

You can change the operational mode of the logic analyzer by using the microprocessor clock to provide the signal to capture a state. Thus, each time the processor clock rises from low to high (0 to 1), you capture the state of the pins of the processor and write that to the logic analyzer memory. In this case, the relative timing information between the signals is lost, but you can see the value of the signals when they are relevant to the processor.

Most logic analyzers are available with software — called disassemblers — that are capable of reducing the raw data recorded by the logic analyzer and representing it in tabular form as an assembly language mnemonic instruction, address information, operand reads and writes, and special status information, such as interrupt service instruction cycles. Figure 6.12 is an example of the logic analyzer data represented in state mode.

Figure 6.12 Logic analyzer data table.

```
    Trace List                Offset=0        More data off screen (ctrl-F, ctrl-G)
    Label:  Address  Data                  Opcode or Status            time count
    Base:     hex    hex                         mnemonic                absolute

    after   004FFA   2700     2700  supr data rd word         ------------
    +001    004FFC   0000     0000  supr data rd word         +  520      nS
    +002    004FFE   2000     2000  supr data rd word         +   1.0     uS
    +003    002000   2479   MOVEA.L 0001000,A2               +   1.5     uS
    +004    002002   0000     0000  supr prog                 +   2.0     uS
    +005    002004   1000     1000  supr prog                 +   2.5     uS
    +006    002006   2679   MOVEA.L 0001004,A3               +   3.0     uS
    +007    001000   0000     0000  supr data rd word         +   3.5     uS
    +008    001002   3000     3000  supr data rd word         +   4.00    uS
    +009    002008   0000     0000  supr prog                 +   4.52    uS
    +010    00200A   1004     1004  supr prog                 +   5.00    uS
    +011    00200C   14BC   MOVE.B  #000,[A2]                 +   5.52    uS
    +012    001004   0000     0000  supr data rd word         +   6.00    uS
    +013    001006   4000     4000  supr data rd word         +   6.52    uS
    +014    00200E   0000     0000  supr prog                 +   7.00    uS
```

Screen capture from a logic analyzer tracing execution on a Motorola 68000 family processor.

In Figure 6.12, you see that the disassembler software reduces the individual clock cycles to instructions and memory reads and writes. The logic analyzer inserts a time count so that the real-time instruction execution times can be easily determined. From the point of view of actual execution, the logic analyzer is totally non-intrusive. The processor runs at full speed, and the logic analyzer records a slice in time of the executed instructions, the accessed memory locations, and the read and written data values.

If the address, data, and status signals for each instruction can be recorded, this flow can be related back to a higher-level language, such as C or C++. If a debugger can relate the C or C++ statements back to the memory locations that represent the corresponding machine language instruction in memory, one should be able to repeat the process with a recorded logic analyzer trace. Figure 6.13 illustrates how — if the compiler's symbol table is valid — a dissasembler can relate the C source statements to the program execution flow.

Figure 6.13 Display with interleaved source code.

```
Trace List                    Offset=0       More data off screen (ctrl-F, ctrl-G)
Label:        Address         Data        Opcode or Status w/ Source Lines       time
Base:         symbols         hex                      mnemonic w/symbols          rel
+009    sysstack:+003FC2      0738      0738   supr data wr word                   520
-010    sysstack:+003FC0      0006      0006   supr data wr word                   480
+011    main:main+00000A      01AA      01AA   supr prog                           520
        ##########main.c - line     104 ##########################################
              initialize_system();
+012    main:main+00000C      4EB9  JSR     |_initialize_sys                       480
+013    main:main+00000E      0000      0000   supr prog                           520
+014    main:main+000010      114A      114A   supr prog                           480
        ##########initSystem.c - line     1 thru     38 ##########################
        void refresh_menu_window();

        void
        initialize_system()
        {
+015    |_initialize_sys      4E56  LINK    A6,#00000                              520
```

Screen capture of a logic analyzer state trace with C source statements and the corresponding assembly language instructions inserted in the trace display.

The trace now gets much busier than before, but at least you can raise the abstraction level of the debugging to something more appropriate than individual machine clock cycles. By post-processing the raw trace, either on the host or in the logic analyzer itself, the information is distilled from the state of all the processor pins on every clock cycle, to bus cycles, to assembly language instructions, and finally to C source statements.

Triggers

In state mode, sophisticated logic analyzers can trace every instruction executed and relate it directly to the associated line in the source. Although this information gives a powerful view into what is happening, a trace that reports every instruction executed quickly becomes overwhelming. Like any trace-based debugging, debugging with a logic analyzer trace is efficient only if the programmer can select which part of the trace to view. The key isn't to trace every instruction but to trace and study the relevant instructions. Triggers are the basic mechanisms for selectively controlling which part of the execution history the logic analyzer reports.

Typically, the trigger system is among the most complex hardware circuitry because the sequence of code execution states and data values that can lead to a trigger event of interest also can be extremely complex and convoluted. The trigger system also must be able to deal with various combinations of the address, data, and status information.

Figure 6.14 is an example of symbolic triggering. Notice how in this example you can set trigger values based on their symbolic names from the C source file.

Figure 6.14 Symbolic triggering.

LABEL >	ADDR	SYMBOL	DATA	STAT	_RAS	_WE	TR
Base >	Hex	Symbol	Hex	Symbol	Binary	Binary	Binary
1	010198	FIB.S:_fib+008	49608602	200. :idle	1110	1	0	1

Symbolic trigger settings for a logic analyzer. Here `fib` **is a symbolic name used in the source file.**

Specifying a Trigger

One of the most difficult tasks for a software developer is to correctly set up the trigger condition for a logic analyzer so that the event of interest can be isolated and captured. The trigger system also can be used as a toggle switch. In this mode, a trigger event turns on the recording feature of a trace system, and another trigger event turns it off. This is particularly useful for debugging a single task in a RTOS. The trace system only is enabled during the execution of that task, thus saving the memory from recording uninteresting tasks. The logic analyzer's trigger system is usually arranged around the concept of resources and state transitions.

It's helpful to record only several states before and after accesses to a certain memory location. In other words, every time a global variable is accessed, a limited number of states around it are recorded. This allows you to easily isolate why the global variable was being mysteriously clobbered by another task.

Trigger Resources

The logic analyzer's trigger system is usually arranged around the concept of resources and state transitions. Think of the resources as logic variables. A resource might be assigned to a condition of the system, such as ADDRESS = 0x5555AAAA. However, just as with C, you can assign a resource so that ADDRESS != 0x5555AAAA. In other words, trigger if the address doesn't equal this value. You also can assign ranges to resources, so that if the address bus has a value in the range of

```
0x50000000 <= ADDRESS <= 0x50000010
```

the logic analyzer triggers. You can also trigger on addresses outside a specific range, as in

```
(0x50000000 <= ADDRESS <= 0x50000010)!
```

You also can save some resources by using a "don't care" form of a resource. The "don't care" just means that those bits are not used in the resource comparisons. Thus, if the trigger condition is

```
ADDRESS = 0x500XXXXX
```

the logic analyzer only uses address bits 20 through 31 in the comparison and ignores bits 0 through 19. In a way, this is similar to declaring a range trigger but without defining an explicit range. Most logic analyzers support a fixed number of resources that can be assigned to trigger conditions. To create a range resource, you must combine two resources so that the trigger occurs on the logical ANDing of RESOURCE1 (0x50000000 <= ADDRESS) and RESOURCE2 (ADDRESS <= 0x50000010).

You also can assign trigger resources to the data bus bits and to the status bus bits. Just as you can logically AND to address resources to create an address range trigger condition, you can create logical AND, OR, and NOT combinations of the processor's buses or individual bits. Thus, one might form a complex trigger condition like this:

```
IF (ADDRESS=0xAAAAAAAA) AND (DATA=0x0034) AND (STATUS=WRITE)
THEN TRIGGER.
```

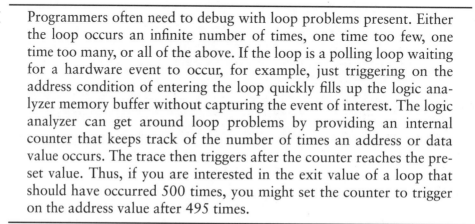

Programmers often need to debug with loop problems present. Either the loop occurs an infinite number of times, one time too few, one time too many, or all of the above. If the loop is a polling loop waiting for a hardware event to occur, for example, just triggering on the address condition of entering the loop quickly fills up the logic analyzer memory buffer without capturing the event of interest. The logic analyzer can get around loop problems by providing an internal counter that keeps track of the number of times an address or data value occurs. The trace then triggers after the counter reaches the preset value. Thus, if you are interested in the exit value of a loop that should have occurred 500 times, you might set the counter to trigger on the address value after 495 times.

How Triggers Work

To understand a trigger, recall that the logic analyzer is a passive device. It records the signals that appear on the microprocessor busses while the processor runs normally. Because the processor might be executing 10 million or more instructions each second and the logic analyzer has finite memory, you need a mechanism to tell the trace memory when to start and stop storing state or timing information. By turning the recording on at the appropriate time, you can record (capture) the actions of the processor around the point of interest. So, just as you use a debugger to set breakpoints in your code, you can use the trigger capabilities of a logic analyzer to record the instruction and data flow at some point in the program execution flow.

The schematic diagram in Figures 6.15 represents a memory system that is one million states deep and 200 bits wide. It is arranged as a circular buffer so that no special significance to memory location 0x00000 or 0xFFFFF exists; they just are adjacent to each other in the buffer. Each time the processor clock is asserted — usually on a rising edge — 200 bits are recorded in the memory, and the address is automatically incremented to the next location.

This process goes on continuously, whether the logic analyzer is supposed to record any information or not. After it records one million states, the logic analyzer just records over what it previously recorded. The key contribution of the trigger circuitry is to tell the logic analyzer trigger when to stop recording information. This simple concept has some powerful debugging implications. With the logic analyzer set up this way, you can see backward in time, up to 1 million states before the trigger signal occurs.

Figure 6.15 Memory system diagram.

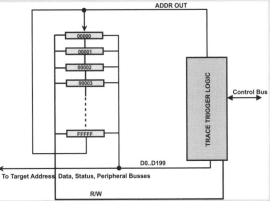

Schematic representation of a logic analyzer trace and trigger system.

State Transitions

Recall that one of the real problems with debugging code is isolating and capturing the event of interest among a complex array of possible pathways. Sometimes specifying address, data, and status values, even with the capability of defining complicated patterns, is just not enough. This is where the state transition trigger capability can be used (see Figure 6.16). With trigger sequencing, the resources have been combined to provide a triggering capability that depends on the path taken through the code.

Figure 6.16 Triggers.

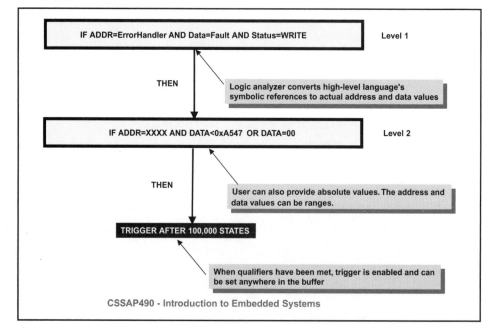

Triggering a logic analyzer after a sequence of trigger states.

Each match that occurs takes you to a new level in the trigger-sequencing system. Eventually, if all the transition conditions are met, the logic analyzer triggers. Setting up such a complex combination of trigger conditions isn't a task for the faint of heart. It usually takes a lot of trial and error before you get the trigger system working properly. Unfortunately, your ability to get the most out of the logic analyzer's triggering capability is often greatly diminished by the logic analyzer's user interface, documentation, or both. It is extremely frustrating when you know exactly what you want to do, but can't figure out how to make your tool do it.

With a logic analyzer, this often means that you set it up to trigger on some complex, low-occurrence fault — occurring perhaps once a day —

and you miss the event because your trigger sequence was set incorrectly. The sad reality is that most engineers hardly ever take advantage of the logic analyzer's complex triggering capabilities because it is just too difficult to set up the logic analyzer with any confidence that you'll be successful the first time you try it.

From the Trenches

I visited a customer once to learn more about how our products were being used. Our logic analyzer had extremely powerful triggering capabilities, a rich set of resources, and eight levels of trigger sequencing. Referring back to Figure 6.16, imagine up to eight of those logical conditions with various kinds of looping back to prior states. The logic analyzer did not have a particularly deep memory and could store a maximum of 1,024 states, which was a source of constant complaint by the customers we visited. The memory was just not deep enough. We would counter their argument by saying that the complex triggering capability made a deep memory unnecessary. Just dial in the trigger condition that you need to isolate the fault, and then you won't need to search through a deep memory buffer for the event, which you have to do if your trigger condition is too simple.

Most, if not all, the customers wanted a simple trigger to capture the event, and then they were willing to search manually through the trace buffer for the event of interest. Several, in fact, were proud of some utilities they wrote to post-process the trace file from the logic analyzer. Because they could upload it as an ASCII text file, they wrote software to find the trace event that they were interested in.

Customer research shows that 90 percent of users triggered their logic analyzer (or ICE) on simple Boolean combinations of address, data, and status information, with perhaps a count qualifier added for loop unrolling.

This apparent disconnect between what the user needs (simple triggering with a deep trace and post-processing) and what the tool vendor supplies (complex triggering with shallow memory) reflects the logic analyzer's roots as a hardware designer's tool. State sequencing is a common algorithm for a hardware designer but less well known for a software developer. Tools such as oscilloscopes and logic analyzers are created by hardware designers for hardware designers. Thus, it's easy to understand the focus on state sequencing as the triggering architecture. In any case, the logic analyzer is a powerful tool for debugging real-time systems. Although this chapter has concentrated on the processor's busses, the logic analyzer easily can measure other signals in your digital system along with the processor so you can see what peripheral devices are doing as the processor attempts to deal with them.

Limitations

By now, you might think the logic analyzer is the greatest thing since sliced bread. What's the down side? The first hurdle is the problem of mechanical connections between the logic analyzer and the target system. If you've every tried to measure a voltage in a circuit, you know that to measure one voltage, you need two probes. One probe connects to the source of the voltage and the other connects to the circuit ground to bring your voltmeter and the circuit to the same reference point. If your processor has 200 I/O pins, which is reasonably common today, you need to be able to make 201 connections to the processor to capture all its I/O signals.

The second problem is that meaningful interpretation of a logic analyzer trace assumes you can relate the addresses and data observed on the bus to sequences of instruction executions. Unfortunately, the on-chip cache and other performance enhancements (such as out-of-order instruction dispatch) interfere with this assumption.

Physical Connections

Logic analyzer manufacturers are painfully aware of the difficulty associated with connecting several hundred microscopic I/O pins to their tools and have built interconnecting systems that enable the logic analyzer and a surface-mounted microprocessor to make a reasonable electrical and mechanical connection. These interconnecting devices are often called preprocessors. For relatively simple pin-grid array packages, where the I/O pins of the processor are designed to plug into a socket with a two-dimensional array of holes located on 0.1 inch centers, the preprocessor plugs into the socket on the target system, and the target microprocessor plugs into the preprocessor. This arrangement is also referred to as an interposer because the preprocessor sits between the target and the processor.

Figure 6.17 shows an example of a preprocessor. The preprocessor can contain some additional circuitry (such as the transition board shown in Figure 6.10) to provide some signal isolation because of the added electrical load created by the preprocessor and the logic analyzer. If you're unlucky and your embedded processor is more like the ColdFIRE chip shown in Figure 6.17, the preprocessor could be a rather fragile and expensive device. In one design, a threaded bolt is glued to the top of the plastic IC package using a special alignment jig and cyano-acrylic glue. The rest of the connector then attaches to this stud and positions the mini-probes on the I/O pins of the processor. It takes a bit of trial and error to get all the preprocessor connections made, but the preprocessor is reliable after it's installed. However, this is not something that you want to attach and remove from the chip at regular intervals.

Figure 6.17 Preprocessor connection sequence.

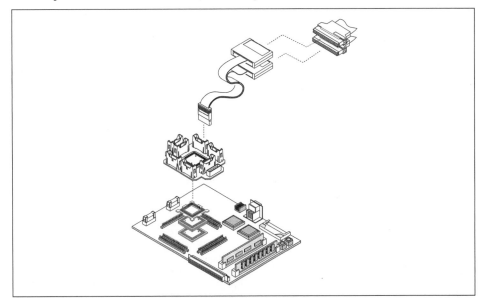

The preprocessor provides over 100 reliable electrical and mechanical connections to the target processor and to the logic analyzer. Drawing courtesy of Agilent Technologies, Inc.

From the Trenches

One company keeps these expensive connectors in a locked cabinet. The group's manager has the key, and engineers are allowed one free replacement. After that, each subsequent replacement requires more and more in-depth analysis of the engineer's design and debugging methods.

Logic Analyzers and Caches

Now that you have this expensive preprocessor probe connected to the microprocessor and you're ready to debug, you might be out of the woods. Suppose your embedded microprocessor has an input pipeline or an on-chip instruction cache (I-cache), data cache (D-cache), or both. It definitely makes triggering a logic analyzer and capturing a trace a much more problematic task. Remember that the logic analyzer is passively "sniffing" the processor's I/O pins on every clock cycle. If every state that is visible on the bus corresponds to what the processor is doing with that instruction, the logic analyzer will accurately capture the instruction and data flow sequence of the processor.

However, if the activity on the bus does not have a 1:1 correspondence to the instructions being executed and the data being accessed, the logic analyzer's usefulness begins to diminish. Most on-chip caches are generally refilled from main memory in bursts. Even if only one byte of data is not available in the cache, the bus control logic of the processor generally fetches anywhere from 4 to 64 bytes of data, called a refill line, from main memory and places the refill line in the cache. The logic analyzer records a burst of memory reads taking place. Where's the data of interest?

If the caches are small, clever post-processing software can sometimes figure out what the processor is actually doing and display the real flow. You might still have a problem with triggering, but it's possible to circumvent it. With small caches, branches in the code generally have at least one possible branch destination located outside the cache. Thus, clever software might be able to use basic block information from the compiler and the address of memory fetches to reconstruct what happened at various branch points. If the caches are large enough to normally hold both possible destinations of a branch, a logic analyzer, with only external bus information available to it, has no way to determine what instructions are being executed by the processor. Of course, most processors allow you to set a bit in a register and turn off the caches. However, as with the debug kernel discussed earlier, the performance degradation caused by the intrusion of the logic analyzer might cause your embedded system to fail or to behave differently than it would if the caches were enabled.

Trace Visibility

Most manufactures of embedded systems understand the importance of real-time traces and add on-chip circuitry to help logic analyzers or other tools decode what is actually going on inside of the processor. Over the years, several different approaches have been taken. National Semiconductor Corporation and Intel Corporation created special versions of their embedded processors called "bond-outs" because additional signals that were available on the integrated circuit die were bonded out to extra I/O pins on these special packages. Thus, a normal package might have 100 pins, but the bond-out version has 140 pins. These extra pins provided additional information about the program counter and cache behavior. With this information, it becomes feasible to post-process the logic analyzer trace to uncover the processor program flow.

Traceable Cache™

AMD took another approach called Traceable Cache™. Rather than create a bond-out version of the chip, certain AMD 29K family processors could be put into a slave mode through the JTAG port. The master processor and slave processor are mounted together on a preprocessor module, and both have their data lines connected to the system data bus. Only the master processor has its address lines connected to the address bus. The two microprocessors then run in lockstep. The unconnected address pins of the slave processor output the current value of the program counter on every instruction cycle. These additional states are captured by the logic analyzer, and, by post-processing the resulting trace, the actual instruction flow can be reconstructed, even though the processor is running out of the cache.

Today, the generally accepted method of providing trace information is to output the program counter value when a non-sequential fetch occurs. A non-sequential fetch occurs whenever the program counter is not incremented to point to the address of the next instruction in memory. A branch, a loop, a jump to subroutine, or an interrupt causes non-sequential fetches to occur. If the debug tools record all the non-sequential fetches, they should be able to reconstruct the instruction flow, but not the data flow, of the processor. Non-sequential fetch information can be output when the bus is idle, so it usually has a minimal impact on the processor's performance; however, tight loops can often cause problems if the data is coming too fast. Some sort of an on-chip FIFO for the non-sequential fetch data usually helps here, but even that can get overrun if the branch destination is being output every few clock cycles.

Caches and Triggering

As noted earlier, triggering might still be a problem. Traditional triggering methods also fail when caches are present, so the semiconductor manufacturers place triggering resources on-chip, as part of their debug circuitry. Often, these resources are called breakpoint registers because they are also available to debuggers for setting breakpoints in the code. A breakpoint register might be set to cause a special code to be output on several status pins whenever the internal breakpoint conditions are met. The code is then interpreted by the logic analyzer as a trigger signal, and the logic analyzer takes the appropriate action, such as starting to capture a trace. Chapter 7 discusses the IEEE ISTO-5001 embedded debug standard, including the various dynamic debugging modes defined in the standard.

In these examples, you've seen that as the processor speed and complexity increases, the type of information that you must record to understand what the processor is doing necessarily changes as well. Today, attempting to capture the external bus states on every clock cycle is generally not possible or necessary. By effectively using the on-chip dynamic debug resources, such as the address information about non-sequential fetched and internal trigger resources, you usually can record enough information from the processor to reconstruct the real-time instruction flow of the processor.

Compiler Optimizations

With optimizations turned on, a good C or C++ compiler can generate code that, at the assembly language level, is almost impossible to relate to the original source code. Even with the C source statements interspersed with the assembly code, critical events might not show up in the trace where you expect them to be. Of course, turning off the optimizations can have the same effect as turning off the caches to gain visibility. The tool becomes intrusive, and performance is compromised, perhaps so much as to cause the embedded system to fail.

Cost Benefit

Even with all the limitations of logic analysis as a debugging tool, the negatives don't outweigh the positives. Although high-performance logic analyzers can be expensive (over $20,000), excellent units are available below $10,000 that will meet your needs for a long time to come. Magazines, such as *Electronic Design* and *EDN*, regularly do feature articles surveying the latest in logic analyzers. One interesting new offering is a logic analyzer on a PCI card that can plug into your desktop PC. Although the performance is modest, compared with the standalone units, this type of a logic analyzer offers a reasonable amount of performance for a modest investment.

Other Uses

Up to now I've been considering the logic analyzer to be a specialized type of debugging tool. The developers define a trigger event that hopefully is related to the fault they are investigating, wait for the trigger event to occur, examine the resultant trace, and fix the problem. This seems to imply that all data is contained within a single trace. However, a logic analyzer also can be used as a key tool for processor-performance measuring and code-quality testing. These topics are discussed in more detail in Chapter 9, so they are only introduced here.

Statistical Profiling

Suppose that instead of waiting for a trigger event, you tell the logic analyzer to capture one buffer full of data. If the logic analyzer is connected to a PC, you can write a fairly simple C program that randomly signals the logic analyzer to start immediately and capture one trace buffer full of data. You're not looking for anything in particular, so you don't need a trigger. You are interested in following the path of the microprocessor as it runs through its operation code under fairly normal conditions.

Each time you tell it to capture a trace buffer full of data, you wait for it to complete and then upload the buffer to a disk file on your PC. After uploading the trace buffer, you start a random time generator, and, when the timer times out, you repeat the process.

Note

The random time generator is necessary because the possibility exists that the time loop from taking and uploading a trace is somehow related to the time it takes to execute a fraction of code in the target system. If the logic analyzer were continuously restarted without the random time delay, you might never see blocks of code executing, or you might get the inverse situation so that all you ever see is the same block of code executing.

Each time you take a trace and upload it to the PC, you get a brief snapshot of what the program has been doing for the last 1 million or so bus cycles. The snapshot includes:

- What instructions were executed and how often they were executed
- What functions were being accessed and how long each function took to run
- What memory locations (instructions, data, stack, and heap) were being accessed
- How big the stack grew
- What global variables were being accessed and by which functions

Because the uploaded trace buffer is an ASCII text file, you can use the standard file-manipulation tools that come with the C or C++ library to gradually build statistics about your program. The longer you allow the embedded program to run with the logic analyzer attached and gathering data, the more accurate the information that you gather will be. From the linker map and symbol tables, you can relate the memory address to your variables, data structures, and functions. For example, you can easily build a graph that shows what percentage of the time is spent in each function.

Importance of Execution Profiling

Most software designers have no idea how long it takes for the various functions in their code to execute. For example, a company thought it would have to do a complete redesign of its hardware platform because the performance of the system wasn't up to standard and the software team adamantly claimed the code had been fine-tuned as much as humanly possible. Fortunately, someone decided to make some performance measurements of the type discussed here and found that a large fraction of the time was spent in a function that shouldn't have even been there. Somehow, the released code was built with the compiler switch that installs the debug support software because it was erroneously included in the final make file. The processor in the released product was spending half its time in the debug loops!

In "The Twenty-Five Most Common Mistakes with Real-Time Software Development," David Stewart[6] notes that the number one mistake made by real-time software developers is the lack of measurements of execution time. Follow his steps to avoid the same trap:

• First, design your system so that the code is measurable!
• Measure execution time as part of your standard testing. Do not only test the functionality of the code!
• Learn both coarse-grain and fine-grain techniques to measure execution time.
• Use coarse-grain measurements for analyzing real-time properties.
• Use fine-grain measurements for optimizing and fine-tuning.

One of the logic analyzer's shortcomings is that it performs a sampling measurement. Because it must capture a discrete buffer each time and then stop recording while it is being uploaded, it might take a long time to gain accurate statistics because extremely short code sections, such as ISRs, might be missed. Chapter 9 discusses other methods of dealing with this problem. For now, it's easy to see that because the logic analyzer often can operate non-intrusively, using it as a quality assurance tool makes good sense.

The logic analyzer can be used to show what memory locations are being accessed by the processor while it runs the embedded program code. If code quality is important to you, knowing how thoroughly your testing is actually exercising your code (i.e., code coverage) is valuable. Code-coverage measurements are universally accepted as one of the fundamental measurements that should be performed on embedded code before it is released. If your coverage results indicate that 35 percent of your code has been "touched" by your test suite, that means that 65 percent of the code you've written has not been accessed by your tests.

Summary

The debug kernel is a powerful part of the embedded system designer's toolkit. In fact, it's arguably the most important tool of all. With a debug kernel, you have a degree of control and an observation window into the behavior of your system, with only moderate overhead demands on the target.

As the complexity (and cost) increases, these hardware tools are asked to address the issue of intrusiveness in their own particular way. With an

Experiment Design

I'm convinced that debugging is the lost art of software development. In the introductory C++ class that I teach, I actually devote class time to discussions and demonstrations on how to debug and use a debugger. What I see is that students (and many practicing engineers) have not a clue as to how you should approach the problem of finding a flaw in a system. Of course, sometimes a bug can be so obscure and infrequent as to be almost impossible to find, even for the best deductive minds. I can vividly remember a scene from my R&D lab days when a group of senior engineers were standing around for hours staring at an FPGA in a complex embedded system. It wasn't working properly, and they could not conjure up an experiment that they could use to test the various hypotheses that they had as to why they were seeing this failure. What was so striking about this scene was I saw them standing there at about 10 A.M., and, when I went by again at around 3:30 P.M. everyone was in exactly the same position with the same expressions on their faces. I assume they had gone to lunch, the restroom, etc., but you couldn't tell from my before and after vignettes.

I think that part of the difficulty of debugging is the amount of time you need to commit to finding the problem. If faced with a choice between trying something "quick and dirty" or setting up a detailed sequence of experiments and observations, most engineers will opt for the quick and dirty approach. This isn't meant to be a criticism, it's just the way people are. Another popular debugging technique is to "shotgun" the problem. Shotgunning the problem means changing everything in sight with the hope that one of the things that you try will fix it. You do this even though you know from your high school geometry proofs that you should progress one step at a time. You should postulate a reason for the failure, based upon careful observations of your system under test. You then design an experiment to test your hypothesis, if it works, you are then able to explain what went wrong, and you have high confidence that you actually fixed the problem. We all do that. Right?

With my students, I often see the antithesis of any attempt at logical thinking. If it doesn't work, they just write their code all over again! It is frustrating for the student, and for me, to try to single-step a timer ISR when the timer ticks every 150 microseconds. What is even more frustrating for me is that I even taught them how to use a logic analyzer.[1]

So what are we trying to accomplish here? The answer lies at the heart of what we are trying to do in debugging an embedded system, and I believe that in many ways it is fundamentally different from how we debug host-based programs. The embedded system is often a complex mix of external stimuli and system responses, controlled by one or more processors and dedicated hardware. Just getting an accurate picture of what's going on is often the crux of the problem. A product marketing manager with whom I once worked summarized it quite succinctly. He referred to this problem of just trying to understand what is going on as, *Time to Insight*. In other words, how long will it take me to figure out what is going on with this !#%$*$#&* embedded system? The problem that you face is akin to the problem face by an electrical engineer trying to debug the hardware without an oscilloscope. You can measure some DC voltages with a digital voltmeter, but that won't tell you if you have serious overshoot or undershoot problems with your bus signals.

embedded system, you need the run control feature set that the debugger provides because examining and modifying memory and registers, single-stepping, and running to breakpoints is fundamental to debugging software of any kind. You can use these debug kernel features to trace program execution but not without intruding on the real-time behavior of the system. The logic analyzer, although more expensive, provides a less intrusive means of tracing program execution.

This chapter has considered the three fundamental tool requirements for integrating hardware and software:

- A debug kernel for controlling the processor during code development
- Substitution memory as a way to rapidly download and replace code images in non-volatile memory
- A non-intrusive way to follow code execution in real time

In the next chapter, you'll learn how to benefit even more by tightly coupling these three tools. In short, you'll examine the in-circuit emulator.

Works Cited

1. Berger, Arnold S. "A New Perspective on Teaching Embedded Systems Design." http://www.embedded.com/story/OEG20010319S0092, 20 March 2001.
2. Berger, Arnold S. "Following Simple Rules Lets Embedded Systems Work With uP Emulators." *EDN*, 13 April 1989, 171.

3. Ledin, Jim A. "Hardware-in-the-Loop Simulation." *Embedded Systems Programming*, February 1999, 42.

4. Ledin, Jim A. "Modeling Dynamic Systems." *Embedded Systems Programming*, August 2000, 84.

5. Smith, M. "Developing a Virtual Hardware Device." *Circuit Cellar Inc.*, November 1995, 36–45.

6. Stewart, Dave. "The Twenty-Five Most Common Mistakes with Real-Time Software Development." A paper presented at the Embedded Systems Conference, San Jose, 26 September 2000.

Chapter 7

BDM, JTAG, and Nexus

Traditionally, the debug kernel has been implemented in firmware. Thus, for the kernel to execute correctly on new hardware, the new design must at least get the processor–memory interface correct. Unfortunately, as clock speeds increase and memory systems grow in size and complexity, this interface has become more and more demanding to engineer, which raises a question "how you can debug the system when you can't rely on the system to execute even the debug kernel?"

Increasing levels of integration create a related problem: How do you modify firmware when it's embedded on a chip in which you can't use a ROM emulator?

To address these and other related issues, chip vendors are beginning to supply hardware implementations of the debug kernel as part of the chip circuitry. When the functionality of the debug kernel is part of the chip circuitry, debugging tools can continue to deliver run control and to monitor system resources even if the processor chip isn't able to communicate with the rest of the board. This robustness makes it much easier to determine whether intermittent "glitches" are hardware or software problems.

Putting debug control directly in the processor solves other problems, too. In chips with sophisticated pipelines and complex caches, integral debug circuitry can report processor state without concern for the cache and pipeline visibility problems that limit logic analyzers. Well-designed debug interfaces can reduce the overall package pin count. Also, when implemented in silicon, the debug core can't be accidentally destroyed by software that has run amok and has written over a debug kernel located in the target system. (Not only is this a nice convenience, it can be a major time-saver if the debug kernel has to be downloaded to the target system every time the system crashes.) As processors and embedded systems become faster and more complex, on-chip debug support becomes more critical.

Finally, when the debug kernel is implemented as a fixed, standard part of the processor, hosted tool vendors can't communicate with the "debug kernel" via a proprietary protocol any longer. Thus, moving the debug kernel into hardware has contributed to the emergence of new standard interface protocols. Three major debug protocols are used today: BDM (Background Debug Mode), IEEE 1149.1 JTAG (Joint Test Action Group), and IEEE-5001 ISTO (Nexus).

Hardware Instability

In general, you will be integrating unstable hardware with software that has never run on the hardware. The instability of the hardware means that the interface between the processor and the memory might be faulty, so that any code, even a debugger, cannot possibly run reliably in the target system.

With today's processors running at frequencies over 1GHz and bus speeds in excess of 200MHz, circuit designers must take into account the dreaded *analog* effects. A printed circuit board that checks out just fine at DC might fail completely at normal bus speeds.

An embedded system that has a marginal timing problem or a cross-talk problem can appear to work correctly for long stretches of time and then just die. When the right combination of 1s and 0s appears on the right bus at the right time, a glitch occurs, and a bit flips where it shouldn't, taking the system down with it. Until recently, these kinds of problems could wreck a project. Unless the processor-to-memory system was stable, the system could not be turned on. The only tool that could overcome this problem was the ICE.

Background Debug Mode

BDM is Motorola's proprietary debug interface. Motorola was the first embedded processor vendor to place special circuitry in the processor core with the sole function of processor debugging. Thus, BDM began the trend to on-chip debug resources. Today, embedded processors or microcontrollers are expected to have some kind of dedicated, on-chip debugging circuitry. The hardware design need only bring the processor's debug pins out to a dedicated connector and the debug tool, called an *n*-wire or *wiggler*.

Figure 7.1 is a schematic representation showing an *n*-wire tool connected to an embedded system.

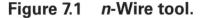

Note

The hardware module that interfaces to the embedded system's *n*-wire debug port is sometimes called a wiggler because it wiggles several pins on the processor to implement the protocol of the debug core being used.

Compared to the cost of a traditional ICE, a wiggler is an incredible bargain. For example, I purchased 10 wigglers for use with the Motorola MF5206e ColdFire processor for about $40 each (including an educational discount). The wiggler, from P&E Micro, connects through the parallel port of a PC and includes a basic debugger that runs on the PC and communicates with the BDM core in the processor. The wiggler is inexpensive because the complex portions of the functionality have been moved into the chip, where circuitry is cheap. The wiggler does little else other than implement the debug core's timing and protocol interface to the CPU.

Figure 7.1   *n*-Wire tool.

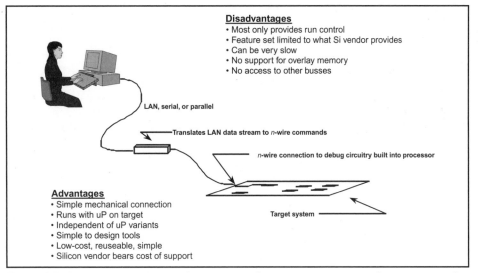

Embedded system connection to a host computer using an *n*-wire connection to the processor debug core.

BDM was first implemented with the 683XX family and is used with the ColdFire processor family. BDM connects to a 26-pin connector that is mounted on the target PC board. Figure 7.2 shows the pinout for the BDM debug interface.

Figure 7.2 Pinout for the Motorola BDM debug interface.

Motorola Recommended BDM Pinout			
RESERVED	1	2	BREAKPOINT
GROUND	3	4	DSCLK
GROUND	5	6	RESERVED
RESET	7	8	DSI
+5 Volts	9	10	DSO
GROUND	11	12	PST3
PST2	13	14	PST1
PST0	15	16	DDATA3
DDATA2	17	18	DDATA1
DDATA0	19	20	GROUND
RESERVED	21	22	RESERVED
GROUND	23	24	CLK_CPU
VCC_CPU	25	26	TEA

Pinout for the Motorola BDM debug interface. The connection is implemented using a standard 26-pin connector to a third-party BDM tool.

BDM is noteworthy because it supports both processor control and a form of real-time trace monitoring. The four bits — DDATA0–DDATA3 — output debug data, and the four bits — PST0–PST3 — output processor status while the processor is running at full speed. Thus, a third-party tool equipped to analyze the information flow from the BDM port can provide the developer with important information about the execution flow of the processor core. Figure 7.3 shows the processor codes output through pins PST0–PST3.

The 14 possible processor status output codes shown in Figure 7.3 are designed to be used in conjunction with a user's or debugger's knowledge of the program's memory image in order to completely track the real-time execution of the code. Notice how codes are provided for change-of-flow instructions, such as 0101 for the execution the first instruction after a taking branch and 1100 for entry into an exception handler.

A complete discussion of the behavior of the PST3-PST0 pins would quickly drive all but the most dedicated readers into "geek overload", so I'll end my discussion here. If you are interested, you can find the details in the Motorola MCF5206e User's Manual.

The ColdFire instruction set also includes special instructions, PULSE and WDDATA. These instructions were specially created to better integrate the debug core operation with the instruction execution flow. PULSE causes the binary code 0100 to be output on the PST pins. This signal might be accepted as a trigger signal by a hardware debug tool, such as a logic or performance analyzer. Similarly, the WDDATA instruction enables the processor to write a byte, word, or long word operand directly to the DDATA port. Thus, the user might want to insert the PULSE instruction at function entry and exit points to perform execution time measurements.

Figure 7.3 Processor codes output.

PST3 - PST0	Definition
0000	Continue execution
0001	Begin execution of an instruction
0010	Reserved
0011	Entry into user mode
0100	Begin execution of PULSE or WDDATA instruction
0101	Begin execution of taken branch
0110	Reserved
0111	Begin execution of RTE instruction
1000	Begin 1-byte transfer on DDATA
1001	Begin 2-byte transfer on DDATA
1010	Begin 3-byte transfer on DDATA
1011	Begin 4-byte transfer on DDATA
1100	Exception processing (asserted for multiple cycles)
1101	Emulator-mode entry exception processing (as above)
1110	Processor is stopped, waiting for interrupt (as above)
1111	Processor is halted (as above)

Status signals output through the BDM debug core.

For example, suppose a certain function normally wouldn't cause a problem. That is, its execution meets the needs of the real-time service it performs. Occasionally, an interrupt occurs while this function is executing, however, and the resulting execution time for this function plus the ISR (interrupt service routine) is now over the allotted time budget. This situation might be impossible to analyze statically, but a tool that can perform a series of time-duration measurements, keyed by the PULSE instruction, would provide a high-accuracy data set for the designer to use. Figure 7.4 is summary of the BDM command set.

Referring to Figure 7.4, it's striking how similar these commands are to the commands that you might issue to any debugger. However, remember that these commands are going directly into the CPU core and operate independently of any program code the user might be trying to execute.

The debug core of the ColdFire processor directly supports real-time debugging by providing additional resources for gathering information and providing some user control without the need to halt the processor. This assumes that some slight intrusion is permitted but halting the CPU core, as is required by some of the BDM commands discussed in Figure 7.4, is not acceptable. This support comes in the form of additional registers that can be programmed via the BDM port to cause breakpoints to occur under various conditions. The breakpoint can cause the processor to HALT execution or can be treated as a high-priority interrupt to the processor. This forces the CPU to enter a user-defined debug ISR. The processor continues to execute instructions when it receives this breakpoint.

Figure 7.4   BDM command set.

Command	Mnemonic	Description	CPU Impact
Read A/D Register	RAREG/RDREG	Read the selected register and return the result via the serial BDM interface.	Halted
Write A/D Register	WAREG/WDREG	The data operand is written to the specified address or data register via the serial BDM interface.	Halted
Read Memory Location	READ	Read the sized data at the memory location specified by the long word address.	Cycle Steal
Write Memory Location	WRITE	Write the operand data to the memory location specified by the long word address.	Cycle Steal
Dump Memory Block	DUMP	Used in conjunction with the READ command to dump large blocks of memory.	Cycle Steal
Fill Memory Block	FILL	Used in conjunction with the WRITE command to fill large blocks of memory.	Cycle Steal
Resume Execution	GO	The pipeline is flushed and refilled before resuming instructions at the current value of the Program Counter (PC register).	Halted
No Operation	NOP	NOP performs no operation and may be used as a null command.	Parallel
Read Control Register	RCREG	Read the system control register.	Halted
Write Control Register	WCREG	Write the operand data to the system control register.	Halted
Write Debug Module Register	WDMREG	Write the operand data to the Debug Module register.	Halted
Notes: General effects of the BDM command upon system operation: 1. Halted - CPU must be halted to perform this command. 2. Cycle Steal - Command generates a bus cycle which is interleaved with CPU accesses. 3. Parallel - Command is executed in parallel with CPU activity.			

BDM command set for the Motorola ColdFire processor family.

Joint Test Action Group (JTAG)

The JTAG (IEEE 1149.1) protocol evolved from work in the PC-board test industry. It represented a departure from the traditional way of doing board tests. PC boards were (and still are) tested on complex machines that use dense arrays of point contacts (called a bed of nails) to connect to every node on the board. A *node* is a shared interconnection between board components. Thus, the output of one device, a clock driver, for example, might connect to five or six inputs on various other devices on the board. This represents one node of the board. Connecting a pin from the board tester to this node (typically a trace on the board) allows the tester to determine whether this node is operating correctly. If not, the tester can usually deduce whether the node is short-circuited to power or to ground, whether it's improperly connected (open-circuited), or whether it's accidentally connected to another node in the circuit.

JTAG was designed to supplement the board tester by connecting all the nodes in the board to individual bits of a long shift register. Each bit represents a node in the circuit.

Note

A shift register is a type of circuit that receives or transmits a serial data stream. A COM port, Ethernet port, FireWire, and USB are examples of serial data streams. Usually, the serial data stream is keyed to a multiple of a standard data width. Thus, an Ethernet port can accept a data packet of 512 bytes. RS232C transmits 1 byte at a time. In contrast, a JTAG serial data stream might be hundreds, or thousands, of bits in length.

For JTAG to work, the integrated circuit devices used in the design must be JTAG-compliant. This means that each I/O pin of a circuit component should contain a companion circuit element the interfaces that pin to the JTAG chain. When enabled, the state of each pin is sampled, or "sniffed," by the companion JTAG cell. Thus, by properly reconstructing the serial bit stream in the correct order, the entire state of the circuit can be sampled at one instance (see Figure 7.5).

Figure 7.5 is a simple schematic representation of a JTAG loop for three circuit elements. The loop consists of an entry point to a device and a separate exit point. Connecting the exit points to the entry points allows you to create a continuous loop that winds through the entire circuit.

A JTAG loop can be active, as well as passive. An I/O pin in the circuit can be forced to a given state by writing the desired bit value to the corresponding JTAG location in the serial data stream. Because the serial data stream can be thousands of bits in length, the algorithms for managing JTAG loops tend to become very complex, very fast. By their nature, JTAG loops can become rather slow as well, because many bits must be shifted each time a value is read or changed.

JTAG gave board test people an alternative to expensive board testers, and, perhaps more significantly, a device equipped with a JTAG loop could be easily tested under field service conditions. Thus, it became a good tool for field maintenance personnel to use when equipment needed to be serviced.

Figure 7.5 JTAG loop.

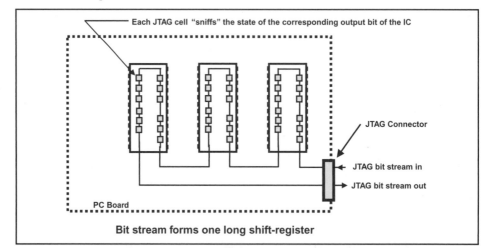

Schematic representation of a JTAG loop for three circuit elements on a PC board.

Embedded processor manufacturers quickly realized that if you can use JTAG on a printed circuit board, you could use it inside a processor core to sample and modify register values, peek and poke memory, and generally do whatever a standard debugger could do.

Early JTAG implementations, such as that used on AMD's 29K family, were simple implementations of the JTAG protocol. With the processor's internal clock stopped, the JTAG loop could be used to modify the processor internals. Accessing external memory was slow because a bus cycle was reconstructed by manually changing all the single bit values for the address, data, and status busses. Figure 7.6 shows a simplified schematic of a debug core implemented using the JTAG protocol.

Other semiconductor companies also began to use the JTAG protocol, or JTAG-like protocols, to connect to their own debug core implementations. Two noteworthy improvements were the addition of addressable loops and JTAG-based commands. The JTAG-based command uses the standard JTAG protocol for moving the serial bit stream but then controls the core through debug commands, rather than by directly jamming in new values.

Thus, instead of a serial loop with 10,000 bits, a bit stream of several hundred bits could be sent to the debug core. The bit stream would be interpreted as a command to the core (such as, "change the value of register R30 to 0x55555555").

Figure 7.6 Debug core using JTAG.

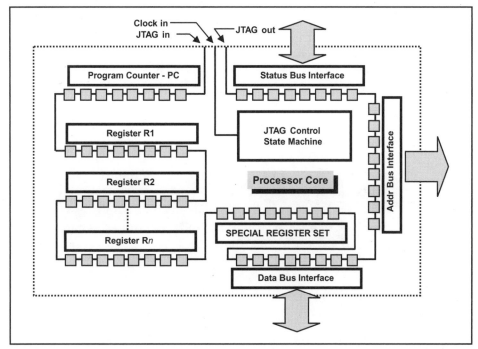

JTAG-based debug core. The JTAG loop sniffs the state of the processor's internal registers.

The other improvement — addressable loops — replaces one long loop with a number of smaller loops. A short JTAG command is sent out to set up the proper loop connection. Then, the smaller loop can be manipulated instead of a single long loop. Addressable loops have another compelling application: multiple processor debugging. For example, suppose you are trying to debug an ASIC with eight embedded RISC processor cores. One long JTAG loop could take tens of milliseconds per command. With a small JTAG steering block added to the design, the user can send a short command to some JTAG steering logic to then direct the loop to the appropriate processing element.

> The ColdFire family is unique in that it supports both BDM and JTAG protocols. The JTAG function shares several of the BDM pins, so the user can enable either JTAG or BDM debug operations.

Because the JTAG implementation is a serial protocol, it requires relatively few of the microprocessor's I/O pins to support a debugger connection. This is a definite plus because I/O pins are a precious resource on a cost-sensitive device, such as an embedded microprocessor. Note that the JTAG pin definition includes both TDI and TDO pins. Thus, the data stream can enter the CPU core and then exit it to form a longer loop with another JTAG device. Also, unlike BDM, the JTAG interface is an open standard, and any processor can use it. However, the JTAG standard only defines the communications protocol to use with the processor. How that JTAG loop connects to the elements of the core and what its command set does as a run control or observation element are specific to a particular manufacturer and might be a closely guarded secret, given only to a relatively few tool support vendors. For example, several companies, such as MIPS and AMD have chosen to define an "extended JTAG" (eJTAG) command set for several of their embedded microprocessors. However, these are proprietary interfaces, and the full extent of their capabilities might only be given to a select few partners.

Figure 7.7 Pin descriptions.

PIN	Description
TCK	A clock input that synchronizes the JTAG port logical operations
TMS	A test mode select input that is sampled on the rising edge of TCK to sequence the internal state machine controller (TAP Controller)
TDI	The input test data stream that is sampled on the rising edge of TCK
TDO	The output test data stream that updates on the falling edge of TCK
TRST	An active low asynchronous reset

Pin descriptions for the IEEE 1149.1 (JTAG) interface.

> Although the previous remarks were a bit ominous, working closely with one, or at most a few, tool vendors can be a good thing. With such a wide spectrum of embedded processors, the number of design starts for a particular device, or family of devices, can be small. In fact, it can be too small a number to support the large number of tool vendors that might want to support it. The dilemma that the semiconductor vendor often faces is how to guarantee high-quality, long-term

support for its past and future products. Often, it's better to keep a small number of partners healthy, rather than allow a large number to starve.

Nexus

The automobile industry provided the motivation for the next attempt at bringing some form of standardization for on-chip debugging. Several of the largest automobile manufacturers conveyed to their semiconductor vendors a simple message: *Either standardize your on-chip debugging technology so we can standardize our development tools, or we'll specify you out of consideration for future automobile designs.*

The automobile manufacturers were tired of having to re-supply their embedded development teams every time they chose a new microprocessor for a new application. Not only is there a steep learning curve for the design engineers to become proficient with yet another processor and another debugging tool, but there is also the reality that the modern automobile contains dozens of embedded microcontrollers. Thus, the variety of development tools in use was becoming a major design and support nightmare and a major impediment to improved productivity.

In 1998, the Global Embedded Processor Debug Interface Standard (GEPDIS) was organized by tool providers Bosch ETAS and HP Automotive Solutions Division and by embedded microcontroller providers Hitachi Semiconductor, Motorola Vehicle Systems Division, and Infineon Technologies. The group's original working name was the Nexus Consortium ("Nexus: a connected group"), but it is now known as the 5001 Forum, in recognition of its affiliation with the IEEE-ISTO. The standard was assigned the designation ISTO-5001, Global Embedded Microprocessor Debug Standard. The standard was formally approved by the IEEE Industry Standards and Technology Organization (ISTO) in early 2000.

> **Note**
>
> Just so you know, at the time of this writing (April 2001), I am a member of the Nexus 5001 Steering Committee and the secretary/treasurer of the organization.

The complete definition of the standard is about 160 pages of rather detailed information, so I'll only touch on some highlights here. The standard is readily accessible from the IEEE-ISTO Web site at `http://www.ieee-isto.org/Nexus5001/standard.html`. The Nexus standard introduces several new concepts to embedded processor debugging. The first is scalability. A processor can comply with the Nexus standard at several levels of compliance. The first level provides for simple run control commands. Each successive level adds more capabilities and requires more pins on the processor to implement. These additional pins allow real-time trace data to be output by the processor without stalling the processor core. Thus, a manufacturer of an 8-bit embedded controller might only need to implement the first level of compliance because I/O pins are precious commodities for a low-cost device. Manufacturers of high-performance 32-bit embedded processors would probably want to implement a higher level of compliance to provide real-time trace and other capabilities.

Also, Nexus used the JTAG protocol (IEEE 1149.1) as the standard protocol for the lowest level of compliance. This means a well-accepted standard protocol, with a rich set of existing tools and software support, is usable for the Nexus methodology.

Figure 7.8 shows the basic structure of the Nexus interface.

Figure 7.8   Nexus interface.

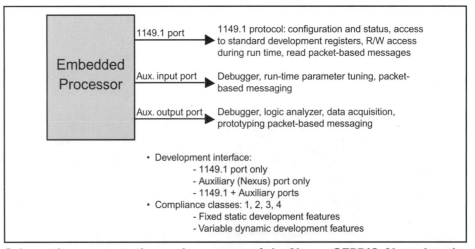

Schematic representation and summary of the Nexus GEPDIS. Note that the interface is scalable from the basic run control feature set through to dynamic debugging (real-time trace).

Figure 7.9 shows compliance Classes 1 through Class 4. The matrix shows the various run control features available at each compliance level. The boxes with an "A" mean that this feature must be implemented according to the APIs defined in section five of the standard. The boxes marked with a "V" mean that the silicon vendor must define the implementation due to the differences in the various processor architectures; however, accessing these features must be in accordance with the defined APIs. Notice that for static debugging — features similar to running under a standard debugger — all compliance classes support the same set of debug behaviors.

Figure 7.9 Compliance classes 1 through 4.

Development Features	Class 1	Class 2	Class 3	Class 4	Nexus Feature
STATIC DEVELOPMENT FEATURES					
Read/write user registers in debug mode	V	V	V	V	Refer to SECTION 5
Read/write user memory in debug mode	A	A	A	A	Read/Write Access
Enter a debug mode from reset	A	A	A	A	Development Control and Status
Enter a debug mode from user mode	A	A	A	A	
Exit a debug mode to user mode	A	A	A	A	
Single-step instruction in user mode and re-enter debug mode					
Stop program execution instruction/ data breakpoint and enter debug mode (minimum two breakpoints)	A	A	A	A	

Note:
"A" indicates a required development feature that must be implemented via the Nexus API.
"V" indicates a required vendor-defined development feature implemented in the Nexus API.

Static debug features of the Nexus interface. Note that certain features, such as reading and writing to the processor registers, are vendor-defined implementations because different processors have different registers.

The Nexus standard also provides for instruction jamming. As the name implies, instructions are "jammed" into the processor via the Nexus port, rather than fetched from memory. Although slow when compared with full-speed operation, instruction jamming is a cost-effective way to edit, compile, assemble, link, download, and debug the embedded code without first having to program a ROM or flash memory chip. For single stepping, jamming is just as efficient as a resident debugger. Figure 7.10 shows the extensive dynamic debugging features available via the Nexus interface. In particular, the Nexus feature called Memory Substitution implements the instruction-jamming feature just discussed. As you can see, this is available only at Class 4-compliance level.

Figure 7.10 Nexus dynamic debugging features.

Development Feature	Class 1	Class 2	Class 3	Class 4	Nexus Feature
DYNAMIC DEVELOPMENT FEATURES					
Ability to set breakpoint or watchpoint	A	A	A	A	Breakpoints/Watchpoints
Device identification	A	A and P	A and P	A and P	Device ID Message (see SECTION 6)
Ability to send out an event occurrence when watchpoint matches	P	P	P	P	Watchpoint Message (see SECTION 6)
Monitor process ownership while processor runs in real-time	-	P	P	P	Ownership Trace
Monitor program flow while processor run in real-time (logical address)	-	P	P	P	Program Trace
Monitor data writes while processor runs in real-time	-	-	P	P	Data Trace (Writes only)
Read/write memory locations while program runs in real-time	-	-	A and P	A and P	Read/Write Access
Program execution (instruction/data) from Nexus port for reset or exceptions	-	-	-	P	Memory Subsitution
Ability to start ownership, program, or data trace upon watchpoint occurrence	-	-	-	A	Development Control and Status
Ability to start memory substitution upon watchpoint occurrence or upon program access of device-specific address	-	-	-	O	Development Control and Status
Monitor data reads while processor runs in real-time	-	-	O	O	Data Trace (Reads and Writes)
LSIO port replacement and HSIO port sharing	-	O	O	O	Port Replacement/Sharing
Transmit data values for acquisition by tool	-	-	O	O	Data Acquisition

Dynamic debugging features of the Nexus interface (from the Nexus Web site).

Finally, the Nexus standard provides an innovative solution to a real problem, namely, if everything is standardized, how can you differentiate between different manufacturer and vendor tools and debug solutions? The answer is the concept of private messages. In effect, the Nexus standard allows for a semiconductor manufacturer and a particular tool vendor to develop a partnership that is mutually beneficial to both companies. Suppose for example, tool company ABC has developed a novel algorithm for measuring code performance in a real-time system. ABC asks a semiconductor company, DEF, to add several special registers that record certain statistics as the processor runs normally. Periodically, these statistics are sent out the Nexus port and analyzed by ABC's software. Perhaps the results are fed to ABC's C++ compiler and used to optimize the code running on the processor.

In this scenario, ABC and DEF want to keep a proprietary control of the link between the information being generated internally by the processor and the compiler optimizations. Nexus allows a private message to be defined to which only ABC and DEF are privy. Other Nexus-based tools from other vendors that might be connected to the Nexus port see these messages as private messages and ignore them.

The concept of a private message is a significant innovation. Until now, debug tools have been closely coupled with the remote debug kernels with which they communicate. Messages that can't be interpreted generally result in the system aborting the debug session. However, as long as all the tools are able to deal with the possibility that private messages might be outputed by the processors' debug core, the messages themselves won't cause the tools to lose synchronization and abort the communications. Tools that understand the messages can interpret them and act on the results. Thus, the private message allows for uniqueness and added functionality within the overall context of an industry-wide standard. Private messaging is the Nexus feature called Data Acquisition in Figure 7.10, shown earlier.

Considering that high-performance processors can generate a large quantity of debugging information in a short time period, it's important to determine how intrusive some of the dynamic debugging features in Figure 7.10 are. In other words, does the generation of the debugging information affect the real-time operation of the processor? With a single IEEE 1149.1 port on the processor, the dynamic data flowing out from the port can't keep up with the processor, and it's likely that the CPU core would have to periodically stop (stall) to allow the JTAG port to catch up. The Nexus developers anticipated this by defining scalability in terms of features and the I/O hardware necessary to support those features. Thus, by adding additional I/O pins to the processor to add "debugging bandwidth," dynamic debugging features can be accommodated with minimal intrusion. (However, "minimal" is a loaded word. What is acceptable for one user might cause unpredictable results in another user's target system.) Figure 7.8 shows this auxiliary I/O port as a schematic representation. Figure 7.11 shows the number of dedicated I/O pins that are necessary for each compliance class. Notice that as many as 16 pins might be necessary for full compliance at Class 4.

Note

The decision to add extra pins to an embedded processor package is not a simple one. Pins are valuable commodities in terms of chip area and package costs.

Figure 7.11 I/O pins.

Compliance Class and Port Type	Number of Device Data Pins				
	1	2	4	8	16
Class 2 input port	X	X	-	-	-
Class 2 output port	X	X	-	-	-
Class 3 or 4 input port	X	X	X	-	-
Class 3 or 4 output port	-	-	X	X	X

Nexus port I/O pin requirements.

The driving force to create the Nexus 5001 standard came from the automobile industry, but the standard is not limited to automotive applications. The original working group of five companies were heavily involved in supplying semiconductors or development tools to the automotive industry; however, that group has now grown to over 25 semiconductor and development-tool support companies that have products supporting a wide range of industrial applications of embedded processors. At the same time, several prominent semiconductor manufacturers are not members of the Nexus 5001 group. These companies might choose to remain outside of the standards group because they view their on-chip debug circuitry as a "market differentiator" for them, as well as a competitive advantage.

Summary

The designers of the Nexus standard did several key things correctly. From a technical point of view, this should make the adoption of the standard fairly straightforward. Eventually, members of the Nexus 5001 group will be able to access suggested interface tool designs, representative implementations in Verilog or VHDL, and a standard set of software APIs.

Nexus is a good thing for the industry and will enable both silicon developers and tool developers to bring better debug systems to the market. This, in turn, will help their common customers bring products to market in a timely manner. As former Hewlett-Packard CEO John Young once said, "Standards by themselves are not particularly interesting, but they allow you to do very interesting things."

Chapter 8

The ICE — An Integrated Solution

Chapter 6 introduced the three key capabilities necessary to hardware/software (HW/SW) integration:

- Microprocessor run control
- Memory substitution
- Real-time trace

So far, you've learned how to address these capabilities using separate tools, namely a debugging kernel, a ROM emulator, and a logic analyzer. In this chapter, you'll see what happens when you design a tool system that addresses these needs in a more integrated fashion.

Traditionally, an in-circuit emulator (ICE) is a single-test instrument that integrates all these functions and more. (Modern on-chip debugging support has changed this somewhat, as the later sidebar "Distributed Emulators" explains.) Emulators are the premier tools for HW/SW integration. An emulator's close coupling of run control, memory substitution, and trace facilities generates a synergism that significantly increases the power of each component.

Even so, the ICE is widely underused. Only about one-third of the embedded system designers, principally firmware developers, use ICE tools. Hopefully, after reading this and the next chapter, you'll appreciate how important the ICE is to HW/SW integration.

165

> In the language of embedded systems, a firmware developer is someone who writes the low-level driver code that interfaces the software directly to the hardware. Because the ICE has been primarily designated as a HW/SW integration tool, firmware designers have been the people most closely associated with it.

Bullet-Proof Run Control

In the most general case, an ICE uses a debug kernel for run-time control but with a difference that eliminates dependence on the target's untested memory/processor interface. Instead of relying on the target's processor and memory, the ICE supplies its own processor and memory. A cable or special connector (see the "Making the Connection" sidebar on page 170) allows the ICE processor to substitute for the target's processor.

The target program remains in the target memory, but the debug kernel is hosted in the ICE memory. When in normal run mode, the ICE processor reads instructions from the target memory; however, when the debug kernel needs control, the ICE switches to its own local memory. This arrangement ensures that the ICE can maintain run control, even if the target memory is faulty, and also protects the debug kernel from being damaged by bugs in the target.

Figure 8.1 shows a straightforward, generic implementation. The key blocks are labeled:

- NMI control logic
- Memory steering logic
- Shadow ROM and RAM

When the user or emulator decides to stop processing the user's code and enter the debugger, the NMI signal is asserted, and the NMI control logic responds as follows:

- The NMI signal from the target system is blocked by the NMI control logic, so that no further NMI-based interrupts are detected by the processor while it's executing the code in the debug kernel.
- The memory steering logic switches off the address and data bus buffers to the target system and enables the emulator's local, or "shadow," memory to connect to the processor. In effect, the context switch occurs by swapping the memory space of the processor.
- The processor then takes the interrupt vector that directs it into the debugger entry point, now located in the shadow ROM.

Thus, with this generic emulation system, the only requirement for processor debug support is that the processor has an external NMI capability.

Figure 8.1   General emulator design.

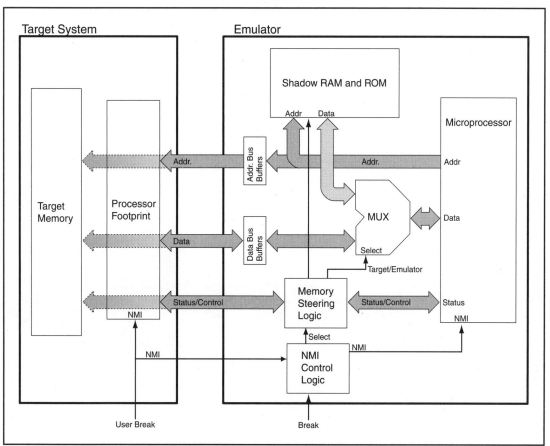

Schematic representation of the architecture of a run control system for a general emulator design.

Note

Most processors have a processor input pin called a *non-maskable interrupt* (NMI). This interrupt signal cannot be ignored (masked) by the processor. It differs from a RESET signal in that the context of the processor can be saved with an NMI but is lost with a RESET. What they have in common is that when either is asserted, the processor must respond to it. In embedded systems, the NMI signal is reserved for catastrophic events, such as a watchdog timer time out or imminent power failure.

Why Emulators Aren't Used More

In many labs, the entire lab has only one emulator. It sits on a mobile cart and has a long, thin wooden pole attached to it. On the top of the pole is a blaze orange, triangular flag that some engineer purchased in a bike shop for his kid's bike a few years ago. Whenever a gnarly problem arises, someone looks for the flag and grabs the emulator. Next, they try to find Joe or Susan — the one or two engineers in the place who actually know how to use it — and hope they can find and fix the problem. The other engineers have been playing with this bug for a week now, and they've finally thrown in the towel and want to bring in the big gun. Up to now, they've resisted the urge to get the ICE because they figured it would take them the better part of a morning to get it hooked up and running. They always had one other quick-and-dirty test to try that would only take 20 minutes or so. This goes on for a few days until the call goes out to send in the cavalry.

It isn't always that bad. But I've heard that exact scenario enough times and seen enough of those flags to know that I'm on to something. What are they really saying?

- Emulators are hard to use. (They certainly can be.)

- Emulators are too fragile. (There is also some truth to this but not universally.)

- Emulators are too expensive. (Compared to what? What did the lost weeks cost in terms of engineering expenses and time-to-market?)

- Emulators won't run in my target system. (This is rarely true but is an excuse that usually covers up all kinds of system design flaws.)

- Emulators don't fit in my process.

- I've been getting by without it, and, now that I really do need it, my development process presents a much too closed environment for the ICE to be used effectively. (This can certainly be the case.)

Because of these prevailing perceptions, for many embedded systems developers, the ICE becomes the tool of last resort, rather than an integral part of the tool suite. Unfortunately, that attitude just perpetuates a self-fulfilling prophecy: The ICE isn't used because it's too hard to use, which means it will never be understood well enough to make it easy to use.

Real-Time Trace

After the generic emulator has been attached to the target, acquiring real-time trace information is almost trivial. The emulator already has connections to the necessary address, data, and status busses. To add real-time trace, you just piggy-back a logic analyzer onto the same connection. Thus, without too much additional complexity, you can use the same target system connection that you used for the logic analyzer to concentrate both run control and trace in one target connection instead of in two.

With your new emulation/trace tool, you can control the processor and observe its behavior in real time. Wait, there's more. Remember that logic analyzers have all this complex circuitry to detect when to begin capturing a trace. Why not use this trigger signal for more than just starting and stopping the trace? Why not also connect it to the NMI control logic so that you can cause the processor to stop program execution and enter the debug monitor program exactly at the place in the code where the event of interest occurs?

Figure 8.2 shows this schematically. The logic analyzer has been added to show how the system functions. The address, data, and status busses are connected to the trace memory and to the trigger system. The trigger system determines when the trace memory should start capturing a trace and when it should stop capturing a trace. It also connects to the NMI control logic block so that you can define trigger conditions that function independently of the trace system. These other trigger conditions control when the processor stops executing user code and enters the debug kernel (also called the monitor program).

Figure 8.2 Emulation control system.

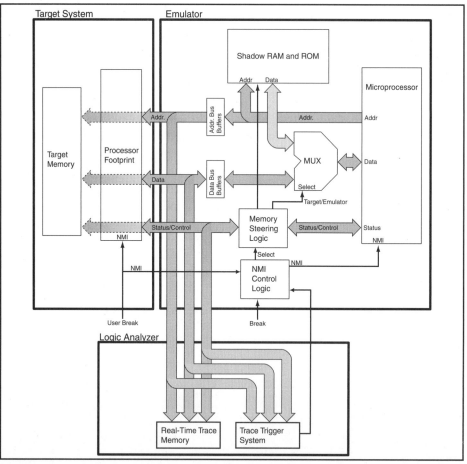

Block diagram of the core of an emulation control system with real-time trace.

Making the Connection

The emulator's steering circuitry must be interposed between the pins of the processor and the target system. This can be done in one of two ways:

- Remove the target microprocessor from the target (unplug it from its socket)

- Disable it in a way that all the pins become open-circuited as far as the target system is concerned (called tri-stated)

If the Target Can Be Socketed Easily

If the footprint of the socket matches the footprint of the microprocessor, it's simple to replace the microprocessor with the appropriate socket and then plug the replacement system into the socket. Of course, the replacement "emulator" must also have some kind of communication port on the board so you can communicate with your emulation debug kernel, but this is easy to implement. Thus, you can easily add a simple RS232 port to this board and connect the interrupt output signal from the port to the NMI control logic of your emulation circuitry. When a new character is received at the serial port, the NMI is asserted, and you're into the debug kernel.

If the Target Can't Be Socketed Easily

Some processors have a dedicated input pin that, when asserted, turns the chip completely off. You can plug the replacement chip (with the emulator signals) into the target system as an overlay. You can do this several ways—some ways are easy, some are not so easy, some are costly, and some are fragile. For example, suppose the target processor is a surface-mounted part with 300 extremely delicate pins mounted around its periphery. This is typical of what you might expect to find today. If the target system has room, the hardware designers might be able to place some high-density sockets on the target PC board so that each pin of the socket intercepts one of the I/O pins of the target processor. Two or three high-density sockets easily can cover the 300 pins of the target processor. If you get the mechanical design just right, you should be able to plug the connectors on the emulator board into the matching sockets of the target system.

If the target processor has a "disable everything" pin, you can turn it off. If it doesn't, you must remove the processor from the target and depend on the emulation processor, mounted on the generic emulation board, to become the target processor. You probably won't have the luxury of sockets on the target system, so go to plan B.

In this situation, you need to find a manufacturer of specialized connection devices (such as Ironwood Electronics Corporation at `www.ironwoodelectronics.com` or Emulation Technology, Inc., at `www.emulation.com`) so you can solder an interface connector to the 300-pin footprint on your target printed circuit board and provide a mating socket into which ou can plug your emulator. This is shown schematically in Figure 8.3, in which a mechanical adapter can be soldered to the target system PC board to replace the embedded microprocessor that you are trying to emulate/control.

With this socket adapter mounted to the PC board, you can plug in the target processor (by mounting it to a small PC board with an SMT footprint on the top side and mating PGA pins on the bottom), or you can plug in your emulator. Adapters such as this cost anywhere from $1 per pin to $5 per pin, so one very fragile adapter might set you back $1,000. Also, because these sockets add some additional length to the electrical interconnections of the target system, some distortion of the waveforms might occur at high bus rates. How this impacts your target system is generally impossible to predict in advance.

Another advantage of this technique is that it's generally usable with many miniature and crowded target systems. That's not to say that it's universal because some perverse mechanical designs are out there that absolutely defy physical access, but, at least in this situation, it's not taking up any more space at the board-level than the actual footprint of the microprocessor itself.

Figure 8.3 Mechanical adapter.

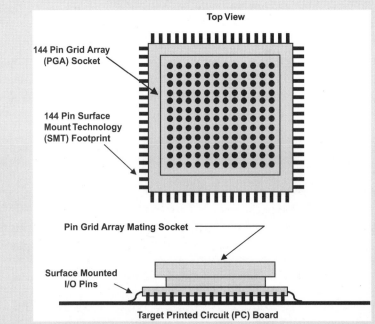

An adapter for converting a surface-mounted package into a pin-grid array style socket.

Hardware Breakpoints

Now you can let the trigger system of the logic analyzer take over some of the functionality that was previously supplied by the debug kernel. You can set a breakpoint, or a complex break condition, in the trigger system and let it signal the breakpoint in real time as the program executes at full speed.

> **Note**
>
> Many discrete logic analyzers have the capability to output a trigger pulse. Often, you can use this pulse as an input to your BDM or JTAG interface to force the debug core to stop execution. However, a large number of instructions might get executed after the break condition occurs (called *skew*), so, if you really want to stop on a dime, this method forces some compromises.

This looks pretty good. Using the combination of the run control functionality of a debugger with the capability to set a breakpoint lets the user halt execution of the code without slowing the processor down the way a real debugger would. Also, you can still set your breakpoint even if the code you are running is located in ROM. As a bonus, the trace capability of the logic analyzer allows you to see what's happening, or what's happened, in real time. If you have an ISR that comes on 0.000000001% of the time, the logic analyzer can capture it when it happens and show you what it's doing.

So what's a good trigger signal?

How you set up the trigger signal depends upon what you're looking for. Let's say that you're interested in debugging a very short and infrequent ISR. In this example system, the interrupt causes the processor to read automatically from memory location 0x00000078 and use the data valued stored there as the memory location of the first instruction of the ISR. This is normally referred to as an exception vector. The vector in this case is a term used for an indirect memory access. In this example, we could set the trigger to be asserted when the processor does a read from memory location 0x00000078. Thus, our trigger condition in this situation is a specific address and a processor-read cycle. In this example, we don't care what the data value happens to be, so we'll only assert the trigger on the address and status bits. Also, we want the system to begin recording states after the trigger occurs and stop recording before we overwrite the states we recorded beginning from the trigger point. Thus, no matter how infrequently the ISR occurs or how short it is, the logic analyzer will continue recording and overwriting until the trigger condition is met, and the logic analyzer captures a trace buffer full of states.

Let's consider a different situation. Suppose that the exception vector is caused by a program fault, such as an illegal op-code, but when the exception processing occurs, it also seems to be failing. In this case, you would want to set the trigger point so that the trigger point occurs in the middle of the trace buffer. In this way, you can see all of the states of the system leading up to the failure and then see what the processor executed once the exception vector is taken. Most logic analyzers allow you to set the trigger event to occur anywhere in the buffer memory.

Thus, you can record all the states that occurred leading up to the trigger event, all of the states following the trigger event, and everything in between.

Our previous example shows that we can easily specify an address as a trigger condition. As a C or C++ programmer, it's usually not convenient to have to find out where the addresses of variables are located. The compiler takes care of those details so we don't have to. Therefore, just as with a source-level debugger, we should be able to use the same logic analyzer soft ware that provides us with symbolic trace information to allow us to create trigger conditions without having to know the low-level details. Thus, if I write a simple function foo():

```
int foo( int, bar)
{
 int embedded =  15;
 bar++;
 return embedded+bar ;
 }
```

Let's assume that for some very strange reason the function that calls foo() sometimes gets an erroneous return value back. When you single-stepped your program on the host, it worked just fine. You suspect that an ISR is overwriting your local variable on the stack. You could look up the symbol table and link map and figure out where the function is located, or, if your LA is suitably appointed, you could tell it to trigger on foo() and have the software figure out where foo() happens to be in memory.

Overlay Memory

Even though triggered breakpoints work on code located in ROM, you still need some kind of substitution memory, if for no other reason than to speed up the edit–compile–link–load–debug cycle. Chapter 6 covered the ROM emulator, a device that plugs into the ROM sockets and replaces the ROM, while providing an easy method of downloading code through an Ethernet or serial port. You could do that here as well. This is called *substitution memory* because it's used to substitute one form of memory, RAM, for another form, ROM. The substitution memory lives in the same space as the ROM that would normally be plugged into the socket.

Today, most emulators don't use substitution memory, although they certainly could. Because the emulator already has steering logic to determine which memory space from which it grabs the next instruction (the target memory or the shadow memory as shown previously in Figure 8.2), it wouldn't be much more complicated to design an emulation memory system that could overlay the target memory system. Thus, for certain memory operations, you could go to the target system to read or write memory. For other operations, such as fetching instructions, you could activate this other memory that is connected to the emulator and is presumably easy to download to with new instructions or data. This other type of memory is called *overlay memory* because it can cover broad areas of the processor's address space, rather than look at the target system through the ROM socket.

Overlay memory is extremely useful. In fact, it's much more useful than substitution memory. Overlay memory uses the same trick that is used with shadow memory. On a bus cycle-by-bus cycle basis, fast buffers and steering logic are used to decide to which block of memory the processor actually connects. The block of memory can exist on the target, in shadow memory, or in overlay memory. In a way, the memory steering logic functions much like an on-chip Memory Management Unit (MMU). The circuitry maps the physical address being output by the processor to various external memories.

Figure 8.4 shows how you can set up an overlay memory system. Suppose your processor has a 32-bit address bus and the smallest block of overlay memory you can map in or out is 16KB. Also, assume that you have a total of 1MB of emulation, or overlay memory. If you divide this memory into 16KB chunks, you have a total of 64 16KB blocks that can be used to overlay or to replace any one of the 256KB blocks in the target memory space. Assuming you have some magical way of programming the memory-mapper RAM, you can then program each 18-bit data value in the mapper RAM to translate the 18-bit input address from the target microprocessor to another value on the output. One address goes in; another goes out as data. If you program every memory location in the mapper RAM with the corresponding address value, the mapper has no apparent effect, other than using up some valuable time that might otherwise be available to the target system's memory.

Because you only have 1MB of emulation memory, you can't map more than you have. The emulation control system limits you to how many unique mapping situations (called *mapping terms*) you can create. Obviously, you can assign several 16KB blocks to consecutive addresses to form larger blocks of emulation memory.

Figure 8.4 Emulation control system.

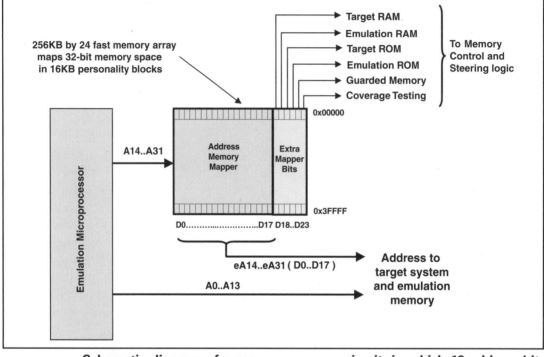

Schematic diagram of a memory-mapper circuit, in which 18 address bits map the 18 high-order address bits from the microprocessor to the addresses of physical memory, either target-system memory or emulation memory. The remaining six bits are used to assign unique personalities to each of the 16KB blocks.

Note

It is certainly possible to design the memory-mapping system in other ways. The emulator with which I'm most familiar actually used a different scheme with custom integrated circuits to build the mapper system. Rather than using a memory block as a logical element, as shown earlier in Figure 8.4, you can design the system around address comparator circuits. These circuits do a hardware comparison between the address coming from the target microprocessor and the address range assigned, for example, to a particular 16KB block. The advantage of this method is that it doesn't require a large, fast memory array, as is required in Figure 8.4. In fact, a comparator-based design is very much like the trigger circuit that you use in the logic analyzer to compare the address, data, and status states to your trigger condition. The disadvantage is that it's harder to explain in a simple picture how this kind of a memory-mapper system works, so this discussion uses the RAM-based architecture.

The mapper memory is actually wider than it needs to be to perform the memory-mapping function. The extra memory bits assign "personalities" to each of the 16KB memory blocks. Thus, you can map memory as emulation RAM or target RAM. This means that the memory system steering logic sends the address, data, and status information to the appropriate memory space, either in the target system or in emulation memory. The other bits allow you to detect error conditions in the code flow. If, for example, you assign an emulation ROM attribute to a 16KB memory block, you can cause the emulation system to stop execution, trigger a trace, or both, if a write signal is asserted to a memory address in that block. However, because each block of emulated ROM really is RAM memory located within the emulator, each block can be easily loaded with new software, much like the ROM emulator.

Figure 8.4 points out an important difference between overlay memory and substitution memory. Because overlay memory is mappable and can be assigned a personality, it can be given precedence over memory in the target system by assigning the selected block of address space to emulation memory instead of the target memory. Substitution memory can be used only to replace a block of memory in the target system that is accessed through the ROM socket.

The two other personality bits of interest in Figure 8.4 allow you to protect a region of memory from being written to, even though it's assigned to be target or emulation RAM. This feature allows you to track any attempts to overwrite a variable defined as const, as usually happens when a pointer goes haywire. The coverage bit is discussed in the next chapter with coverage testing. For now, the coverage bit enables you to gather statistics about what distinct memory locations in that 16KB block have been accessed by the user's program code.

Overlay memory completes the design of the generic emulator. In contrast to the individual tools described in earlier chapters, the emulator offers:

- A single connection to the target board
- Reliable run control even in unreliable systems
- Cross-triggering of the run control system, allowing trace and breakpoint facilities to work together
- Real-time monitoring of illegal memory accesses

Despite these advantages, the emulator is only slightly more complex than a logic analyzer.

Timing Constraints

Unfortunately, emulators can't be used with every system. The two main obstacles are timing constraints and physical constraints. The physical constraints are similar to those limiting the use of logic analyzers and were discussed in the "Making the Connection" sidebar. The timing constraints, however, are a direct consequence of the emulator's steering logic.

The fact that a RAM circuit is needed to map the memory regions has a serious implication for the target system's capability to work properly with the emulator. If the target system is designed with very little timing margin between the processor and the target memory, or other memory-mapped I/O devices in the target, you could have a problem.

Note

Hardware designers aren't wrong to design very close to the edge with respect to timing constraints. For example, according to the data book, a particular memory chip might have a minimum access time of 45ns, a typical access time of 55ns, and a maximum access time of 70ns. This data represents a statistical sampling by the manufacturer that, over the appropriate temperature range for that version of the device, most of the devices would be able to work at 55ns, and almost all of them (six sigma) would work at 70ns. This also implies that almost none of them would work at access times less than 45ns.

However, it would be possible to get a lot of parts and painstakingly sort through them until you find some that actually worked reliably below 45ns. Alternatively, if you could guarantee that the part never got warmer than room temperature, then a processor with an access time of 41ns might actually work with a memory chip that had a maximum access time of 70ns. Thus, you could save some money by buying a part that is less costly but slower than the part that a conservatively designed system might demand.

Recall that the hardware designer is trying to do the right thing and not overdesign the hardware. Thus, if the processor-to-memory-system-interface timing specification calls for a minimum of 55ns and you use a memory chip with a typical specification of 50ns, you should be safe. The design might not pass a stringent hardware design review, but it will most likely work. However, your emulator might need to steal 10ns from the 50ns because the memory-mapper RAM needs 10ns to do the address translation. After all, it's RAM memory as well. Suddenly, the 55ns access time becomes 45ns, and the system stops working when the emulator is substituted for the actual processor.

Several possible solutions exist. If the hardware designer added the capability to the design or the feature was already built into the microcontroller, you could add one or more *wait states* to the memory access time. Another possibility is to slow down the processor clock so that the access times increase. This might work, but it probably won't.

> **Note**
>
> A wait state is a method of stretching the memory access time by one or more clock cycles. For example, the Motorola MF5206e ColdFire processors that are used in my Embedded Systems class have an on-chip wait state generator that can add from one to 16 wait states onto a memory access. This is convenient because the experiment boards and cables tend to mess things up a bit, and three wait states are required for reliable access to the experiment boards.

Last, you might be able to use faster parts in your development boards and go with the slower ones in the released product. Of course, the downside is that you've started on a slippery slope. Your emulator now has intruded upon your target system by forcing it to run slower (a wait state takes time). Your target system might not run properly because the time to execute critical code segments has increased beyond some critical threshold. The emulator designers are aware of this, and they can sometimes choose processors that have been selected for speed to compensate for the access time used up by the mapping memory. However, sometimes it just won't work.

Distributed Emulators

Earlier in this chapter, I mentioned the concept of constructing an emulator from these separate pieces:

- Run control

- Real-time instruction and data trace

- Memory substitution

The generic emulator used a debug kernel instead of a debug core. You can still build the ICE and integrate the three functions even if you have a debug core. In this case, much of the run control circuitry is simplified, but the three elements pretty much function in the same relative way.

A JTAG or BDM debugger, a ROM emulator, and a logic analyzer can be brought together and used to provide similar functionality to an ICE. When properly interconnected, these generic tools can do a lot of what a full-function ICE does, but they don't do everything. They have the following limitations:

- Cross-triggering is difficult to do with distributed emulation because the logic analyzer must be able to output a signal that the trigger event has occurred, the JTAG or BDM debugger must be able to accept that asynchronous signal, and the code execution must halt. Some JTAG devices can accept these signals, but some can't.

- ROM emulators provide substitution memory, but that memory is limited to what can be seen through the ROM socket. You can't assign personality bits to the ROM emulator, so you might not be able to detect a write-to-ROM error unless you program the logic analyzer to look for it.

- Distributed systems often take time for a "break" signal to flow from the logic analyzer to the debug core. This results in the processor continuing to run on past the breakpoint, which is called *skew*. It might or might not be a problem in your application.

All ICEs suffer from the same limitations that logic analyzers have with respect to modern microprocessors and microcontrollers. They need some kind of window into the processor busses, or they lose a significant amount of their effectiveness. The behavior of a processor with on-chip instruction and data caches is just as invisible to an ICE as it is to a logic analyzer, so most emulators are designed to take advantage of all the on-chip trace and breakpoint circuitry provided by the chip manufacturer. Fortunately for the user, the postprocessing of the data is taken care of by the emulator manufacturer, so the trace that you see has already been cooked to fill in the information that has to be inferred, rather than directly measured.

Thus, if the processor has several on-chip breakpoint registers, you might be able to set up a simple combination of address, data, and status in these resisters, so the trace receives a trigger signal through an I/O pin on the processor or the processor stops code execution. If you really want to set up a complex breakpoint, however, you will probably have to turn off the on-chip caches and take the performance hit that goes along with it.

(In 1995, Larry Ritter and I[1] wrote an article discussing the concept of "distributed emulation." Our premise was that the complexity of the ICE is, in part, a result of the fact that it integrates the functions of run control, substitution memory, and real-time trace to such an extent that the resultant tool becomes expensive, fragile, complex, and processor-specific. As in Chapter 6, we argued that the real need is to be able to perform these three tasks, and the ICE happens to be a tightly integrated method of doing just that. Suppose, we argue, you break the ICE apart into its component pieces and then use them independently. By doing that, you lose the tight integration but gain because you can use more generic and cost-effective tools in place of the ICE. This argument certainly has merit. In fact, devious to fault, I made that argument in the previous chapter. However, as with most engineering endeavors, we have trade-offs that must be evaluated. Hopefully, this chapter will explain some of these trade-offs.)

Usage Issues

Despite the fact that the emulator implements much of the same functionality as the more commonly used combination of a debug kernel, ROM emulator, and logic analyzer, the ICE still has a reputation for being hard to use. It isn't difficult to teach someone to use an emulator as they would use any kind of debugger. The difficult part is the initial exercise of setting up the emulator to run in a specific target system.

In part, emulators are difficult to set up because they are designed to be adaptable to a wide range of use models and target situations. If all the emulator ever had to do was plug into a compact PCI card cage or VXI card cage, its design would be much simpler than it is. However, because we didn't know how it would be used, it had to be designed with a lot of flexibility. The flexibility meant the user would have to make many functional decisions to make the emulator run in the target. Overall, most engineers are reluctant to use ICEs because of the difficulty in setting them up to work properly in a particular target system.

Another difficulty is the need to know the memory map of the system to correctly overlay emulation memory onto your target system. It's a relatively easy thing to do, but, surprisingly, it's often ignored.

Setting the Trigger

The last setup barrier to overcome is setting up and using the trigger and trace capability of the emulator. Much of this discussion applies equally to a logic analyzer.

Perhaps the most exasperating experience that you can have is to try to set up the trace tool to capture an extremely infrequent event and then learn that you killed the day because the trigger condition wasn't set right. It's happened to me more times than I want to admit. Sometimes, I try to get around the problem by setting a general trigger condition — such as trigger on a read operation from a certain address — and hope that the event I was looking for occurred within that window. This situation usually results in the logic analyzer triggering on the wrong event and then filling the trace buffer so that the real event is never observed.

Some emulators or logic analyzers allow you to use one trigger condition to turn on the trace and another to turn it off. With this feature, you can set up a trace so that only a few states are captured each time the trigger event occurs. Then you have to search through 50,000 events to find the one for which you're looking. Thus, you have either to set up the trace specification as a complex sequence that has a high probability of not capturing the event of interest or to set up a simple tracespec and manually search the trace buffer for the event of interest.

> One technique that has worked for me is to write a simple test program and load it into the target system as a test program for the trace system. The test program can use different address locations and data values, but the logical flow should approximate the real situation that you want to track and set the trigger on. It's extra work to write and debug your test program, but it lowers the risk that you'll miss a once-a-week failure with an erroneous tracespec.

Additional Reading

This list is representative of recent articles on the state of in-circuit emulation. With great modesty, I've decided not to include my own articles. I'll simply liberally sprinkle the ideas throughout this chapter, and you'll never know the difference.

- Ganssle, Jack G. "Debugging Modern Embedded Systems." *Embedded Systems Programming*, March, 2000 87.
- Ganssle, Jack G. "ICE Technology Unglugged." *Embedded Systems Programming*, October, 1999 103.
- Ganssle, Jack G. "In-Circuit Emulators." *Embedded Systems Programming*, October, 1998 75.
- Ganssle, Jack G. "Trends in Debugging." *Embedded Systems Programming*, September, 1999,34.
- Mann, Daniel. "The State of Embedded Software Debug." *Microsoft Embedded Review*, 1998 8.
- Laengrich, Norbert. "New Concepts Required for Debugging Embedded Software." *Computer Design*, Septermber, 1997 55.

Summary

The emulator is a powerful tool for HW/SW emulation, but it imposes enough demands on the target physical layout, the memory timing margin, and the user's skills that some advance planning is warranted. The worst scenario is to be in a time crunch and have a bug that you can't figure out, only to discover that it's another one-or-two week project just to modify your target system so you can use an emulator to find the problem.

Even if you don't plan to make the emulator a primary integration tool, you should design for the possibility. That way, when you encounter that project-killing bug, you'll at least have the option of "bringing in the big guns." These are my suggestions:

Design for emulation.   In other words, design with your development tools in mind. If you anticipate a need for an emulator, even if you don't plan to use it as a primary design tool, make sure it is mechanically and electrically compatible with your target. This might be as simple as putting a socket adapter on your development boards or as involved as locating the processor in a particular spot and orientation on the target.

Design with worst-case timing margins.   Designing with typical parameters might be more economical, but you might get erratic results when the emulator steals some of your valuable cycle time.

Take the time to understand your target hardware.   Talk to the hardware designers. They can help you understand what parameters need to be set in the emulator for it to work reliably. For example, when the emulator is running in its internal debug monitor (shadow memory), do you want the bus cycles to be visible to the target system? Some target systems need to see bus activity, or they will generate an NMI or RESET signal. Others use dynamic RAM (DRAM) memory and need to see these signals to retain their memory contents.

Understand the real-time constraints.   Do you have watchdog timers or other real-time events that must be serviced for the system to run? The emulator might work just fine, but it can crash the target if it isn't used in the proper mode.

Research the software compatibility issues.   Can the emulator download your file format? Is it RTOS aware?

Learn to use it before you need it.   Don't wait until you are in a time crunch to become familiar with the tool.

Work Cited

1. Berger, Arnold and Larry Ritter. "Distributed Emulation: A Design Team Strategy for High-Performance Tools and MPUs." *Electronic News*, 22 May 1995, 30.

Chapter 9

Testing

Embedded systems software testing shares much in common with application software testing. Thus, much of this chapter is a summary of basic testing concepts and terminology. However, some important differences exist between application testing and embedded systems testing. Embedded developers often have access to hardware-based test tools that are generally not used in application development. Also, embedded systems often have unique characteristics that should be reflected in the test plan. These differences tend to give embedded systems testing its own distinctive flavor. This chapter covers the basics of testing and test case development and points out details unique to embedded systems work along the way.

Why Test?

Before you begin designing tests, it's important to have a clear understanding of why you are testing. This understanding influences which tests you stress and (more importantly) how early you begin testing. In general, you test for four reasons:

- To find bugs in software (testing is the only way to do this)
- To reduce risk to both users and the company
- To reduce development and maintenance costs
- To improve performance

To Find the Bugs

One of the earliest important results from theoretical computer science is a proof (known as the Halting Theorem) that it's impossible to prove that an arbitrary program is correct. Given the right test, however, you can prove that a program is incorrect (that is, it has a bug). It's important to remember that testing isn't about proving the "correctness" of a program but about finding bugs. Experienced programmers understand that every program has bugs. The only way to know how many bugs are left in a program is to test it with a carefully designed and measured test plan.

To Reduce Risk

Testing minimizes risk to yourself, your company, and your customers. The objectives in testing are to demonstrate to yourself (and regulatory agencies, if appropriate) that the system and software works correctly and as designed. You want to be assured that the product is as safe as it can be. In short, you want to discover every conceivable fault or weakness in the system and software before it's deployed in the field.

Developing Mission-Critical Software Systems

Incidents such as the Therac-25 radiation machine malfunction — in which several patients died due to a failure in the software monitoring the patients — should serve as a sobering reminder that the lives of real people might depend on the quality of the code that you write. I'm not an expert on writing safety-critical code, but I've identified some interesting articles on mission-critical software development:

- Brown, Doug. "Solving the Software Safety Paradox." *Embedded Systems Programming*, December 1998, 44.

- Cole, Bernard. "Reliability Becomes an All-Consuming Goal." *Electronic Engineering Times*, 13 December 1999, 90.

- Douglass, Bruce Powel. "Safety-Critical Embedded Systems." *Embedded Systems Programming*, October 1999, 76.

- Knutson, Charles and Sam Carmichael. "Safety First: Avoiding Software Mishaps." *Embedded Systems Programming*, November 2000, 28.

- Murphy, Niall. "Safe Systems Through Better User Interfaces." *Embedded Systems Programming*, August 1998, 32.

- Tindell, Ken. "Real-Time Systems Raise Reliability Issues." *Electronic Engineering Times*, 17 April 2000, 86.

To Reduce Costs

The classic argument for testing comes from *Quality Wars* by Jeremy Main.

> In 1990, HP sampled the cost of errors in software development during the year. The answer, $400 million, shocked HP into a completely new effort to eliminate mistakes in writing software. The $400M waste, half of it spent in the labs on rework and half in the field to fix the mistakes that escaped from the labs, amounted to one-third of the company's total R&D budget...and could have increased earnings by almost 67%.[5]

The earlier a bug is found, the less expensive it is to fix. The cost of finding errors and bugs in a released product is significantly higher than during unit testing, for example (see Figure 9.1).

Figure 9.1   The cost to fix a problem.

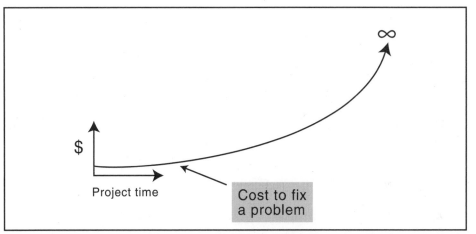

Simplified graph showing the cost to fix a problem as a function of the time in the product life cycle when the defect is found. The costs associated with finding and fixing the Y2K problem in embedded systems is a close approximation to an infinite cost model.

To Improve Performance

Testing maximizes the performance of the system. Finding and eliminating dead code and inefficient code can help ensure that the software uses the full potential of the hardware and thus avoids the dreaded "hardware re-spin."

When to Test?

It should be clear from Figure 9.1 that testing should begin as soon as feasible. Usually, the earliest tests are module or unit tests conducted by the original developer. Unfortunately, few developers know enough about testing to build a thorough set of test cases. Because carefully developed test cases are usually not employed until integration testing, many bugs that could be found during unit testing are not discovered until integration testing. For example, a major network equipment manufacturer in Silicon Valley did a study to figure out the key sources of its software integration problems. The manufacturer discovered that 70 percent of the bugs found during the integration phase of the project were generated by code that had never been exercised before that phase of the project.

Unit Testing

Individual developers test at the module level by writing stub code to substitute for the rest of the system hardware and software. At this point in the development cycle, the tests focus on the logical performance of the code. Typically, developers test with some average values, some high or low values, and some out-of-range values (to exercise the code's exception processing functionality). Unfortunately, these "black-box" derived test cases are seldom adequate to exercise more than a fraction of the total code in the module.

Regression Testing

It isn't enough to pass a test once. Every time the program is modified, it should be retested to assure that the changes didn't unintentionally "break" some unrelated behavior. Called *regression testing*, these tests are usually automated through a test script. For example, if you design a set of 100 input/output (I/O) tests, the regression test script would automatically execute the 100 tests and compare the output against a "gold standard" output suite. Every time a change is made to any part of the code, the full regression suite runs on the modified code base to insure that something else wasn't broken in the process.

From the Trenches
I try to convince my students to apply regression testing to their course projects; however, because they are students, they never listen to me. I've had more than a few projects turned in that didn't work because the student made a minor change at 4:00AM on the day it was due, and the project suddenly unraveled. But, hey, what do I know?

Which Tests?

Because no practical set of tests can prove a program correct, the key issue becomes what subset of tests has the highest probability of detecting the most errors, as noted in *The Art of Software Testing* by Glen Ford Myers[6]. The problem of selecting appropriate test cases is known as *test case design*.

Although dozens of strategies exist for generating test cases, they tend to fall into two fundamentally different approaches: *functional testing* and *coverage testing*. Functional testing (also known as *black-box testing*) selects tests that assess how well the implementation meets the requirements specification. Coverage testing (also known as *white-box testing*) selects cases that cause certain portions of the code to be executed. (These two strategies are discussed in more detail later.) Both kinds of testing are necessary to test rigorously your embedded design. Of the two, coverage testing implies that your code is stable, so it is reserved for testing a completed or nearly completed product. Functional tests, on the other hand, can be written in parallel with the requirements documents. In fact, by starting with the functional tests, you can minimize any duplication of efforts and rewriting of tests. Thus, in my opinion, functional tests come first. Everyone agrees that functional tests can be written first, but Ross[7], for example, clearly believes they are most useful during system integration … not unit testing.

The following is a simple process algorithm for integrating your functional and coverage testing strategies:

1. Identify which of the functions have NOT been fully *covered* by the functional tests.

2. Identify which sections of each function have not been executed.

3. Identify which additional coverage tests are required.

4. Run new additional tests.

5. Repeat.

Infamous Software Bugs

The first known computer bug came about in 1946 when a primitive computer used by the Navy to calculate the trajectories of artillery shells shut down when a moth got stuck in one of its computing elements, a mechanical relay. Hence, the name *bug* for a computer error.[1]

In 1962, the Mariner 1 mission to Venus failed because the rocket went off course after launch and had to be destroyed at a project cost of $80 million.[2] The problem was traced to a typographical error in the FORTRAN guidance code. The FORTRAN statement written by the programmer was

```
DO 10 I=1.5
```

This was interpreted as an assignment statement, DO10I = 1.5.

The statement should have been

```
DO 10 I=1,5.
```

This statement is a DO LOOP. Do line number 10 for the values of I from one to five.

Perhaps the most sobering embedded systems software defect was the deadly Therac-25 disaster in 1987. Four cancer patients receiving radiation therapy died from radiation overdoses. The problem was traced to a failure in the software responsible for monitoring the patients' safety.[4]

When to Stop?

The algorithm from the previous section has a lot in common with the instructions on the back of every shampoo bottle. Taken literally, you would be testing (and shampooing) forever. Obviously, you'll need to have some predetermined criteria for when to stop testing and to release the product.

If you are designing your system for mission-critical applications, such as the navigational software in a commercial jetliner, the degree to which you must test your code is painstakingly spelled out in documents, such as the FAA's DO-178B specification. Unless you can certify and demonstrate that your code has met the requirements set forth in this document, you cannot deploy your product. For most others, the criteria are less fixed.

The most commonly used stop criteria (in order of reliability) are:

- When the boss says
- When a new iteration of the test cycle finds fewer than X new bugs
- When a certain coverage threshold has been met without uncovering any new bugs

Regardless of how thoroughly you test your program, you can never be certain you have found all the bugs. This brings up another interesting question: How many bugs can you tolerate? Suppose that during extreme software stress testing you find that the system locks up about every 20 hours of testing. You examine the code but are unable to find the root cause of the error. Should you ship the product?

How much testing is "good enough"? I can't tell you. It would be nice to have some time-tested rule: "if method Z estimates there are fewer than X bugs in Y lines of code, then your program is safe to release." Perhaps some day such standards will exist. The programming industry is still relatively young and hasn't yet reached the level of sophistication, for example, of the building industry. Many thick volumes of building handbooks and codes have evolved over the years that provide the architect, civil engineer, and structural engineer with all the information they need to build a safe building on schedule and within budget. Occasionally, buildings still collapse, but that's pretty rare. Until programming produces a comparable set of standards, it's a judgment call.

Choosing Test Cases

In the ideal case, you want to test every possible behavior in your program. This implies testing every possible combination of inputs or every possible decision path at least once. This is a noble, but utterly impractical, goal. For example, in *The Art of Software Testing*, Glen Ford Myers[6] describes a small program with only five decisions that has 10^{14} unique execution paths. He points out that if you could write, execute, and verify one test case every five minutes, it would take one billion years to test exhaustively this program. Obviously, the ideal situation is beyond reach, so you must use approximations to this ideal. As you'll see, a combination of functional testing and coverage testing provides a reasonable second-best alternative. The basic approach is to select the tests (some functional, some coverage) that have the highest probability of exposing an error.

Functional Tests

Functional testing is often called black-box testing because the test cases for functional tests are devised without reference to the actual code — that is, without looking "inside the box." An embedded system has inputs and outputs and implements some algorithm between them. Black-box tests are based on what is known about which inputs should be acceptable and how they should relate to the outputs. Black-box tests know nothing about how the algorithm in between is implemented. Example black-box tests include:

- **Stress tests:** Tests that intentionally overload input channels, memory buffers, disk controllers, memory management systems, and so on.
- **Boundary value tests:** Inputs that represent "boundaries" within a particular range (for example, largest and smallest integers together with –1, 0, +1, for an integer input) and input values that should cause the output to transition across a similar boundary in the output range.
- **Exception tests:** Tests that should trigger a failure mode or exception mode.
- **Error guessing:** Tests based on prior experience with testing software or from testing similar programs.

- **Random tests:** Generally, the least productive form of testing but still widely used to evaluate the robustness of user-interface code.
- **Performance tests:** Because performance expectations are part of the product requirement, performance analysis falls within the sphere of functional testing.

Because black-box tests depend only on the program requirements and its I/O behavior, they can be developed as soon as the requirements are complete. This allows black-box test cases to be developed in parallel with the rest of the system design.

Like all testing, functional tests should be designed to be *destructive*, that is, to prove the program doesn't work. This means overloading input channels, beating on the keyboard in random ways, purposely doing all the things that you, as a programmer, know will hurt your baby. As an R&D product manager, this was one of my primary test methodologies. If 40 hours of abuse testing could be logged with no serious or critical defects logged against the product, the product could be released. If a significant defect was found, the clock started over again after the defect was fixed.

Coverage Tests

The weakness of functional testing is that it rarely exercises all the code. Coverage tests attempt to avoid this weakness by (ideally) ensuring that each code statement, decision point, or decision path is exercised at least once. (Coverage testing also can show how much of your data space has been accessed.) Also known as white-box tests or glass-box tests, coverage tests are devised with full knowledge of how the software is implemented, that is, with permission to "look inside the box." White-box tests are designed with the source code handy. They exploit the programmer's knowledge of the program's APIs, internal control structures, and exception handling capabilities. Because white-box tests depend on specific implementation decisions, they can't be designed until after the code is written.

From an embedded systems point of view, coverage testing is the most important type of testing because the degree to which you can show how much of your code has been exercised is an excellent predictor of the risk of undetected bugs you'll be facing later.

Example white-box tests include:

- **Statement coverage:** Test cases selected because they execute every statement in the program at least once.
- **Decision or branch coverage:** Test cases chosen because they cause every branch (both the true and false path) to be executed at least once.

- **Condition coverage:** Test cases chosen to force each condition (term) in a decision to take on all possible logic values.

Theoretically, a white-box test can exploit or manipulate whatever it needs to conduct its test. Thus, a white-box test might use the JTAG interface to force a particular memory value as part of a test. More practically, white-box testing might analyze the execution path reported by a logic analyzer.

Gray-Box Testing

Because white-box tests can be intimately connected to the internals of the code, they can be more expensive to maintain than black-box tests. Whereas black-box tests remain valid as long as the requirements and the I/O relationships remain stable, white-box tests might need to be re-engineered every time the code is changed. Thus, the most cost-effective white-box tests generally are those that exploit knowledge of the implementation without being intimately tied to the coding details.

Tests that only know a little about the internals are sometimes called gray-box tests. Gray-box tests can be very effective when coupled with "error guessing." If you know, or at least suspect, where the weak points are in the code, you can design tests that stress those weak points. These tests are gray box because they cover specific portions of the code; they are error guessing because they are chosen based on a guess about what errors are likely. This testing strategy is useful when you're integrating new functionality with a stable base of legacy code. Because the code base is already well tested, it makes sense to focus your test efforts in the area where the new code and the old code come together.

Testing Embedded Software

Generally the traits that separate embedded software from applications software are:

- Embedded software must run reliably without crashing for long periods of time.
- Embedded software is often used in applications in which human lives are at stake.
- Embedded systems are often so cost-sensitive that the software has little or no margin for inefficiencies of any kind.
- Embedded software must often compensate for problems with the embedded hardware.
- Real-world events are usually asynchronous and nondeterministic, making simulation tests difficult and unreliable.

- Your company can be sued if your code fails.

Because of these differences, testing for embedded software differs from application testing in four major ways. First, because real-time and concurrency are hard to get right, a lot of testing focuses on real-time behavior. Second, because most embedded systems are resource-constrained real-time systems, more performance and capacity testing are required. Third, you can use some real-time trace tools to measure how well the tests are covering the code. Fourth, you'll probably test to a higher level of reliability than if you were testing application software.

Dimensions of Integration

Most of our discussion of system integration has centered on hardware and software integration. However, the integration phase really has three dimensions to it: hardware, software, and real-time. To the best of my knowledge, it's not common to consider real time to be a dimension of the hardware/software integration phase, but it should be. The hardware can operate as designed, the software can run as written and debugged, but the product as a whole can still fail because of real-time issues.

Some designers have argued that integrating a real-time operating system (RTOS) with the hardware and application software is a distinct phase of the development cycle. If we accept their point of view, then we may further subdivide the integration phase to account for the non-trivial task of creating a board support package (BSP) for the hardware. Without a BSP, the RTOS cannot run on the target platform. However, if you are using a standard hardware platform in your system, such as one of the many commercially available single-board computers (SBC), your BSP is likely to have already been developed for you. Even with a well-designed BSP, there are many subtle issues to be dealt with when running under an RTOS.

Simon[8] does an excellent job of covering many of the issues related to running an application when an interrupt may occur at any instant. I won't attempt to cover the same ground as Simon, and I recommend his book as an essential volume in any embedded system developer's professional library.

Suffice to say that the integration of the RTOS, the hardware, the software and the real-time environment represent the four most common dimensions of the integration phase of an embedded product. Since the RTOS is such a central element of an embedded product, any discussion about tools demands that we discuss them in the context of the RTOS itself. A simple example will help to illustrate this point.

Suppose you are debugging a C program on your PC or UNIX workstation. For simplicity's sake, let's assume that you are using the GNU compiler and debugger, GCC and GDB, respectively. When you stop your application to examine the value of a variable, your computer does not stop. Only the application being debugged has stopped running; the rest of the machine is running along just fine. If your program crashes on a UNIX platform, you may get a core dump, but the computer itself keeps on going

Now, let's contrast this with our embedded system. Without an RTOS, when a program dies, the embedded system stops functioning—time to cycle power or press RESET. If an RTOS is running in the system and the debugging tools are considered to be "RTOS aware," then it is very likely that you can halt one of the running processes and follow the same debugging procedure as on the host computer. The RTOS will keep the rest of the embedded system functioning "mostly normally" even though you are operating one of the processes under the control of the debugger. Since this is a difficult task to do and do well, the RTOS vendor is uniquely positioned to supply its customers with finely tuned tools that support debugging in an RTOS environment. We can argue whether or not this is beneficial for the developer, certainly the other tool vendors may cry, "foul," but that's life in the embedded world.

Thus, we can summarize this discussion by recognizing that the decision to use an RTOS will likely have a ripple effect through the entire design process and will manifest itself most visibly when the RTOS, the application software, and the hardware are brought together. If the tools are well designed, the process can be minimally complex. If the tools are not up to the task, the product may never see the light of day.

Real-Time Failure Modes

What you know about how software typically fails should influence how you select your tests. Because embedded systems deal with a lot of asynchronous events, the test suite should focus on typical real-time failure modes.

At a minimum, the test suite should generate both typical and worst case real-time situations. If the device is a controller for an automotive application, does it lock up after a certain sequence of unforeseen events, such as when the radio, windshield wipers, and headlights are all turned on simultaneously? Does it lock up when those items are turned on rapidly in a certain order? What if the radio is turned on and off rapidly 100 times in a row?

In every real-time system, certain combinations of events (call them *critical sequences*) cause the greatest delay from an event trigger to the event response. The embedded test suite should be capable of generating all critical sequences and measuring the associated response time.

For some real-time tasks, the notion of deadline is more important than latency. Perhaps it's essential that your system perform a certain task at exactly 5:00P.M. each day. What will happen if a critical event sequence happens right at 5:00P.M.? Will the deadline task be delayed beyond its deadline?

Embedded systems failures due to failing to meet important timing deadlines are called hard real-time or time-critical failures. Likewise, poor performance can be attributed to soft real-time or time-sensitive failures.

Another category of failures is created when the system is forced to run at, or near, full capacity for extended periods. Thus, you might never see a `malloc()` error when the system is running at one-half load, but when it runs at three-fourths load, `malloc()` may fail once a day.

Many RTOSs use fixed size queues to track waiting tasks and buffer I/O. It's important to test what happens if the system receives an unusually high number of asynchronous events while it is heavily loaded. Do the queues fill up? Is the system still able to meet deadlines?

Thorough testing of real-time behavior often requires that the embedded system be attached to a custom hardware/simulation environment. The simulation environment presents a realistic, but virtual, model of the hardware and real world. Sometimes the hardware simulator can be as simple as a parallel I/O interface that simulates a user pressing switches. Some projects might require a full flight simulator. At any rate, regression testing of real-time behavior won't be possible unless the real-time events can be precisely replicated.

Unfortunately, budget constraints often prohibit building a simulator. For some projects, it could take as much time to construct a meaningful model as it would to fix all the bugs in all the embedded products your company has ever produced. Designers do not spend a lot of time developing "throw-away" test software because this test code won't add value to the product. It will likely be used once or twice and then deleted, so why waste time on it?

In Chapter 3, I discussed HW/SW co-verification and the way that a VHDL simulator could be linked to a software driver through a bus functional model of the processor. Conceptually, this could be a good test environment if your hardware team is already using VHDL- or Verilog-based design tools to create custom ASICs for your product. Because a virtual model of the hardware already exists and a simulator is available to exercise this model, why not take advantage of it to provide a test scaffold for the software team? This was one of the great promises of co-verification, but many practical problems have limited its adoption as a general-purpose tool. Still, from a conceptual basis, co-verification is the type of tool that could enable you to build a software-test environment without having to deploy actual hardware in a real-world environment.

Measuring Test Coverage

Even if you use both white-box and black-box methodologies to generate test cases, it's unlikely that the first draft of the test suite will test all the code. The interactions between the components of any nontrivial piece of software are just too complex to analyze fully. As the earlier "shampoo" algorithm hinted, we need some way to measure how well our tests are covering the code and to identify the sections of code that are not yet being exercised.

The following sections describe several techniques for measuring test coverage. Some are software-based, and some exploit the emulators and integrated device electronics (IDE) that are often available to embedded systems engineers.

Because they involve the least hardware, I'll begin with the software-based methods. Later I'll discuss some less intrusive, but sometimes less reliable, hardware-based methods. Despite the fact that the hardware-based methods are completely nonintrusive, their use is in the minority.

Software Instrumentation

Software-only measurement methods are all based on some form of execution logging. Statement coverage can be measured by inserting trace calls at the beginning of each "basic block" of sequential statements. In this context, a basic block is a set of statements with a single entry point at the top and one or more exits at the bottom. Each control structure, such as a goto, return, or decision, marks the end of a basic block. The implication is that after the block is entered every statement in the block is executed. By placing a simple trace statement, such as a printf(), at the beginning of every basic block, you can track when the block — and by implication all the statements in the block — are executed. This kind of software-based logging can be an extremely efficient way to measure statement coverage.

Of course, printf() statements slow the system down considerably, which is not exactly a low-intrusion test methodology. Moreover, small, deeply embedded systems might not have any convenient means to display the output (many embedded environments don't include printf() in the standard library).

If the application code is running under an RTOS, the RTOS might supply a low-intrusion logging service. If so, the trace code can call the RTOS at the entry point to each basic block. The RTOS can log the call in a memory buffer in the target system or report it to the host.

An even less-intrusive form of execution logging might be called *low-intrusion* printf(). A simple memory write is used in place of the printf(). At each basic block entry point, the logging function "marks" a unique spot in excess data memory. After the tests are complete, external software correlates these marks to the appropriate sections of code.

Alternatively, the same kind of logging call can write to a single memory cell, and a logic analyzer (or other hardware interface) can capture the data. If, upon entry to the basic block, the logging writes the current value of the program counter to a fixed location in memory, then a logic analyzer set to trigger only on a write to that address can capture the address of every logging call as it is executed. After the test suite is completed, the logic analyzer trace buffer can be uploaded to a host computer for analysis.

Although conceptually simple to implement, software logging has the disadvantage of being highly intrusive. Not only does the logging slow the system, the extra calls substantially change the size and layout of the code. In some cases, the instrumentation intrusion could cause a failure to occur in the function testing — or worse, mask a real bug that would otherwise be discovered.

Instrumentation intrusion isn't the only downside to software-based coverage measurements. If the system being tested is ROM-based and the ROM capacity is close to the limit, the instrumented code image might not fit in the existing ROM. You are also faced with the additional chore of placing this instrumentation in your code, either with a special parser or through conditional compilation.

Coverage tools based on code instrumentation methods cause some degree of code intrusion, but they have the advantage of being independent of on-chip caches. The *tags* or markers emitted by the instrumentation can be coded as noncachable writes so that they are always written to memory as they occur in the code stream. However, it's important to consider the impact of these code markers on the system's behavior.

All these methods of measuring test coverage sacrifice fine-grained tracing for simplicity by assuming that all statements in the basic block will be covered. A function call, for example, might not be considered an exit from a basic block. If a function call within a basic block doesn't return to the calling function, all the remaining statements within the basic block are erroneously marked as having been executed. Perhaps an even more serious shortcoming of measuring statement coverage is that the measurement demonstrates that the actions of an application have been tested but not the reasons for those actions.

You can improve your statement coverage by using two more rigorous coverage techniques: Decision Coverage (DC) and Modified Condition Decision Coverage (MCDC). Both of these techniques require rather extensive instrumentation of the decision points at the source code level and thus might present increasingly objectionable levels of intrusion. Also, implementing these coverage test methods is best left to commercially available tools.

Measuring More than Statement Execution

DC takes statement coverage one step further. In addition to capturing the entry into the basic blocks, DC also measures the results of decision points in the code, such as looking for the result of binary (true/false) decision points. In C or C++, these would be the `if`, `for`, `while`, and `do/while` constructs. DC has the advantage over statement coverage of being able to catch more logical errors. For example, suppose you have an `if` statement without an `else` part

```
if (condition is true)
{
< then do these statements>;
}
< code following elseless if >
```

You would know whether the TRUE condition is tested because you would see that the then statements were executed. However, you would never know whether the FALSE condition ever occurred. DC would allow you to track the number of times the condition evaluates to TRUE and the number of times it evaluates to FALSE.

MCDC goes one step further than DC. Where DC measures the number of times the decision point evaluates to TRUE or to FALSE, MCDC evaluates the terms that make up the decision criteria. Thus, if the decision statement is

```
if (A || B)
{
< then do these statements>;
}
```

DC would tell you how many times it evaluates to TRUE and how many times it evaluates to FALSE. MCDC would also show you the logical conditions that lead to the decision outcome. Because you know that the `if` statement decision condition would evaluate to TRUE if A is TRUE AND B is also TRUE, MCDC would also tell you the states of A and B each time the decision was evaluated. Thus, you would know why the decision evaluated to TRUE or FALSE not just that it was TRUE or FALSE.

Hardware Instrumentation

Emulation memories, logic analyzers, and IDEs are potentially useful for test-coverage measurements. Usually, the hardware functions as a trace/capture interface, and the captured data is analyzed offline on a separate computer. In addition to these three general-purpose tools, special-purpose tools are used just for performance and test coverage measurements.

Emulation Memory

Some vendors include a *coverage bit* among the attribute bits in their emulation memory. When a memory location is accessed, its coverage bit is set. Later, you can look at the fraction of emulation memory "hits" and derive a percent of coverage for the particular test. By successively "mapping" emulation memory over system memory, you can gather test-coverage statistics.

One problem with this technique is that it can be fooled by microprocessors with on-chip instruction or data caches. If a memory section, called a *refill line*, is read into the cache but only a fraction of it is actually accessed by the program, the coverage bit test will be overly optimistic in the coverage values it reports. Even so, this is a good upper-limit test and is relatively easy to implement, assuming you have an ICE at your disposal.

Logic Analyzer

Because a logic analyzer also can record memory access activity in real time, it's a potential tool for measuring test coverage. However, because a logic analyzer is designed to be used in "trigger and capture" mode, it's difficult to convert its trace data into coverage data. Usually, to use a logic analyzer for coverage measurements, you must resort to statistical sampling.

For this type of measurement, the logic analyzer is slaved to a host computer. The host computer sends trigger commands to the logic analyzer at random intervals. The logic analyzer then fills its trace buffer without waiting for any other trigger conditions. The trace buffer is uploaded to the computer where the memory addresses, accessed by the processor while the trace buffer was capturing data, are added to a database. For coverage measurements, you only need to know whether each memory location was accessed; you don't care how many times an address was accessed. Thus, the host computer needs to process a lot of redundant data. For example, when the processor is running in a tight loop, the logic analyzer collects a lot of redundant accesses. If access behavior is sampled over long test runs (the test suite can be repeated to improve sampling accuracy), the sampled coverage begins to converge to the actual coverage.

Of course, memory caches also can distort the data collected by the logic analyzer. On-chip caches can mask coverage holes by fetching refill lines that were only partly executed. However, many logic analyzers record additional information provided by the processor. With these systems, it's sometimes possible to obtain an accurate picture of the true execution coverage by post-processing the raw trace. Still, the problem remains that the data capture and analysis process is statistical and might need to run for hours or days to produce a meaningful result.

In particular, it's difficult for sampling methods to give a good picture of ISR test coverage. A good ISR is fast. If an ISR is infrequent, the probability of capturing it during any particular trace event is correspondingly low. On the other hand, it's easy to set the logic analyzer to trigger on ISR accesses. Thus, coverage of ISR and other low-frequency code can be measured by making a separate run through the test suite with the logic analyzer set to trigger and trace just that code.

Software Performance Analyzers

Finally, a hardware-collection tool is commercially available that facilitates the low-intrusion collection method of hardware assist without the disadvantage of intermittent collection of a logic analyzer. Many ICE vendors manufacture hardware-based tools specifically designed for analyzing test coverage and software performance. These are the "Cadillac™" tools because they are specifically designed for gathering coverage test data and then displaying it in a meaningful way. By using the information from the linker's load map, these tools can display coverage information on a function or module basis, rather than raw memory addresses. Also, they are designed to collect data continuously, so no gaps appear in the data capture, as with a logic analyzer. Sometimes these tools come already bundled into an ICE, others can be purchased as hardware or software add-ons for the basic ICE. These tools are described in more detail later in the following section: "Performance Testing."

Performance Testing

The last type of testing to discuss in this chapter is performance testing. This is the last to be discussed because performance testing, and, consequently, performance tuning, are not only important as part of your functional testing but also as important tools for the maintenance and upgrade phase of the embedded life cycle. Performance testing is crucial for embedded system design and, unfortunately, is usually the one type of software characterization test that is most often ignored. Dave Stewart, in "The Twenty-Five Most Common Mistakes with Real-Time Software Development,"[9] considers the failure to measure the execution time of code modules the number one mistake made by embedded system designers.

Measuring performance is one of the most crucial tests you need to make on your embedded system. The typical response is that the code is "good enough" because the product works to specification. For products that are incredibly cost sensitive, however, this is an example of engineering at its worst. Why overdesign a system with a faster processor and more and faster RAM and ROM, which adds to the manufacturing costs, lowers the profit margins, and makes the product less competitive, when the solution is as simple as finding and eliminating the hot spots in the code?

On any cost-sensitive embedded system design, one of the most dramatic events is the decision to redesign the hardware because you believe you are at the limit of performance gains from software redesign. Mostly, this is a gut decision rather than a decision made on hard data. On many occasions, intuition fails. Modern software, especially in the presence of an RTOS, is extremely difficult to fully unravel and understand. Just because you can't see an obvious way to improve the system throughput by software-tuning does not imply that the next step is a hardware redesign. Performance measurements made with real tools and with sufficient resources can have tremendous payback and prevent large R&D outlays for needless redesigns.

How to Test Performance

In performance testing, you are interested in the amount of time that a function takes to execute. Many factors come into play here. In general, it's a nondeterministic process, so you must measure it from a statistical perspective. Some factors that can change the execution time each time the function is executed are:

- Contents of the instruction and data caches at the time the function is entered
- RTOS task loading
- Interrupts and other exceptions
- Data-processing requirements in the function

Thus, the best you can hope for is some statistical measure of the minimum, maximum, average, and cumulative execution times for each function that is of interest. Figure 9.3 shows the CodeTEST performance analysis test tool, which uses software instrumentation to provide the stimulus for the entry-point and exit-point measurements. These tags can be collected via hardware tools or RTOS services.

Dynamic Memory Use

Dynamic memory use is another valuable test provided by many of the commercial tools. As with coverage, it's possible to instrument the dynamic memory allocation operators `malloc()` and `free()` in C and `new` and `delete` in C++ so that the instrumentation tags will help uncover memory leakages and fragmentation problems while they are occurring. This is infinitely preferable to dealing with a nonreproducible system lock-up once every two or three weeks. Figure 9.2 shows one such memory management test tool.

Figure 9.2 Memory management test tool.

Function	Source File	Line	# XEQ	Type	Min	Max	Avg	Bytes	Bytes Allocated Histogram
makeSuper	memMgmt.	295	93	malloc	20	984	315	0	
getSymNod	memMgmt.	245	171	calloc	24	992	314	696	
extendNod	memMgmt.	255	559	realloc	20	1000	325	798	
initializeSy	memMgmt.	270	109	malloc	18	1000	362	0	
makeUser	memMgmt.	280	305	malloc	22	992	369	738	
getHdrSym	memMgmt.	285	102	calloc	26	984	315	150	
makeDefau	memMgmt.	290	90	malloc	16	952	293	0	
userProgra	ctdemo.c	181	6	malloc	4	8	4	0	
enlargePac	memMgmt.	300	610	realloc	20	1008	351	1004	
createUser	memMgmt.	320	87	malloc	20	984	290	582	
createNull	memMgmt.	325	100	malloc	28	1000	307	0	
createSupe	memMgmt.	330	89	malloc	18	968	384	0	
addRecExt	memMgmt.	335	621	realloc	20	1008	343	544	
addRecExt	memMgmt.	340	601	realloc	20	1008	333	730	

The CodeTEST memory management test program (courtesy of Applied Microsystems Corporation).

Figure 9.3 CodeTEST test tool.

Function	#XEQ	Min(uS)	Max(uS)	Avg(uS)	Cumulative(uS)	% Time	% Time Histogram
extendNod	1580	2710.6	7491.7	4491.6	7096680.0	9.52%	
addRecExt	1506	2544.9	7784.6	4504.7	6784080.0	9.10%	
addRecExt	1487	2994.8	7497.3	4502.5	6695190.0	8.98%	
enlargePac	1475	2636.1	7235.1	4482.2	6611270.0	8.87%	
getCmdFro	71926	86.6	90.3	89.4	6433550.0	8.63%	
returnCmd	71927	45.9	47.7	46.9	3370760.0	4.52%	
parseCmd	71927	45.3	47.7	46.7	3360930.0	4.51%	
memMgmt	775	138.1	10342.4	3922.2	3039710.0	4.08%	
makeUser	685	1277.0	4085.9	3155.1	2161210.0	2.90%	
handleCmd	152	2805.6	21865.0	12978.2	1972690.0	2.65%	
getSymNod	502	1713.5	4239.9	3274.0	1643550.0	2.20%	
badExit	483	11.1	10745.1	3011.1	1454340.0	1.95%	
freeSuperP	264	2783.4	8948.3	5066.0	1337430.0	1.79%	

CodeTEST performance analysis tool display showing the minimum, maximum, average, and cumulative execution times for the functions shown in the leftmost column (courtesy of Applied Microsystems Corporation).

From the Trenches

Performance testing and coverage testing are not entirely separate activities. Coverage testing not only uncovers the amount of code your test is exercising, it also shows you code that is never exercised (dead code) that could easily be eliminated from the product. I'm aware of one situation in which several design teams adapted a linker command file that had originally been written for an earlier product. The command file worked well enough, so no one bothered to remove some of the extraneous libraries that it pulled in. It wasn't a problem until they had to add more functionality to the product but were limited to the amount of ROM space they had. Thus, you can see how coverage testing can provide you with clues about where you can excise code that does not appear to be participating in the program. Although removing dead code probably won't affect the execution time of the code, it certainly will make the code image smaller. I say probably because on some architectures, the dead code can force the compiler to generate more time-consuming long jumps and branches. Moreover, larger code images and more frequent jumps can certainly affect cache performance.

Conceptually, performance testing is straightforward. You use the link map file to identify the memory addresses of the entry points and exit points of functions. You then watch the address bus and record the time whenever you have address matches at these points. Finally, you match the entry points with the exit points, calculate the time difference between them, and that's your elapsed time in the function. However, suppose your function calls other functions, which call more functions. What is the elapsed time for the function you are trying to measure? Also, if interrupts come in when you are in a function, how do you factor that information into your equation?

Fortunately, the commercial tool developers have built in the capability to unravel even the gnarliest of recursive functions.

Hardware-based tools provide an attractive way to measure software performance. As with coverage measurements, the logic analyzer can be programmed to capture traces at random intervals, and the trace data — including time stamps — can be post-processed to yield the elapsed time between a function's entry and exit points. Again, the caveat of intermittent measurements applies, so the tests might have to run for an extended period to gather meaningful statistics.

Hardware-only tools are designed to monitor simultaneously a spectrum of function entry points and exit points and then collect time interval data as various functions are entered and exited. In any case, tools such as these provide unambiguous information about the current state of your software as it executes in real time.

Hardware-assisted performance analysis, like other forms of hardware-assisted measurements based on observing the processor's bus activity, can be rendered less accurate by on-chip address and data caches. This occurs because the appearance of an address on the bus does not necessarily mean that the instruction at that address will be executed at that point in time, or any other point in time. It only means that the address was transferred from memory to the instruction cache.

Tools based on the instrumentation of code are immune to cache-induced errors but do introduce some level of intrusion because of the need to add extra code to produce an observable tag at the function's entry points and exit points. Tags can be emitted sequentially in time from functions, ISRs, and the RTOS kernel itself. With proper measurement software, designers can get a real picture of how their system software is behaving under various system-loading conditions. This is exactly the type of information needed to understand why, for example, a functional test might be failing.

From the Trenches

From personal experience, the information, which these tools provide a design team, can cause much disbelief among the engineers. During one customer evaluation, the tool being tested showed that a significant amount of time was being spent in a segment of code that none of the engineers on the project could identify as their software.

Upon further investigation, the team realized that in the build process the team had inadvertently left the compiler switch on that included all the debug information in the compiled code. Again, this was released code. The tool was able to show that they were taking a 15-percent performance hit due to the debug code being present in the released software. I'm relatively certain that some heads were put on the block because of this, but I wasn't around to watch the festivities.

Interestingly, semiconductor manufacturers are beginning to place additional resources on-chip for performance monitoring, as well as debugging purposes. Desktop processors, such as the Pentium and AMD's K series, are equipped with performance-monitoring counters; such architectural features are finding their way into embedded devices as well. These on-chip counters can count elapsed time or other performance parameters, such as the number of cache hits and cache misses.

Another advantage of on-chip performance resources is that they can be used in conjunction with your debugging tools to generate interrupts when error conditions occur. For example, suppose you set one of the counters to count down to zero when a certain address is fetched. This could be the start of a function. The counter counts down; if it underflows before it's stopped, it generates an interrupt or exception, and processing could stop because the function took too much time. The obvious advantages of on-chip resources are that they won't be fooled by the presence of on-chip caches and that they don't add any overhead to the code execution time. The downside is that you are limited in what you can measure by the functionality of the on-chip resources.

Maintenance and Testing

Some of the most serious testers of embedded software are not the original designers, the Software Quality Assurance (SWQA) department, or the end users. The heavy-duty testers are the engineers who are tasked with the last phases of the embedded life cycle: maintenance and upgrade. Numerous studies (studies by Dataquest and *EE Times* produced similar conclusions) have shown that more than half of the engineers who identify themselves as embedded software and firmware engineers spend the majority of their time working on embedded systems that have already been deployed to customers. These engineers were not the original designers who did a rotten job the first time around and are busy fixing residual bugs; instead, these engineers take existing products, refine them, and maintain them until it no longer makes economic sense to do so.

One of the most important tasks these engineers must do is understand the system with which they're working. In fact, they must often understand it far more intimately than the original designers did because they must keep improving it without the luxury of starting over again.

From the Trenches

I'm often amused by the expression, "We started with a clean sheet of paper," because the subtitle could be, "And we didn't know how to fix what we already had." When I was an R&D Project Manager, I visited a large telecomm vendor who made small office telephone exchanges (PBX). The team I visited was charged with maintaining and upgrading one of the company's core products. Given the income exposure riding on this product, you would think the team would have the best tools available. Unfortunately, the team had about five engineers and an old, tired PBX box in the middle of the room. In the corner was a dolly with a four-foot high stack of source code listings. The lead engineer said someone wheeled that dolly in the previous week and told the team to "make it 25 percent better." The team's challenge was to first understand what they had and, more importantly, what the margins were, and then they could undertake the task of improving it 25 percent, whatever that meant. Thus, for over half of the embedded systems engineers doing embedded design today, testing and understanding the behavior of existing code is their most important task.

It is an unfortunate truth of embedded systems design that few, if any, tools have been created specifically to help engineers in the maintenance and upgrade phases of the embedded life cycle. Everyone focuses on new product development. Go to any Embedded Systems Conference™, and every booth is demonstrating something to help you improve your time to market. What if you're already in the market? I've been to a lot of Embedded System Conferences™ and I've yet to have anyone tell me his product will help me figure out what I'm already shipping to customers. Today, I'm aware of only one product idea that might come to market for a tool specifically focusing on understanding and categorizing existing embedded software in a deployed product.

Additional Reading

- Barrett, Tom. "Dancing with Devils: Or Facing the Music on Software Quality." *Supplement to Electronic Design*, 9 March 1998, 40.
- Beatty, Sean. "Sensible Software Testing." *Embedded Systems Programming*, August 2000, 98.
- Myers, Glenford J. *The Art of Software Testing.* New York: Wiley, 1978.
- Simon, David. *An Embedded Software Primer.* Reading, MA: Addison-Wesley, 1999.

Summary

In a way, it's somewhat telling that the discussion of testing appears at the end of this book because the end of the product development cycle is where testing usually occurs. It would be better to test in a progressive manner, rather than waiting until the end, but, for practical reasons, some testing must wait. The principal reason is that you have to bring the hardware and software together before you can do any kind of meaningful testing, and then you still need to have the real-world events drive the system to test it properly.

Although some parts of testing must necessarily be delayed until the end of the development cycle, the key decisions about what to test and how to test must not be delayed. Testability should be a key requirement in every project. With modern SoC designs, testability is becoming a primary criterion in the processor-selection process.

Finally, testing isn't enough. You must have some means to measure the effectiveness of your tests. As Tom DeMarco[3], once said, "You can't control what you can't measure."

If you want to control the quality of your software, you must measure the quality of your testing. Measuring test coverage and performance are important components but for safety critical projects, even these aren't enough.

Works Cited

1. Hopper, Grace Murray. "The First Bug." *Annals of the History of Computing*, July 1981, 285.
2. Horning, Jim. *ACM Software Engineering Notes*. October 1979, 6.
3. DeMarco, Tom. *Controlling Software Projects*. New York: Yourdon, 1982.
4. Leveson, Nancy and Clark S. Turner. "An Investigation of the Therac-25 Accidents." *IEEE Computer*, July 1993, 18–41.
5. Main, Jeremy. *Quality Wars: The Triumphs and Defeats of American Business*. New York: Free Press, 1994.
6. Myers, Glenford J. *The Art of Software Testing*. New York: Wiley, 1978.
7. Ross, K.J. & Associates. `http://www.cit.gu.edu.au/teaching/CIT2162/991005.pdf`, p. 43.
8. Simon, David. *An Embedded Software Primer*. Reading, MA: Addison-Wesley, 1999.
9. Stewart, Dave. "The Twenty-Five Most Common Mistakes with Real-Time Software Development." A paper presented at the Embedded Systems Conference, San Jose, 26 September 2000.

Chapter 10

The Future

The previous chapters have focused on tools and techniques that you need to do your job today. This chapter looks beyond the job as it is today to the future. First, I want to describe a new technology — reconfigurable hardware — that has the potential to completely redefine the process of creating an embedded system.

The closing half of this chapter is devoted not so much to what might come, as to what I heartily wish would come.

Reconfigurable Hardware

The ultimate solution to the partitioning problem might be a new technology known as *reconfigurable hardware*. Reconfigurable hardware might be the future of computing systems in general, whether they are desktop PCs or embedded systems. Reconfigurable hardware is circuitry that can be changed dynamically so that its very structure changes at run time.

Imagine, for example, a microcontroller that consists of a standard microprocessor core, a big block of this reconfigurable hardware, and nothing else. Unlike current SoC solutions, this imaginary part wouldn't include any dedicated peripheral devices, such as timers, parallel ports, serial ports, Ethernet ports, and so on. Instead, when the application calls for a parallel port, part of the reconfigurable logic would be configured to be a parallel port. If a serial port is needed, the same thing happens. If the design requires high-speed data steering logic, as you might find in a telecommunications application, the hardware block is reconfigured to be a steering block.

What is this magic hardware? The basis of this "brave new world" of computing hardware is a device that has been around for more than 10 years, the Field Programmable Gate Array (FPGA). Figure 10.1 shows a conceptual model of an FPGA. The device consists of the following:

- A "sea of gates," such as general purpose AND gates, OR gates, NOT gates, and EXCLUSIVE OR gates
- A matrix of programmable interconnection elements
- General-purpose memory
- General-purpose registers
- A configuration memory that, when programmed, connects the devices into the desired circuit blocks

Figure 10.1 FPGA.

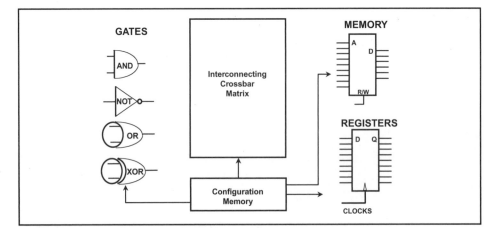

Conceptual diagram of an FPGA.

In Figure 10.1 each element from the sea of gates is represented by a traditional logic gate. In actuality, FPGAs do not implement the logic function as traditional, dedicated gates. Instead each individual logic element is actually a small read/write memory array that is programmed directly with the desired function's truth table.

Figure 10.2 shows how this structure can be used to implement a simple AND gate. In this representation, a and b are the address bits to the memory cells. The output, x, is just the data bit stored in each memory cell. Thus, the AND gate can be generated by a simple, four-cell memory that contains the following stored data:

ADDR(0,0) = 0   ADDR(0,1) = 0   ADDR(1,0) = 0   ADDR(1,1) = 1

Figure 10.2 Gates.

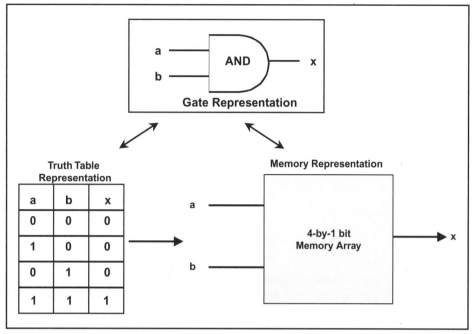

Representing an AND **function in a logic design**.

With the logic table stored directly in the memory array, the output is TRUE, or 1, if and only if both inputs are TRUE. Of course, this structure easily can be expanded to functions with more than just two inputs. For example, you could have an *n*-input AND gate, and output would be TRUE if, and only if, all *n*-input variables were TRUE.

In real life, these memory arrays have five or six input variables each and two or more independent output variables. The advantage of this approach is that any logical expression that can be represented as a function of five or six independent input variables can be programmed into each logic cell array.

Figure 10.3 shows the pieces in more detail. The unlabeled, small gray squares are programmable cross-point switches, the key elements of the interconnection matrix of Figure 10.1. Each switch can be programmed to connect a vertical signal wire to a horizontal signal wire by programming the corresponding control bit in the configuration memory. The circuit block labeled "D Latch or FF" is the elemental version of a register. Sending the appropriate clock signal or logic level to the block causes the output of the logic cell array to be stored in the register. Thus, as every electrical engineering student must realize by now, you have all the elements that are necessary to build hardware state machines.

Figure 10.3 Interconnecting Elements of FPGA.

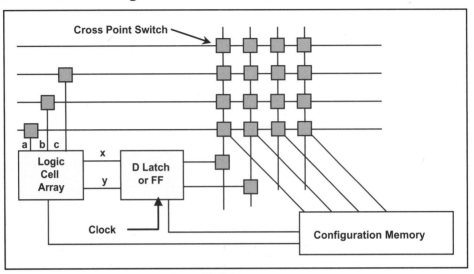

Interconnecting elements of the FPGA.

FPGA technology is not particularly new to hardware design. FPGAs have been used for more than 10 years as a prototype part in the design of ASICs and other custom-made integrated circuits (ICs). The advantage was that an FPGA could be substituted for the actual IC until the correct hardware performance could be verified, and then the FPGA-based design would be transferred to the silicon manufacturer for production. Some silicon manufacturers were even able to read the FPGA configuration files and generate the ASIC directly from that.

The early use of FPGAs was limited because the algorithms used to route the device were slow and computationally intensive. It would commonly take a week of computer time to find a route (correct configuration file) for a particularly dense FPGA design. As the use of the FPGA's resources rose above 50 to 60 percent, the routing time began to increase dramatically. So even if an FPGA has a theoretical capacity of 1,000 gates, perhaps a real design of less than 700 gates would actually be able to fit into the device.

Another problem was cost. FPGAs were five to 10 times more costly than an equivalent size ASIC, so production use was prohibitively expensive. However, many applications were found that were not particularly cost sensitive, and the use of the devices increased rapidly. Several new companies formed that arranged large matrices of individual FPGAs to create equivalent FPGAs of much larger capacity, in one case, over a million equivalent gates[3].

This imaginary processor plus reconfigurable hardware isn't all imaginary. In 1998, a new company called Triscend[2] introduced a microcontroller based on the industry-standard 8032 that contained an array of reconfigurable elements. At the September 2000, Embedded Systems Conference, the leading FPGA manufacturer, Xilinx (www.xilinx.com), announced that standard RISC cores would be available for its FPGAs.

Today, we are just at the threshold of finding new and exciting ways to use the concepts of reconfigurable hardware. Almost all modern embedded processors contain dedicated blocks of circuitry for debugging the application and for performance measurements in some cases. This circuitry is carried by every processor that is shipped to a customer, even if the design was completed many thousands of shipments ago. If the debug core was implemented in reconfigurable hardware, the chip real-estate now "wasted" on debug logic could become available for "soft" field hardware upgrades. There would be a limitless opportunity to load specialized hardware into the arrays as needed.

In Chapter 3, I discussed partitioning an embedded system between hardware (fast but inflexible) and software (slower but flexible). The technology of reconfigurable hardware now blurs this distinction even further. Researchers at HP Laboratories[1] have shown that specialized computational hardware, even running at modest speeds, such as 1MHz, can often outperform the capabilities of supercomputers running thousands of times faster.

Now, factor in the reality that in the near future most embedded systems will be attached to some distributed system, such as the Internet. Suppose you have thousands of Internet appliances on a network. You want to measure various types of performance parameters of your system as it runs during actual use. For a given node in the system, there might be 20 separate and distinctive measurements that you want to make at various times. Rather than design the specialized hardware for each of these separate measurements, you could simply download measurement configurations to the appliance via the Internet and then collect the data locally. After the data is uploaded, you could then download another measurement configuration.

Finally, really let your mind expand. With reconfigurable hardware, the entire embedded system is designed and controlled as a software image. Today, several vendors of IP-based microprocessor cores have parameterized their designs so that much of the architecture of the microprocessor is user configurable. Why not use the flexibility of reconfigurable hardware to enable a next-generation compiler to compile a source file into the traditional software image and into the optimal hardware configuration to execute the code most efficiently?

In today's press, one can read article after article discussing the advantages of DSPs and RISC in embedded applications. SoC designers are combining multiple DSP and RISC cores in their latest designs. With reconfigurable hardware, the distinctions among RISC, CISC, and DSP can go away completely. Just load the correct hardware configuration that is needed at that point in time. It's easy to do because it's only software.

Some Comments on the Tool Business

As someone involved in the development tool side of embedded systems for many years I've had my share of frustrations trying to build tool chains that benefited both the customers, the tool vendors and semiconductor manufacturers. It is clear that the semiconductor vendors don't always supply the quality of development tools that they could. This is not meant as a criticism of the semiconductor companies per se. For the semiconductor vendors, support tools represent the cost of doing business. Tools exist to sell silicon. Without support tools you can't sell your silicon to the embedded designers who design your silicon into their products.

However, if you bear with me for a few pages and indulge me a little trip into the land of fiction, I'll try to paint you a picture of how it could be if tools really did become a competitive edge. I should also give credit to the semiconductor companies and tool vendors because almost all of the products that I'll describe in my little story already exist in one form or another.

Our story opens in a small, windowless conference room at ComDelta, a leading supplier of LAN communications hardware and software for the rapidly growing wireless-network industry. Sue Mason, one of the founders of ComDelta and its chief hardware designer/system architect, is meeting with her design team to discuss the requirements for ComDelta's next-generation product. The model CD700 is going to be ComDelta's flagship wireless LAN bridge, servicing 100 simultaneous users.

The team is at a major decision point. Should they move to a higher performance RISC processor from Integrated Micro Everything (IME) or attempt to squeeze their existing 68060 design one more time? Clearly, using the Im46880 would enable them to easily meet their feature set goals but as Ralph, the software team leader, says, "Trying to do a software schedule with a 46880 processor would be a joke. Garbage in, garbage out. We spent years getting to know the best way to design for the 68K architecture. We know all the tools and their warts. And, to top it off, we've got to have a prototype running by the Wireless World conference next spring. No way!"

Sue had to admit that Ralph was right. In fact, as the only hardware designer supporting a team of nine computer scientists and firmware engineers (EE retreads), she wasn't so sure that she could learn enough about the Im46K family to have hardware for them when they needed it.

The uneasy silence was broken by Chin Lei, the newest employee of ComDelta and a Cornell graduate with an MS/CS degree, who says, "I did my Master's thesis on a graphics engine design that used a bunch of

Im46840s tied together. I was really impressed with the way IME supported our efforts. Here we were, a bunch of university geeks, and they treated us like we were some big laser printer company. Not only that, their embedded design tools are first-rate, and their application literature helped us understand the chip and design requirements. I wrote the multiprocessor OS, and there was this IME software performance superguru, Jerry Flemming, who wouldn't let me screw up. I didn't always understand him, but he meant well. Those guys really have their act together."

Sue went for a walk around the building, thinking about their dilemma. After about an hour, she went back inside and spent the rest of the afternoon doing administrivia. As she peddled home, she continued to think about Chin's obvious enthusiasm for IME.

The next morning, Sue called the local IME sales office. When Sue identified her company, the IME Sales Administrator for the region checked it against her online database of IME's targeted accounts. ComDelta was one of the hot new companies that IME wanted to penetrate. Her call was put through to the field sales engineer for that account, and an automatic request was transmitted to IME's headquarters in Oregon for the ComDelta company profile.

As Ed Rosen spoke with Sue, he entered her data onto his computer. He focused his questions on her knowledge of the Im46K product family and ComDelta's time-to-market needs. He clicked on the box that caused a Im46K Knowledge Box and an Im46880 Evaluation Kit to be rushed to Sue and several other members of her design team. It also started a chain of events in Portland and the IME Field Sales Office. These events culminated in a presentation that Ed hoped to make at ComDelta in the near future.

At work the following day, when Sue opened the Knowledge Box, some clever packaging caused a DVD to rise to the top. "**Watch me first**" it said in bold letters. Sue slipped the DVD into her drive. It presented an overview of how a team of designers, new to the Im46K, could become proficient in a minimum amount of time. It went through the tool chain, recommending certain vendors for particular embedded applications. Sue was impressed. "No hype. Just facts," she thought. The presentation suggested a path to follow to specify the design and identify key areas. It also contained a set of metrics taken from other Im46880 designs.

Sue was particularly intrigued by the System Design Assistant (SDA) software package in the Knowledge Box. SDA is a program based on some of the latest work in expert systems technology. Through a set of questions about her design requirements, SDA provided Sue with some general design parameters, system trade-offs, and references to several specific articles in IME's extensive library of applications notes.

The next day at work, Ralph blasted into her cubicle. "Sue, you've got to try out this evaluation kit; it is awesome. In about an half hour, I was running benchmarks of my data packet compression algorithm. They have this piece of software that analyzed the routine and told me how long it would run on a 66MHz 68060. I didn't believe it, so I ran it on the '060 VXI card. Dead on! And, get this, it includes a graphical analysis package that knows about real-time operating systems. Oh, by the way, the RISC chip ran it 105.8 percent faster, give or take a little."

Ralph's enthusiasm was catching. Sue phoned the IME office and asked if someone could come out and discuss her project in more depth. IME was ready; the hook was about to be set.

The next day, Ed and his field application engineer (FAE), Jon Turner, came out loaded for bear. Ed casually suggested that he could make a brief presentation that ComDelta might find valuable. Sue agreed to get the right people together. Ed's presentation was the sum total of IME's research about the ComDelta project. Ed presented a market analysis of ComDelta and its competitors. He showed how designing with the Im46K family provided a code-compatible upgrade path. He outlined the services IME provided and its support plan for its tool chain. Finally, he gave ComDelta the pricing and availability information that he had prepared. In short, he concluded, "You will not fail in your market because IME has failed to meet your needs."

While Ed's presentation was going on, Jon was meeting with the rest of the design team. He showed them how to best analyze the throughput requirements for their project. Together, their analysis showed that as long as their product specs stayed close to what it was, they could avoid doing a custom ASIC. This alone could save them several months in their schedule. However, just to be sure, Jon brought along a demo version of the RTOS-check evaluation package. This software, which Ralph had briefly played with a few days earlier, allowed Jon to model the RTOS behavior of the project trying different RTOSs, processors, and real-time user data loads. Because the team was basically keeping the same architectural structure for the project, the only variables that they needed to consider were the maximum number of users that could be accommodated before data-packet integrity began to fall off too rapidly.

Jon also spent time going through the IME tool chain. The team was understandably concerned about committing to an aggressive schedule with a brand-new tool chain. Jon covered the various elements of IME's Blend3D tool strategy. He went over the philosophy of System Debug Interface (SDI) and how it allowed a seamless integration of tools for the design team. Mike, a graying hippie-type with a long ponytail was particularly acerbic. "I've seen that story a bazillion times already. It's the holy grail of embedded design. Why should I believe that you guys got it when every booth at the Embedded Systems Conference has a bunch of Marketing types in Polo™ shirts telling me that they have the inside track on time to market?"

Jon smiled and told Mike that he had every right to be skeptical. He then told the team about IME's commitment to the tool chain through the Interoperability Lab (IO Lab) support team back at the factory. John said, "The IO Lab can replicate any problem that you can wring out of the tools."

He told them of one IME customer in Asia who was having problems optimizing a compression algorithm for a photographic-image scanner. The algorithm was sent to IME for analysis by the IO Lab. Their simulations showed that it should be running in one-fifth of the time. IME shipped out a loaner software performance analyzer with real-time profiling capability built-in. The IME-Singapore FAE flew out to the plant and set up the analyzer to gather software performance data on that algorithm. In one hour, they had the answer.

The object code for this algorithm filled about 75 percent of the cache. With both caches and interrupts enabled, the OS task switch, which occurred with each clock tick, was just large enough to cause a full cache flush and refill. The system was thrashing. The scanner design team then split the algorithm into two parts, which stopped the thrash situation, and re-ran the tests. Performance improved by 600 percent.

Mike said, "IME really did that? No bull?" Jon smiled. They were his.

The next day Sue called Ed and asked for quantity pricing information. Informally, she told him that IME was awarded the contract.

About a week later, a big IME box appeared on Sue's desk. In it, were three sets of videotapes entitled, "Designing with the Im46K Family." There were four tapes in the series. Also included was a set of CD-ROMs with the following titles:

- Online Im46K Help
- Communications Algorithms for Im46K Designers
- Conversion Software for RISC-Based Systems
- Im46K Design and Integration Tools, for Evaluation
- CASE Tools for Embedded Systems Design
- Im46K Hardware Design Guide

A full set of traditional manuals was included, as well as six sets of volumes I, II, and III of Dr. Jerry Flemming's book, *Programming the Im46K RISC Family*. Sue also found a book of coupons for free pizzas from ComDelta's favorite take-out shop with a little note from Ed wishing the team good luck and thanking them for their confidence in IME.

The next week, Jon came by and met with the design team. Together they undertook an in-depth analysis of the design tools that ComDelta already had in their possession and suggested additional tools that would help their productivity. They debated the purchase of an in-circuit emulator (ICE).

They had done their previous designs without one. Why should they incur the additional expense? Jon showed how one emulator, with real-time software performance analysis, would be good insurance for the problems that might crop up.

Jon also demonstrated the new software on CD-ROM, *Conversion Software for RISC-Based Systems*, which had come in the developer's kit the previous week. This was a package that IME had developed with ComSoft-Sys, Ltd., a small software company from Israel. The main program, CISC2RISC46K, was a C and C++ source code browser that scanned a source listing written for 68K processors and found code segments that could be modified to take advantage of superior RISC constructs.

Just for fun, they scanned some of ComDelta's packet-switching algorithms through CISC2RISC46K. It highlighted several data structures and suggested that these could be modified to take advantage of the Im46K's rich register set. It also keyed on several interrupt service routines (ISRs) and, using its hyperlink and code generation facility, created some alternative code segments for the old CISC code.

With Sue's permission, the list of tool vendors that Jon suggested were given information about the ComDelta project. Each arranged for an on-site demonstration. Each demonstration was professionally done and focused on the unique problems of the ComDelta project. Obviously, everyone had done their homework on this one. IME shared their ComDelta information with the key partners, and it showed. Each vendor's presentation echoed and reinforced a consistent theme, "We won't let you fail. IME stands behind the performance of these tools. All the tools in the recommended tool chain work together with seamless integration through SDI. We are fully SDI-compliant."

Three months later

The pizza coupons were finally used up. Ralph joked that they needed another IME presentation to refresh their coupon supply.

The first cut of PC boards had come back, and Sue was busy powering them up. The software team had ported most of the code that they wanted to re-use, stubbed-out the new code, and were waiting for real hardware to run it on. They found the development environment to be everything that IME had promised. Using the software simulator, along with the evaluation boards, they had most of the new software ready for real hardware. The OS had been configured using the RTOS-check software, and the team was pretty confident that the integration phase was under control.

They were right. Two weeks after the hardware and software were brought together, the team did a full software build and downloaded 33MB of code into their target through their sysROM ROM Emulator. Sue fired up the CD700. It went through its self-test and announced to the world that it was ready (a green light came on). Sue sat down with her laptop and attempted to log on to their network through the CD700.

What happened then was almost anticlimactic: she logged on. Not wanting to tempt fate any further, Sue declared a team holiday. The CD700 development team headed out in all directions.

Over the course of the next several weeks, the CD700 came closer to its design goals. The ComDelta testing lab was able to simulate 78 users before the system would bog down. Then all progress seemed to stop. Sue called Jon and asked for some help. Jon suggested a one-month rental of the tool systems ICE to do some performance analysis. He also asked if they would be willing to beta test the newest revision of the IME C++ Im46K software tool chain. This revision featured ActiveAlgorithm technology. ActiveAlgorithm is IME's exclusive real-time algorithm analysis compiler technology, jointly patented by Twenty-First Century Compilers Corporation and IME.

ActiveAlgorithm compilation allows an emulator or logic analyzer to act as a real-time, traceable cache instruction-flow probe into a target system. The output of the analyzer feeds back to the compiler, which can then call upon several optimization techniques to tune the performance of the compiled code.

With the hardware in place, the CD700 was run at a 78-user level for about three hours. The tool systems ICE gathered the trace statistics and the compiler preprocessor chewed on the results. A new object file was built on the feedback data and the system was restarted. The system bogged down again, but this time at 107 users. This time, Sue treated Jon and the team to Caribbean pizza at their favorite dine-in restaurant.

With one week to go until the Wireless World show, the team felt pretty good. Then disaster struck. Phase7 Systems, ComDelta's chief competitor, planned to pre-announce its latest product. Their HyperX80 serviced 80 users at half the cost of the CD700. The team huddled. Desperate phone calls went to IME. The team decided to try to wring every last ounce of performance out of the Im46880 processor. Jerry Flemming flew out from Portland to assist in fine-tuning the code.

Now improvements came in little chunks, but they came. Using the tool systems Sys46K as a software performance analyzer, they were able to fine-tune module after module. They reached 175 users but felt they needed more. Then Ed stepped back into the picture. He had been in contact with IME's . WCG had a two-channel, wireless LAN chip in development which was nearly pin-compatible with the existing part that ComDelta was already using. As ever, IME delivered. The chip appeared the next day. The team kludged-up a second channel in record time. Jerry helped integrate the ISR and add the additional tasks to the OS.

The next problem that the team faced was a pleasant one. Their simulation lab hardware could not simulate more than 200, users and the Com-Delta was still chugging away.

The CD700 won the Best New Product Award at the Wireless World exhibition. Sue Mason was so pleased with IME's program execution that she volunteered to appear on any future marketing or sales video that IME might produce.

Tool/Chip Tension

Why don't we have the kind of comprehensive, integrated tool support and customer support illustrated by this story? You would think that with such a co-dependency, the tool vendors and chip vendors would be the model of cooperation and collaboration. In fact, the relationship between tool and chip vendors is more akin to a family with working parents, five teenagers, two dogs, a cat, and one bathroom.

A number of basic differences exist between the semiconductor manufacturers and the tool vendors that support their chips. These differences tend to weigh heavily on the world-views of both groups and create tension between them.

The semiconductor manufacturer wishes that every new processor would hit it big with in a few major accounts with incredible volumes (the vertical singularity in Figure 10.4). It is the dream of every semiconductor salesperson to win any of the following:

- An inkjet printer
- Automobile engine management computer
- Video game box

With a few customers, the semiconductor manufacturer can lavish attention and make sure the tools for that customer are the best. In the semiconductor manufacturer's view, the desirable metric is known as *time to money*. This is the point that product shipments begin and volume purchases of microprocessors begin to take place. It is in the semiconductor manufacturer's best interest to help the big volume customer (design team) get the product designed, debugged, tested, and shipped in quantity. Problems with the development tools usually translate to delays in realizing volume shipments of processors. That's the reason I was hired. It was my responsibility to make sure the design process ran smoothly. If almost the entire volume of shipments of a microprocessor goes to a few mega-VIP customers, my job was straightforward. However, under these ideal conditions, my real problem became the tool vendors.

Figure 10.4 Worldviews.

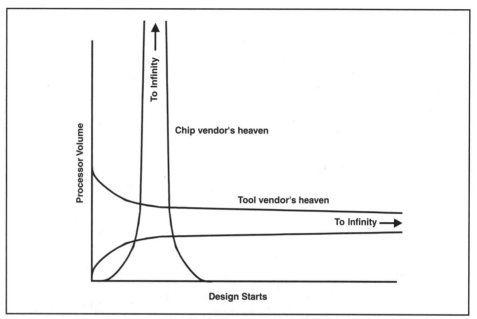

The world view of chip vendors and development tool vendors.

It's the Fabs

Shortly after arriving at my new employer, I was asked to present an informal seminar on the state of tool development as I saw it. Being basically naïve and honest, I proceeded to describe how I could design a pretty credible laser printer with anybody's embedded processor. Furthermore, in my opinion, the differentiating factor was how quickly I could bring a new design to market. I remember making the point that it wouldn't do any good if my hot, new laser printer is almost ready to go when Comdex rolled around. If I missed the Comdex introduction, I might as well kill the project.

The conclusion of my talk was met with stony silence. Afterwards, my supervisor explained that I completely missed the point. In short, my mantra was to become:

It's the fabs, stupid!

The goal of any major semiconductor manufacturer, such as one that builds high-performance microprocessors for the embedded market, is to keep silicon flowing through the foundry. That was the focus, not the quality of the tools. The tools had to be good enough to support the new design wins. I had to be able to go to a customer with a list of tools that supported our embedded microprocessors. It was not my province to expound on improving the state of embedded-tool development. As long as I had all the boxes on my product support matrix appropriately checked off, life was good.

It took me about two years of effort, but I think that I finally changed some minds, although it was probably wishful thinking on my part. Unfortunately, we did have some real situations in which the quality of our development-support tools were not up to the requirements of our customers, and my group had to step in and help. If some of the chip folks did eventually see the wisdom in my words, they never admitted it to my face.

From the perspective of the tool vendor, the semiconductor manufacturer's ideal situation is a bad business arrangement.

Coming from a background in tool development, I tend to think of processors as a necessary evil. Each new processor brings its own quirks to the task of designing the best development tools. Having a deep pipeline on the bus interface unit means that the tool vendor must design a clever state machine to mimic the pipeline behavior in the emulator so that the tool can accurately display real-time trace information.

For a tool vendor to develop a new product, such as a compiler, debugger, or ICE, to support a new processor, there must be a good probability of return on investment (ROI). Suppose the tool vendor invests $750,000 to develop several enhancements to existing products to support the new processor. (Although $750,000 might seem like a lot, good engineers don't come cheap these days. This represents the cost of about five engineers for six to 12 months, depending on how you do your bookkeeping.)

The tool vendor might sell 50 seats of the debugger, if they are lucky, to the two big volume customers using this processor. At $5,000 per seat, their expected ROI is all of $250,000, leaving the tool vendor in the hole for $500,000. Therefore, in the tool vendor's view, targeting a few big customers is a bad business plan. They aren't going to risk their company's money on a brand-new processor with only two or three design wins. A better strategy for them would be to wait a few months to see how well the new processor is accepted by the broader market. If their field sales offices get many phone calls from potential customers asking if they support the XYZ6000, the engineering team will crank up pretty quickly.

A *design win* is a customer making a firm commitment to use a specific processor.

This wait-and-see attitude is not what the semiconductor manufacturer wants. Unless tools are available significantly before the first silicon reaches the general marketplace, they will not be available to the mega-VIP customers who want to be far into their development cycle.

Figure 10.4 show how these two players have conflicting goals. The tools vendor wants to see many design starts. (These design starts could be within the same company. A major telecommunication vendor buying 1,000 seats of a new debugger wouldn't be too bad for business, but that's usually rare.) The semiconductor manufacturer is primarily interested in a few critical, high-volume design wins.

The ideal solution is for the semiconductor manufacturer to provide the tool vendor additional funding to remove some or all of the riskof developing a new tool before there is good marketing data supporting the project.

Basically, the semiconductor manufacturer ends up giving the tool vendor non-refundable engineering (NRE) payments to help balance the risk versus reward analysis that would normally tell them to stay away from this project. The size of this subsidy is heavily dependent on the customers and whether they already like the other products enough to require them for this new design. If you are a tool vendor, getting "spec'd in" by the customer is the only way to travel.

Anyway, all this behind-the-scenes intrigue is usually invisible to the customers, who have their own problems. If you are interested in which tools will support which processors, the way to find out is to see who is lunching together at the Embedded Systems Conference™.

Note

Today, most semiconductor vendors provide you with incredibly attractive data in the form of slick PowerPoint™ presentations describing in vague terms the large number of design starts forecast for this processor. However, if you ask them to name one, you are often told that this is proprietary information and they must protect their customer's privacy.

From the Trenches

I once had the uncomfortable task of speaking to the Tool Support Group of a large telecommunications company that was in the process of evaluating a new processor (my company's new embedded chip). The Tool Support Group had to evaluate the availability and the quality of the supporting tool suite that backed our processor. I was trying to convince them that, of the available compilers that supported our processor, their compiler of choice came out a distant third place out of three compilers that we evaluated. The compiler they preferred to use had performed satisfactorily with their old design, but the code generator section was a simple port from the old processor, with 16 registers, to our RISC processor, with many more registers. In our tests, their old compiler took about twice as long to run comparable sections of code as the best compiler. Naturally, I wanted them to switch to the new compiler.

I was politely, but firmly, informed that they had several million lines of code that they knew would compile with their current compiler, and they also owned several thousand seats of the old compiler. Furthermore, if my company and I really wanted them to switch to our processor, it was our job to improve the performance of their compiler to the point that it was reasonably close to the performance of the best compiler. I went back to the factory with the recommendation that we fund their compiler vendor's improvement of the code-generator section of their compiler.

Summary

Especially when coupled with pervasive network connectivity, reconfigurable hardware has the potential to revolutionize the industry. I've described reconfigurable hardware in terms of a processor coupled to a sea of gates, but, as Xilinx has demonstrated, the processor itself can be implemented within the sea of gates. What happens to the "processor selection" issue if the processor is just downloadable IP? If the entire program can be compiled directly to VHDL and then downloaded to an FPGA, will anyone care about the processor instruction set? Doesn't the existence of a processor just become a cost optimization issue that can be solved by the silicon compiler? The compiler identifies the low performance portions of the algorithm and implements them as firmware executed by a processor, where the microcode for the processor is generated using something akin to a compression algorithm: most frequent operations in shortest opcode. Perhaps that's far flung, but it's not too far from what happens now in some resource scheduling tools available to IC designers.

If nothing else, widespread use of reconfigurable hardware could improve the likelihood of getting some good development tools. After all, FPGAs are pretty much a commodity product; one looks pretty much like another. Widespread use of commodity-class reconfigurable hardware would create a market in which tool vendors could focus on refining a small set of tools instead of continuously working to retarget their tool for the latest and greatest processor.

Unfortunately, the intrinsic difference between FPGA and other IC process costs might always favor fixed logic solutions. Still, if the toolset for reconfigurable hardware became refined and standardized enough, the promise of reduced development costs and improved time-to-market would be more than enough to offset the differential in hardware costs for projects with small-to-medium production runs. It could be that a few standard reconfigurable designs will eventually dominate the low-volume end of embedded systems (much as ARM and PowerPC now dominate the IP market). Who knows, perhaps some new process discovery will remove even the cost barrier.

At any rate, reconfigurable hardware is a technology to watch in the future.

Works Cited

1. Culbertson, W. Bruce et al. "Exploring Architectures for Volume Visualization on the Teramac Custom Computer," in *Proceedings of the 1996 IEEE Symposium on FPGA's for Custom Computing Machines*. Napa Valley, CA, 1996, 80–88.
2. Gott, Robert A. "Reconfigurable Processor Reincarnates the Venerable 8032." *Computer Design*, October 1998, 38.
3. Snider, Greg et al. "The Teramac Configurable Computer Engine," in Will Moore and Wayne Luk, editors, *Field Programmable Logic and Applications*. Berlin: Springer-Verlag, 1995, 44.

Index

Symbols

#pragma 90
_asm 90
_getmem() 81
_main 75, 78

Numerics

5001 Forum
See Nexus

A

absolute address 86
access time 178
address spaces
    code 71
    data 71
    I/O 72
    system 71
    unpopulated 72
addressing mode 86
algorithm
    laser printer 8, 48
    partitioning 8
allocation
    dynamic 71
architectural simulator 101, 115
arguments
    passing 90
ARM 56
ASIC 50, 55, 62, 92
    revision cost 58
assembly
    generating 76
    inline 38, 90
    pseudo-instruction 83
atomic code 99
automata
    See statechart
automatic variables 71

B

back annotation 107
background debug mode
    See BDM

227

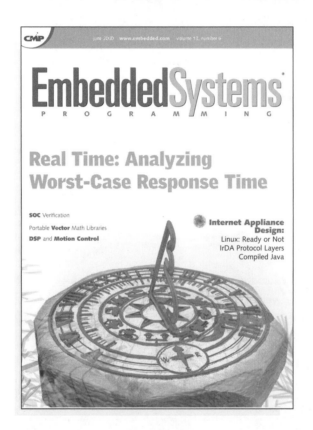

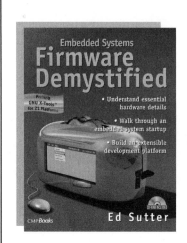